Urban Society in Roman Italy

Urban Society in Roman Italy

Edited by

T. J. Cornell
University of Manchester

&

Kathryn Lomas
University of Newcastle upon Tyne

UCL
PRESS

First published in 1995 by UCL Press
First published in paperback in 1996

UCL Press Limited
University College London
Gower Street
London WC1E 6BT

The name of University College London (UCL) is a registered trade mark used by
UCL Press with the consent of the owner.

ISBN:
1-85728-644-8 PB

British Library Cataloguing in Publication Data.

A catalogue record for this book is available from the British Library.

Typeset in Garamond.
Printed and bound by
Biddles Ltd., Guildford and King's Lynn, England.

Contents

Preface   vii
List of contributors   ix
Abbreviations   xi

Introduction   1
Kathryn Lomas

1 Do theories of the ancient city matter?   9
  C. R. Whittaker

2 The limits of the ancient city and the evolution of the
  medieval city in the thought of Max Weber   27
  L. Capogrossi Colognesi

3 Public honour and private shame:
  the urban texture of Pompeii   39
  Andrew Wallace-Hadrill

4 The organization of space in Pompeii   63
  Ray Laurence

5 The Insula of the Paintings at Ostia i.4.2–4:
  Paradigm for a city in flux   79
  Janet DeLaine

6 Urban elites and cultural definition: Romanization in
  southern Italy   107
  Kathryn Lomas

7 Warfare and urbanization in Roman Italy   121
  T. J. Cornell

8 Religion and rusticity   135
  J. A. North

CONTENTS

9   The Roman *villa* and the landscape of production   151
    Nicholas Purcell

10 The idea of the city and the excavations at Pompeii   181
    Martin Goalen

11 "Slouching towards Rome": Mussolini's imperial vision   203
    Luisa Quartermaine

    Index   217

Preface

The majority of papers in this volume were initially presented at a conference on Urban Society in Roman Italy, which was held at the Institute of Classical Studies of the University of London, in July 1991. This took place as part of a continuing research project on cities and urbanism in ancient Italy, which is funded by the Leverhulme Trust. The editors would like to thank the Director and Secretary of the Institute of Classical Studies for their assistance in hosting the conference, and the Leverhulme Trust for their financial contribution.

List of contributors

Luigi Capogrossi Colognesi
Professor of Roman Law
Istituto di Diritto Romano
Università di Roma "La Sapienza"

T. J. Cornell
Professor of Ancient History
University of Manchester

Janet DeLaine
Lecturer in Archaeology
University of Reading

Martin Goalen
Lecturer in Architecture
University College London

Ray Laurence
British Academy Research Fellow
University of Reading

Kathryn Lomas
Research Fellow
University of Newcastle upon Tyne

John North
Professor of History
University College London

Nicholas Purcell
Fellow of St John's College, Oxford

Luisa Quartermaine
Senior Lecturer in Italian
University of Exeter

Andrew Wallace-Hadrill
Professor of Classics
University of Reading

C. R. Whittaker
Lecturer in Ancient History
Churchill College, Cambridge

Abbreviations

AC *Archeologia Classica*
AE *L'Année Épigraphique*
AJA *American Journal of Archaeology*
Ant. Afr. *Antiquités Africaines*
BAR British Archaeological Reports
BCH *Bulletin de Correspondance Hellénique*
BEFAR Bibliothèque de l'École Française de Rome
Bull. Comm. Bullettino della Commissione Archeologica Comunale di Roma
CAH² *Cambridge ancient history*, 2nd edition
CEFR Collection de l'École Française de Rome
CIL Corpus Inscriptionum Latinarum
DdA *Dialoghi di Archeologia*
GdS *Giornale degli Scavi*
ILLRP *Inscriptiones Latinae Liberae Rei Publicae*
JBAA *Journal of the British Archaeological Association*
JRA *Journal of Roman Archaeology*
JRS *Journal of Roman Studies*
IG Inscriptiones Graecae
ILS Dessau, *Inscriptiones Latinae Selectae*
L'Ant. Class. *L'Antiquité Classique*
MAAR *Memoirs of the American Academy in Rome*
MAL *Monumenti Antichi dell'Accademia dei Lincei*

MAMA Monumenta Asiae Minoris Antiquae
MDAI (R) *Mitteilungen des Deutschen Archäologischen Instituts, Römische Abteilung*
Mem. Linc. *Memorie della Classe di Scienze Morali, Storiche, Filologiche dell'Accademia dei Lincei.*
MEFRA *Mélanges d'Archéologie et d'Histoire de l'École Française de Rome*
NSc. *Notizie degli Scavi dell'Antichità. Atti dell'Accademia dei Lincei*
ORF² H. Malcovati, *Oratorum Romanorum Fragmenta*, 2nd edn.
PCPS *Proceedings of the Cambridge Philological Society*
PdP *La Parola del Passato*
RE *Real-Encyclopädie der classischen Altertumswissenschaft*, eds A. Pauly *et al.*
Riv. Stud. Pomp. *Rivista di Studi Pompeiana*
SCO *Studi Classici e Orientali*
SEG *Supplementum epigraphicum Graecum*
TAPA *Transactions of the American Philological Association*
TLL *Thesaurus Linguae Latinae*
YCS *Yale Classical Studies*
ZPE *Zeritschrift für Papyrologie und Epigraphik*

Introduction

Kathryn Lomas

The city is one of the central phenomena of the ancient world, and one which has generated an unparalleled level of scholarly debate. From Marx, Sombart and Weber to the more recent analyses of Finley,[1] the essential nature of the ancient city and its relation to later European urbanism has been dissected by specialists from many disciplines in an attempt to build a single coherent model of urban development.

The ultimate impossibility of creating a valid model for urban development at all times and in all places, the stated aim of the Chicago school of urban studies, was exposed by Moses Finley in his review of the history of urban theory.[2] However, this has not deterred historians and urban sociologists from constructing global models for the origins and development of the ancient city, based on the Graeco-Roman town, but sometimes including urban settlements in the ancient Near East. Economists, sociologists, historians and archaeologists have contributed to the debate about the nature and economic basis of the city, and its relationship to its surroundings, ranging from Marx, through Sombart, Pirenne, Weber and Childe. Most recently and influentially, Moses Finley, influenced by Weber's notion of ideal types, has sought to identify types of city in accordance with their economic rôle. The ancient city, he argued, was almost entirely a consumer city, living off the resources of its territory, trading its surpluses, manufacturing on a small scale with the needs of the locality principally in mind, and always dominated by a *rentier* class. In contrast, the medieval and early modern city was a producer city, less immediately tied to the countryside and with a much greater emphasis on the mechanisms of large-scale trade and production.[3]

One aspect, however, which all these disparate views have in common is that they are based much more on the Greek than the Roman city. Finley takes the classical Greek *polis* as the purest representation of the ancient city – an independent political unit with a fully autonomous existence and, in most cases, a high degree of economic self-sufficiency based on domination and

1

exploitation of the surrounding territory.[4] The Hellenistic and Roman city, a unit which retained a high degree of local autonomy while ceding overall control of its affairs to a central authority – a monarch, or during the Roman republic, the senate – receives much less emphasis, both from Finley and from the principal object of his discussion, Weber. Indeed, the extent to which the perceived dichotomy between the nature of the 5th century Greek (primarily Athenian) *polis* and that of the Hellenistic city has shaped modern perceptions of the ancient city as a whole, has recently been highlighted by Oswyn Murray.[5]

While it is understandable that the type closest to a Weberian ideal type should receive most emphasis, it also represents, at least for Roman historians, a major omission. Over 80 years ago, Nissen[6] identified 400 urban sites in Italy in his classic account, *Italische Landeskunde*. Since then, evidence for Italian and Roman urbanism has been augmented even further by a vast, and ever growing, body of archaeological material. Although the Roman city shares many of the characteristics of the Greek *polis* (and of the Hellenistic Greek city), it is, nevertheless, a distinct entity which deserves to be studied in its own right. It emphatically should not be regarded as a watered-down version of the Greek city. The development of urbanism in Italy also raises the complex question of whether there is an Italian type of city, distinct from both the Greek *polis* and the Roman, legalistically defined, city.[7] The papers in this volume cannot claim to be a definitive reassessment of urban theory, but instead seek to explore and illuminate aspects of the Italian city in the light of the most recent research.

Having said that this volume is not intended as a challenge to the theories of the ancient city, it is perhaps paradoxical to begin with two papers which concern themselves with precisely this. However, this is highly necessary, given the recent upsurge of interest in theoretical models of urbanism. Over the past five years, there has been an explosion in the number of books concerned with the ancient city, including Rossi's *Modelli della città* (Turin, 1987), a collection of papers on the work of M. I. Finley, edited by Andreau & Hartog and published as *Opus* 1987–89, and Rich & Wallace-Hadrill's *City and country in the ancient world* (1991). Many of these illustrate the extent to which the debate, particularly in the English-speaking world, is still dominated by Weber's ideal type of the city, emphasizing the producer/consumer city, at the expense of Durkheim's model (described by Murray as "holistic") which takes ritual and social behaviour as its starting point.[8]

A strong recent trend has been towards expressions of scepticism over the possibility, and indeed the value, of attempting to construct unified models of the ancient city. However, the debate on the consumer city has reopened with a vengeance as a result of Donald Engels's construction of a model of the ancient city not as a consumer, but as a service city. In his view, ancient Corinth functioned not as a consumer city but as a centre for providing services and administrative functions for its hinterland, generating wealth by provision of services for a wider clientele.[9] Even the supporters of the service city must admit that a model based on Roman Corinth – which was a more overtly commercial and less agrarian community than most – may not necessarily be valid for all cities. Whittaker also casts doubt on much of the economic data from which the model is evolved, and reasserts both the validity of urban theory and the notion of the consumer city. Nevertheless, the model of the service city does suggest ways in which the Weber-Finley duality of the producer versus the consumer city may be developed.

There has also been renewed interest in the evolution of Weber's ideas on the city and of the notion of an ideal type as the basis for modern urban theory. Capogrossi highlights the extent to which *The city*, much the most influential and widely read of Weber's works, is a late and unrepresentative essay, which does not accurately reflect his views on urbanism. He traces the development of Weberian thought on the agrarian economies of ancient civilizations and the ways in which an understanding of how Weber's views changed can influence our understanding of his ideal type.[10]

The primary concern of this collection of papers, however, is not theory but examination of the actual nature of urban society in Roman Italy. Evidence, particularly archaeological evidence, for the Italian city has grown enormously over the last 20 years, and the imposition of some structure on this material is essential if we are to avoid the descent into antiquarianism which was condemned by Finley.[11] Archaeologists and historians have increasingly turned, in recent years, to techniques drawn from other disciplines. Some of the most exciting and innovative research in recent years has been in the field of urban space.[12] The analysis of space and its functions in the ancient city, frequently using techniques developed by urban geographers, has proved very illuminating for the study of social structures and interactions. Spatial analysis has already borne fruit in studies of domestic architecture and the functioning of the Roman household as a social unit,[13] but it is proving increasingly useful as a tool for dissecting the social structures of cities. Wallace-Hadrill reevaluates the evidence for the distribution of bars and brothels in Pompeii – as a means not only of clarifying use of space, but also of exploring the ways in which moral values, in this case the opposition between the honour of participation in public life and the shame attached to establishments associated with vice, modified use of urban space. Another study of the ways in which layout of space affects social interaction, that of Laurence, uses a different technique. Distribution of features such as different types of Pompeian doorway may act as an indicator of house function and of ways in which inhabitants interacted with the community as a whole. On a wider level, distribution of graffiti can be an indicator of the function and frequency of use of particular streets.[14]

The importance of both interdisciplinary techniques and a stringent reevaluation of material first published earlier in the 20th century cannot be overstated. However, it is all too easy to err towards too much theorizing and lose sight of the realities of urban development and its impact. DeLaine produces an architectural study of the Insula of the Paintings at Ostia, illuminating construction techniques, cost, source of materials and manpower, and changes in function. This enables a more realistic reconstruction of the probable form of the insula, in contrast to the extravagant suggestions of Calza,[15] and gives valuable insights into the nature of urban renewal at the most fundamental level.

Inevitably, it is tempting to concentrate on the urban development of Pompeii and Ostia, indubitably the best preserved and most extensive urban sites in Italy. However, any serious analysis of urban society must come to grips with aspects of that society in general, not confining itself to a small number of cities. Italy is so strongly regional in character, even as late as the 2nd century AD, that it is difficult to justify the privileging of a particular site as typical. It is hard to see how conclusions drawn from Pompeii can be regarded as having greater universal significance than those from any other region of Italy, or even from the sprawling metropolis of Rome itself. A recent (as yet unpublished) paper by Mouritsen has highlighted major differences of social and political structure even within Campania, between the neighbouring cities of Pompeii and Herculaneum. Having said this, the sheer quantity of evidence from Pompeii and Ostia makes these sites invaluable for study of the Italian city.

The rôle of the elite and its behaviour is an inescapable element in any study of urban society. It is undoubtedly a disproportionate element, but the lack of reliable evidence for popular culture, particularly in the literary and epigraphic record, makes this weighting difficult, if not impossible, to avoid. The central rôle of military matters in both the cultural and political world of the Roman elite is well known,[16] but this can be extended to cities other than Rome. The demands of virtually constant warfare and the military needs of Rome in terms of troops, supplies and support given by her Italian allies, played an important part in city formation and city development in republican Italy. The economic and social structures required to support such a military machine provide an additional tool for evaluating the consumer city model.

In terms of social structure, study of the elite should not be the beginning and end of the study of urban society, but the balance of evidence is strongly tilted towards the upper end of the social scale, and there are also some questions which can be usefully approached by a consideration of elite behaviour. In a post-conquest situation, such as existed in Italy during the republic and early empire, urban elites and their ideology are vital to our understanding of the processes of acculturation within the cities of Italy.[17] In any city, they are the group most exposed, and receptive, to external contacts, but also the group with the greatest need to control these outside influences. In the Greek and Hellenized cities of southern Italy, this can be observed with particular clarity, as the Romanized elite developed ways of manipulating the Greek heritage of the region to validate its own position and relations with Rome.

One of the areas of greatest research interest in recent years has been the relationship between the city and the surrounding countryside.[18] The central-ity of this subject to the study of urbanism is powerfully articulated by Strabo,[19] who defines the distinction between civilized life and barbarism as lying in the adoption of settled agriculture and urban life, and is fundamental to the mind-set of most other Greek and Roman authors. In modern terms, the theme of urban/rural relations reappears in the work of Adam Smith and continues to be central to that of Marx, Sombart, Weber and many other his-torians of the ancient city.[20]

In recent years, the increasing use of survey archaeology, both in Italy and in other parts of the Mediterranean, has enabled scholars to study patterns of rural habitation and land use with much greater precision, illuminating, amongst other things, the processes of city formation and dissolution and the economic interaction of city and country.[21] However, despite this wealth of evidence, the whole concept of a division between the city and its territory is a problematic one. The essence of the ancient city-state is that there was a symbi-otic relationship between urban centre and outlying countryside. This renders the idea of a division between city and territory in terms of economic and social structures largely meaningless. Nevertheless, the moral values attached to a perceived urban/rural divide by the Romans themselves, and the need to gain a greater understanding of the ways in which a city related to its territory, mean that this subject is still central to the study of Roman urbanism.

As the most visible sign of elite activity and urban exploitation of the coun-try, the villa has received a great deal of attention. Excavation of a number of villas over recent years has given us a substantial body of evidence to work from, but there is considerable tension between this archaeological data and the pattern suggested by ancient writers on agrarian matters. Purcell attempts to resolve this by considering the villa as an embodiment of urban elite values, a phenomenon which must combine agricultural productivity with conform-ity to moral and cultural expectations of the elite about rural life. Thus the elite villa is a productive estate, but cultural expectations lead to the prioritization of some activities – notably wine and oil production – over oth-ers. The rôle of urban expectations in shaping understanding of the country-side is also reflected by North's discussion of the rôle of rustic cults in a substantially urbanized Italy, revealing the exploitation of such cults by the urban population and the lack of any meaningful division between urban and rural religious practices.

One of the most notable features of the ancient city is the powerful influ-ence which it has exercised over the development of architecture and concepts of urban form in more recent times. Since the Renaissance, quotations from classical culture and iconography have been used to validate contemporary issues. Goalen illustrates the powerful influence of the rediscovery and excava-tion of Pompeii in the 18th and 19th centuries. This transformed ideas about the ancient city and was instrumental in changing the very idea of the city in the architecture and town-planning of 19th and 20th century France. On a similar theme, Quartermaine discusses the manipulation of Roman history to validate Mussolini's imperialism and programmes of social and moral reform. Key themes from Roman history were integrated into both popular culture and public architecture. In particular, references to the Augustan period were used to validate social reforms, and the art and architecture of imperial Rome provided inspiration for his creation of a new – fascist – imperial city.

Inevitably, any series of papers of this type raises many questions as well as, it is hoped, providing some answers. The debate on the producer versus the consumer city is far from over. Despite Whittaker's optimism over the possibility of developing a globally valid theory of the ancient city, some scepticism must remain, but there are many avenues still to be explored. The ever increasing body of archaeological data and new techniques of analyzing it give us the possibility of new insights into the relation between city and territory, and into social structures and interactions within the city.

Notes

1. Finley, M. I. The ancient city: from Fustel de Coulanges to Max Weber and beyond, in *Economy and society in ancient Greece*, eds B. D. Shaw & R. P. Saller (London, 1981), pp. 3–23. (Also published in *Comparative Studies in History and Society*, **29**, 1977, pp. 305–27.)
2. *Ibid.*, p. 6; J. Burchard & O. Handlin (eds) *The historian and the city*. (Cambridge, Mass. 1963), p. 2.
3. Finley, The ancient city, pp. 12–13.
4. *Ibid.*, pp. 4–6.
5. O. Murray, Cities of reason, in *The Greek city: from Homer to Alexander*, eds O. Murray & S. R. F. Price (Oxford, 1990), pp. 1–25.
6. H. Nissen, *Italische Landeskunde* (Berlin, 1902).
7. E. Gabba, La città italica, in *Modelli di città*, ed. P. Rossi (1987), pp. 109–26; K. Lomas, The city in south-east Italy: ancient topography and the evolution of urban settlement, 600–300 BC, *Accordia Research Papers* **4**, 1993.
8. Murray, Cities of reason.
9. D. W. Engels, *Roman Corinth* (Chicago, 1990).
10. M. Weber, *Die römische Agrargeschichte* (Stuttgart, 1981), crit. edn J. Deininger (ed.) (Tübingen, 1986); M. Weber, *Agrarverhältnisse im Altertum* (Tübingen, 1909) tr. R. I. Frank as *The agrarian sociology of ancient civilizations* (London, 1976); M. Weber, *Die Stadt* (Tübingen, 1921), tr. *The city* (New York, 1958).
11. Finley, The ancient city, p. 20.
12. D. L. Clarke (ed.), *Spatial archaeology* (London, 1977); Y. Thébert, *L'urbs: espace urbain et histoire* (Paris & Rome, 1987); D. Perring, Spatial organisation and social change in Roman towns, in *City and country in the ancient world*, eds J. Rich & A. Wallace-Hadrill (London, 1991), pp. 273–93.
13. Thébert, *L'urbs*; A.Wallace-Hadrill, The social structure of the Roman house, *PBSR* **56**, 1988, 43–97.

14. On the distribution of electoral *progammata* as a tool for studying Pompeian political life, see also H. Mouritsen *Elections, magistrates and municipal elite: studies in Pompeian epigraphy* (Analecta Romana Instituti Danici, 15) (Rome1988).
15. G. Calza, La preminenza dell' "insula" nella edilizia romana, *Monumenti Antichi*, **23**, 1914 pp. 543–608.
16. W. V. Harris, *War and imperialism in republican Rome 327–70 BC* (Oxford, 1979).
17. W. V. Harris, *Rome in Etruria and Umbria* (Oxford, 1971); P. Bruun (ed.) *Studies in the Romanisation of Etruria* (Rome, 1975); P. Castren, *Ordo populusque Pompeianus: polity and society in Roman Pompeii* (Acta Inst. Romani Finlandiae, 8) (Rome, 1975); J. R. Patterson, Settlement, city and elite in Samnium and Lycia, in *City and country in the ancient world*, eds J. Rich & A. Wallace-Hadrill (London, 1991), pp. 147–68; Lomas, The city in south-east Italy.
18. J. Rich & A. Wallace-Hadrill (eds), *City and country in the ancient world*.
19. Strabo, 4.1.5.
20. Finley, The ancient city, pp. 6–7.
21. J. Rich & A. Wallace-Hadrill (eds), *City and country in the ancient world*; G. Barker & J. A. Lloyd (eds) *Roman Landscapes: archaeological survey in the Mediterranean region* (London, 1991).

1

Do theories of the ancient city matter?

C. R. Whittaker

Introduction: a plethora of books

In his recent excellent book, *Cities, capitalism and civilization*, R. J. Holton[1] says:

> The "city" appears as such a prominent feature of social life in so many contrasting cultures and historical epochs that one might have supposed the question of what all such "cities" have in common to be long settled. Yet this supposition is quite unwarranted.

The theme of more or less irredeemable confusion in the general theory of the ancient city in particular is reflected in many of the publications in recent years, which seem to have reached a crescendo in the last decade. In the last two or three years alone we have had, from Italy, Pietro Rossi (ed.) *Modelli della città* – (1987), a study of ancient and modern cities from the oriental antique to recent American; from France (though printed in Italy) the papers edited by Andreau & Hartog, *La città antica? La cité antique* – the result of a *table ronde* held in Paris in 1988 in memory of Moses Finley and published in 1991 as *Opus 1987–89*; and from Britain, out of that excellent Nottingham-Leicester stable, comes *City and country in the ancient world* (1981), edited by Rich & Wallace-Hadrill. All this is not to mention a spate of monographs like Wim Jongman's *Economy and society of Pompeii* (1988), Donald Engels's *Roman Corinth* (1990), Philippe Leveau's slightly older *Caesarea de Maurétanie* (1984) and Burnham & Wacher's *Small towns of Roman Britain* (1990).

Every one of these works I have selected for mention because they concern themselves with, or challenge, the Bücher-Sombart-Weber-Finley economic model of the consumer city. Probably there are many others that I have missed. Certainly there are others which deal with the ancient city and indirectly or to a lesser extent with its economy – works such as Gros & Torelli,

Storia della urbanistica (1988), Bedon, Chevallier & Pinon's (1988) study of urbanism in Gaul, Becker-Nielsen's *Geography of power* (1988), Patterson's *Samnites, Ligurians and Romans* (1988) and Vittinghoff's *Europäische Wirtschafts – und Sozialgeschichte* (1990). It seemed to me, therefore, that it would be helpful to review some of these more recent studies, partly to clear my own mind. I have confined myself more strictly to economic theories of the city and in doing so I have reverted to a question which I and Jean Andreau independently posed at the *table ronde* in Paris: "Do theories of the ancient city matter?" But the question and the question mark really go back to Finley's last work on *Ancient history: evidence and models*, where he voiced serious objections to Weber's theory of the Greek city.

What is striking in all the studies I have mentioned is how each begins with a ritual disclaimer that anyone can understand or even discover a respectable model for the city. Rossi[2], for example, talks of the "insuperable plurality of models". "What does the 'ancient city' mean?", asks Wallace-Hadrill,[3] and "Is it a phenomenon about which useful generalisations can be made?" In the recent Barker-Lloyd book on Roman landscapes,[4] Simon Keay's introduction to the section on towns and territories is more optimistic but claims the relationship is "only partially understood". But Rihill & Wilson quickly check any premature joy, and at the same time take a swipe at the Gordian knot, by saying it is better to disregard urban theory because of "the futility of this difficult and often sophistic literature for students of ancient society".[5]

The picture, in short, is one of confusion not unmixed with pessimism. Worshippers at the postmodernist Gallic shrines will no doubt tell us that this is one of those power-laden "metanarratives", which have become far too prescriptive, lost in their own language, and have failed to problematize their own legitimacy.[6] Or perhaps, rather, we should agree with those who tell us that obsession with "the city" is a legacy of Whig history, which associated urbanism with economic progress or the fruits of industrial capitalism; and that it was this which stimulated the great names such as Marx, Weber, Durkheim and Pirenne into believing that the city was somehow an independent phenomenon which constituted a causal factor of social change.[7]

On the other hand we can also take heart from theorists such as Abrams[8] or Wallerstein,[9] who urge urban students to transcend the urban–rural dichotomy foisted onto modern historiography by Adam Smith's stress on the importance of commerce of the towns for the improvement of the countryside; instead, modern historians are told, they should return to "the city-state writ large" – that is to the model of the ancient integrated *polis*, though with the proviso that we understand urban-rural as dramatic representations of more fundamental social relations.

Weber and the consumer city

What it is important to note in this contemporary debate is that studies in the 19th century, and especially those of Marx and Weber, were characterized by interest not so much in the city itself as in the rise of capitalism and the question of power in society. Categories such as consumer city and producer city served only to identify a particular historical function of a city in relation to this question, not to produce a general theory of the city.[10] A quite excellent survey of Weber's views on the ancient city by Hinnerk Bruhns[11] points out the "embarrassing" changes in Weber's perspective from the *Agrarverhältnisse* to the posthumous publication of *Die Stadt* after its extraction from *Economy and society*.

The pity is, in my view, that those who launch unguided missiles against the consumer city model do not follow these perspectives, since it is clear that by the time that Weber reached *Die Stadt*, which is the usual object of the attack, he had really lost the interest in the ancient city that he had shown in his earlier work. It was in the *Agrarverhältnisse* that Weber displayed his deep knowledge of relations between town and country in the ancient city, in which he stressed again and again the way the large, aristocratic families controlled political power and used it to increase their wealth by rents or by commercializing their surpluses. In *Die Stadt* his interest had shifted to the central question of why the ancient city, in contrast to the medieval city, never laid the foundations of capitalism, and it is only in this context – a fact often misunderstood by modern commentators – that he used the much over-quoted tag of *homo politicus* to distinguish the ancient citizen's incapacity to turn to rational, productive investment, as opposed to the medieval *homo economicus*.

Whether or not Weber was right about medieval man, it is a caricature of Weber's, followed in this respect by Finley's, thought to say that both denied that ancient landlords had an interest in making money or in maximizing the sale of their urban produce. Those who allege this have either not understood the context of the model or, more often, have failed to read even the translation of Weber's *The city*, described recently[12] as "one of the best-known and least-read contributions to sociology". The observation by Osborne,[13] in a most interesting study of 4th century Athens, that the rich of Athens were "heavily involved in the market" and that this goes "against firmly held modern convictions" is one such example. Another is that by Arthur,[14] who in discussing wine production in northern Campania, believes that the stamping of names of aristocrats on amphorae disproves the supposed orthodoxy of their "apparent reluctance to advertise their involvement in the mechanics of trade".

Since Osborne's paper is claimed to be a critique of Finley's rather than Weber's consumer city model, it is worth elaborating the point. On several occasions in the *Ancient economy*[15] Finley explicitly discusses "estates farmed for cash incomes" and in response to misunderstanding on exactly this score, he quotes[16] with approval the statement:

> The idea that rich landowners were not involved or interested in the profits from the produce of their land . . . is quite simply absurd.[17]

This to him, he said, was "self-evident", yet in no way support for "profit-motivated capitalist exploitation". I am unable to discover in the operations of Phainippos of Athens (whom Osborne uses as an example), whether through his sale of estate produce, or through his renting of public land or in his silver-mining operations, which were undertaken to satisfy his consumption needs, anything which undermines the consumer model, as is claimed.[18]

Wallace-Hadrill[19] in the same volume, in his discussion of elites and traders in Roman towns, correctly quotes Weber[20] that the Roman elites "were as eager for gain as any other historic class" and he usefully demonstrates how the rich were as much involved in urban as in rural property management. But I cannot see how that fact, or the letting out of such property to traders, in any way undercuts the important distinction which Weber made, in the same paragraph from which Wallace-Hadrill quoted, between the acceptable face of property investment by the rich and the unacceptable face of entrepreneurial capital profit.

The service city

One of the most explicit, detailed defences of the consumer city model in recent years has been Jongman's study of Pompeii,[21] which has sought the aid of a battery of econometric searchlights to illuminate the twilight. It is not my intention to discuss that work, but simply to say that the book has not been received with unalloyed enthusiasm everywhere. Among the more hostile reviews is that by Bruce Frier in vol. 4 of the *Journal of Roman Archaeology*, who for the second time in a review commends to our attention an "alternative model" to the consumer city of what is called the "service city", as developed by Engels in his recent book on Roman Corinth.[22]

The bare bones of the service city are relatively simply to trace and, since they will already be known to many, I shall be brief. The city-state of Corinth, comprising a population of some 100,000 persons, was maintained by a territory of some 800 km^2, of which only about a quarter was agricultural land, capable of supporting with its rural produce a maximum population of only 17,500 bodies – less than 20 per cent of the total population. The town of Corinth and Lechaion port alone, covering an area of over 700 hectares, was residence for about 80,000 persons of which no more than 1,500 landlords could have been sustained by the rents paid by the rural population. Therefore, says Engels, the city of Corinth must have earned a massive 80 per cent of its income from manufacture, trade and "services". But since Engels is not inclined to think that manufacture played a "dominant rôle" he is left with the greater part of the revenue of Corinthians to be derived from a very high level of rural food surpluses – as much as 50 per cent, he reckons, sold to foreign visitors and tourists; and above all from the dues taken from the transshipment of goods across the isthmus.

I am in no position to comment on the plausibility of Engels's guesstimates for the rural and urban population, upon which so much of the service city theory depends. But a number of his base assumptions make me uneasy. His per capita consumption figures, for instance, are double those used by other standard studies,[23] which automatically halves the hypothetical number of citizens capable of support from rural produce. The level of 50 per cent rural surpluses produced by peasants is enormously high by most modern studies[24] and Engels's argument that this is proved by the subsequent rise in levels of tax extraction in the later empire will not impress those who believe that it was precisely the impossibility of such payments which led to the problems of the later period.[25]

Furthermore, the unusually large area of 700 plus hectares for the residences of the urban population appears to have been measured by a personal "informal" site survey (p. 80) without any detailed investigation of building use.[26] In Bologna a study of the buildings of the *suburbium* has shown them to be some of the most dense and productive rural installations in the territory. In Roman Africa just such early "informal" surveys of urban sites such as Thelepte and Diana produced large urban areas of between 400 and 500 hectares, which later more scientific surveys reduced to 50–100 hectares.[27]

All those are perhaps instinctive reactions, which have nothing to do with the main point. For it is upon the huge invisible earnings of the Corinthian *diolkos* that Engels lays most stress – "the most important basis of Corinth's economy" (p. 51). So it is worth while trying to get some idea of the scale of the operation and how far it really could have provided earnings for 80,000 townsmen. A minimum *per diem* wage of HS 3 implies an annual salary bill of HS 90 million (80,000 × 3 × 365), which, as a hypothetical 10 per cent *ad valorem* service charge, implies a volume of trading goods to the tune of HS 900 million p.a. Is that credible?

The largest known bulk commodity trade in the ancient world is the export of wine between Italy and Spain/Gaul in the late republic, identified by Tchernia[28] and estimated on the basis of shipwrecks to have been 100,000 hectolitres p.a. = *c.* 450,000 amphorae. Obviously wine varied enormously in quality and therefore price – in the bar at Pompeii by a factor of four and more for luxury wines, which were relatively rare. But let us accept figures of between 8 and 15 HS per amphora for standard new wines.[29] The wholesale value of the Italian wine export would on this calculation have been valued at between HS 3.5 million and 7 million p.a. Even if all the wine was top quality at the highest known price of HS 88 per amphora the value of HS 35 million is nowhere near our hypothetical HS 900 million cargo. Double the figure for a return cargo of an improbable equally valuable commodity, double the *ad valorem* service charge to 20 per cent and we are still at a figure far short of the required revenue.

Indeed, in order to collect the high revenue required by Engels's figures, the Corinthians would have needed to transport so many ships each day that they could hardly have been fitted on the *diolkos*. I lay no store, of course, by the accuracy of my figures but – as it is the fashion to say these days – they provide orders of magnitude, which really means comforting, pseudo-mathematical reasons for rejecting what instinctively we could say was an implausible idea.

There is, of course, nothing impossible about a major commercial port in the ancient world having a population of 100,000 or more and it compares with the quarter of a million often supposed for cities such as Alexandria, Antioch and Carthage. Theories of the consumer city have never excluded such exceptions. Ironically Marx, whom Engels attacks, had made this point precisely.[30] But Carthage, about which I shall say more in a minute, had a massive territory and Antioch's rich hinterland is usually reckoned to have provided for its large population.[31] Alexandria – if we can trust Diodorus' figure of 300,000 – was wholly exceptional in the extraordinary wealth of the oriental luxury trade which was conducted by merchants from that city.

But if we accept the proposition that Corinth earned unusually high invisibles from its services, which is not an unreasonable supposition, even if nothing like as high as those suggested by Engels, can we go on to say that "there were scores of populous city-states with geographic locations along the coast similar to Corinth"?[32] In other words, is this really an economic model which could be applied, say, to Pompeii?

This still leaves us, however, with the puzzle from which Engels began of how a poor and rocky territory such as Corinth's could have sustained a relatively large urban population. The answer, I am convinced, lies partly in the relationship between territoriality and citizenship, which will crop up again later. Although Alexandria had virtually no *chora*, this did not preclude Alexandrians from owning quite extensive amounts of land in other regions. In Theadelphia, for instance, in the 1st century AD, more than two-thirds of the vineyards and garden lands were owned by Romans and Alexandrians. Leveau's studies around the Étang de Berre in Provence have found evidence that rich villas in the territory of Arles were owned by Aixois.[33]

Similar examples of *pagi* communities detached from the *territorium* have long been known in Africa belonging, significantly, to Carthaginians. They are thought to have primarily been means of economic control by the metropolis over the surrounding *civitates*[34] but they represent property owning elites receiving revenues from lands beyond the city-state in which they lived – Carthage, a port city like Corinth, which earned high dues from its services. As it happens we do have at least one similar example from Corinth of a very rich decurion with land in other territories – Cn. Claudius Pulcher with estates in Epidamnus and, perhaps, Troezen, whom Plutarch admired.[35] My conclusion is that the service city, as a new model, is less satisfactory than the consumer city.

La cité organisatrice

Another alternative to the consumer city has been proposed by Leveau and before him by Wacher in the form of "la cité organisatrice",[36] which, despite criticism,[37] Leveau continues to maintain and to clarify. The crux of his argument lies in the proposition that Romanization of the provinces brought with it a Roman mode of exploitation of the land around the newly formed *civitates* and *municipia* centres – more precisely through the villas where Roman elites farmed their estates and which were imposed upon the countryside.[38]

With all this I have no quarrel in the sense that villas became an instrument in the hands of the Romanizing elite to extract surpluses from the rural hinterland, although studies such as that by Hingley[39] show that we have as yet only a very imperfect knowledge of the difference between villa and non-villa or native establishments in the provinces. There is still even a good deal of argument about whether *civitas* capitals really did attract villas or whether *vici* centres exercised an equal pull, although the most recent, systematic analysis in Britain confirms that the older theory was true.[40] That must mean that the "organizing rôle" of the elites, therefore, was largely social and political – with an economic facet, to be sure, in the sense that production of cash crops became commoner on large estates.

But what has this to do with urban production and capital formation? In his most recent contribution to the debate, Leveau agrees that "the Roman provincial city certainly lived off rural rent".[41] But, he adds, we must go further. Urban aristocracies had management skills which created rural wealth as well as exploited it.

Again it is hard to quarrel with the statement. But it in no way alters the fact that maintenance of the civic centres depended almost entirely upon this increased rural wealth and in the end what is demonstrated is the ambiguity between town and country: the villa was an urban phenomenon yet a rural investment. Is this not exactly what Weber's consumer city model proposed? "Roman villas", said Weber in the *Agrarverhältnisse*, "brought with them methods of cultivation which were unquestionably more advanced than the indigenous traditions." But Weber goes on to say that the expansion of country estates in this way resulted in "the disarming of the cities . . . which meant the loss of all those opportunities for profit which depended on the cities and promoted capitalism".[42] It is Weber's cola which is crucial to the debate about the economy of the town. In terms of understanding the economic balance between town and country, "la cité organisatrice" was less important than "la villa productrice", since one could and did survive without the other.

Although the cities benefited financially from the villa "boom" it is a different and debatable question whether this new urban wealth brought material benefits to the rural population. But it has some relevance to the theory of the "organizer city" and is therefore worth mentioning here. While it may be correct that the commercialization of rural surpluses enriched the countryside overall,[43] it does not follow that the *rustici* benefited. Let me explain what I mean in a rather roundabout way.

What is being brought increasingly into focus through recent excellent studies of Romanization, such as those by Millett and Woolf,[44] is the social and political rôle of urbanization – or, rather, of the *civitas-municipia* organization. They stress that we should not so readily accept the traditional theory that these institutions were deliberately fostered by Rome to deal with provincial administration; economic and administrative explanations of town foundations are firmly rejected in favour of a theory of cultural choice: a choice made by consciously Romanizing elites competing for the favours and rewards of patronage.

Attractive as I find these explanations, they contrast quite sharply with the views of a number of scholars on the effect of Romanization in certain parts of Italy. The impact of Rome on Umbria and pre-Apennine Campania accelerated the natural progress towards urban structures: but in Lucania and Apulia it interrupted the process by artificial foundations, which we must regard as instruments of Roman conquest.[45] Gabba has for a number of years argued that the artificial urbanization of the Centro-Sud of Italy was "un fatto politico-amministrativo", which ultimately led to decline, since it did not correspond with any real needs.[46]

I do not have enough expertise to give a satisfactory resolution to these contrasting theories and I shall not spend long on them, since they concern the function of the whole *civitas* more than urbanization itself. But there is an important economic dimension to the debate. I note that contributions by British studies of Italian urbanization take a rather more cultural view, nearer to the Millett-Woolf view than those of the Italians. In Samnium, for example, we are told how the local elite transferred their attention from the *vicus-pagus* centres to the new *municipia*, while simultaneously competing for patronage links with Roman politicians and emperors.[47] The effect, so it is argued, was vastly to increase the landholdings of the rich and to drive the poor off the land into banditry, emigration or, perhaps, into the towns. The poor agricultural workers, in other words, disappear. The last suggestion I find puzzling, although the same scenario is now also suggested for the Ager Falernus.[48] I wonder whether, as has already been suggested in the Ager Tarraconensis survey for a similar phenomenon, this is not perhaps a case where extreme poverty simply gives the impression of an archaeological "disappearance". The general trend in all Italian surveys, such as those of Tuscia or in the Albegna valley, is to rediscover more and more of the population in the countryside.[49]

Before I leave the debate on imposed or voluntary urbanism, it is worth drawing attention to a recent discussion on the Tabula Banasitana, which has some relevance to the discussion.[50] This has revived the observations made by Dessau on the function of attribution as a major instrument of administration in Roman North Africa. The purpose was to attach to *civitas* centres seminomadic *nationes* and *gentes* such as the Numidae, the Cinithii and (at Banasa) the Zegrenses who inhabited peripheral zones – called *provinciae* on the inscription – beyond the territory of the *civitas*. The parallels with the Tabula Clesiana from Trento in north Italy are obvious.

Although most of this is irrelevant to the strictly economic debate on town and country, it both illustrates the administrative functions of the *civitas* and, in so far as it offered rewards to the *principes gentis*, provides an example of the channels towards Romanization on offer to competing native elites, who were thereby detached economically and socially from their rural *gentiles*. The next stage was their installation in rural villas around the *civitas* centres and a change in the relations of production, which parallels the Italian examples and, perhaps also, the changes in Lycia and Arcadia.[51] It is not unlike the radical social transformation, and consequent deterioration in clansmen's land rights, which took place in the Scottish Highlands after Culloden, which was triggered, in part at least, by the attractions of English city life and politics for the highland chiefs and by their desire to extract greater dues from the land to pay for their new social opportunities.[52] "The highland chiefs", said Dr Johnson, "should not be allowed to go further south than Aberdeen."

The processor city

Last but far from least, I come to the tax and trade cycle, in which the towns through urban manufacturers are alleged to play a pivotal rôle as "processors" in the transfer of cash from state consumers to rural producers.[53] There is no need to elaborate on what is well known to all, although I only recently discovered that the cycle was foreshadowed 200 years ago by Gibbon:[54]

> The provinces would soon have been exhausted of their wealth if the manufacturers and consumers of luxury had not insensibly restored to the industrious subjects the sums which were extracted from them by the arms and authority of Rome. As long as the circulation was confined to the bounds of the empire, it impressed the political machine with a new degree of activity.

The strength of the model of the processor city is its simplicity and it continues to command respect and credibility.[55]

I shall not repeat in detail what I have already said in print about the value of the model,[56] which depends entirely upon the medium in which taxes were levied and the modes of commercialization of rural surpluses – neither of which can be proved. I am now more inclined than I was to believe that sale or supply of rural produce to the military and imperial sector was often transacted directly without the agency of the towns or urban traders. The recent work on *annona militaris* in Spain[57] seems to demonstrate that individual military units on the Rhine negotiated with estates for their own oil contracts, as apparently did the Moesian unit recorded on Hunt's Pridianum, (P. Lond 2851), which sent its supply officers to Gaul for clothing and corn.

Certainly the processor-town model offers no explanation for the doubling of numbers of towns in Italy under the empire, while the country was tax free; nor for their decline in the later empire after Diocletian's imposition of tax – when, on the contrary, the new Trinitapolis inscription shows a revival of the administrative function of the *pagi* in the fiscal regime.[58]

But the major objection to the processor model is that the rôle of the town in marketing and manufacture is overshadowed by the villa and the village (confusingly, for these arguments, sometimes called "small town"). It is precisely this ambiguity between town and rural production which led me to question the value of the consumer city model. The point is made now with great clarity by the recent study of "small towns" in Britain, with many examples of manufacturing and extractive activities in the *vici*[59] – to which we ought to add the very considerable interest being shown in oriental villages, which always in antiquity seemed to have had a more explicit proto-urban function while remaining firmly rural in status and definition.[60]

But however much we may liken these centres to urban "cores", with advanced economic and specialist rôles, they remain incontrovertibly rural in context. "Most small towns", we are told, "were closely connected with agricultural production, even those with an apparently industrial base. Braintree, Brampton, Godmanchester, all show signs of field systems and agriculture in association with craftsmen, and even a huge pottery production site such as Water Newton is described as "workshops . . . everywhere interspersed with agricultural features and a number of substantial extra-mural houses or villas".[61] Whether or not, therefore, the industrial or craft surpluses of the *civitas* – that is, the town together with its territory – were sufficient to earn foreign currency, as was surely true in some cases, the rôle of the urban centre as "processor" was negligible. *Vici* were not part of the town. Ideologically, ancient writers such as Strabo and Tacitus are clear that those who lived *kata komas* were *agrioi* (Strabo, 3.4.13); only barbarians lived in scattered houses and villages (Tac. *Germ.* 16).

The same is true of villas, whose industrial or craft activities in spinning, weaving, ceramics and metal work are too well known to need further discussion. A recent survey of Gallic production of amphorae finds the majority on villa sites. A study of north Campania shows that amphora kilns moved progressively closer to villa production sites as the empire progressed. In the Tunisian Sahel kilns have been found in both urban and rural villa contexts.[62] The rich, in short, were indiscriminate about the precise location of their productive activities, and the distinction between urban and rural production is irrelevant economically. Production of these rural manufactures did not disappear as towns grew. On the contrary, the Monte Forco rural habitations in the Ager Capenas have iron clinker during the urban boom of the Augustan period.[63] The same is true of estates around Piacenza and Bologna which indicate "real industrial production".[64] We hardly needed archaeology to confirm what Varro had already told us, that the rich owners of *latifundia* had domestics as smiths and other necessary artisans, such as doctors and fullers (*RR* 1.16.4). But the essential point is that the location of the production was irrelevant for the GPD of the *civitas*.

The ambiguity of the urban phenomenon of *vici* and villas in a rural setting is matched by the perspective from the other end of the telescope. If, following Wallace-Hadrill's splendid new study of households and "housefulls" in Pompeii,[65] the great majority of urban inhabitants were attached to a quite small number of "big" men, either through *familia*, employee or client status, the economic consequences are potentially enormous. I take it for granted that the majority, if not all, of the *patresfamiliae* were the same as the great villa and estate owners of the territory, as the studies of Cherchel and of Pompeii suggest, though cannot prove. The implication is inescapable. A large part of the urban households were fed and clothed by surpluses supplied direct from the rural settlements.

This does not, of course, exclude exchange and market transactions. We cannot wipe out the 900 odd "commercial" premises of Pompeii attached to the big households and it is impossible to be sure of the economic relationship between *paterfamilias* and client. But it must surely diminish the rôle of the market and also mean that a large part of the profits of petty production and sales returned to the landowners in rents. Once again it is the complete intermeshing of urban and rural property and production which makes me unsure of the usefulness (rather than the correctness) of the consumer city model to illuminate this aspect. After Trimalchio's friend Niceros fell in love with the beautiful wife of the innkeeper in his town, he seized his chance to court her when her husband died "out on the estate" – *ad villam* (Petronius, *Sat.* 61). Does this make the family urban or rural?

Theories and problems of the economic city

I end, however, on a more positive note with what remains for me a central paradox of the urban-rural relationship. It is implied in Weber's phrase about "the disarming of the cities", which seems to me insufficiently brought out by the consumer city model. I refer to the means and extent to which the towns *qua* towns benefited economically from the rural surpluses and rural activities of the majority of their citizens. Since the countryman did not pay a land tax to the town but only to the state,[66] the most direct form of rural revenue came from the rents of *ager publicus* and from the sales taxes on urban or rural markets and fairs, of which I have no doubt that the former was by far the more important, except perhaps in large ports. Cicero's example of Atella's income describes the public land rent as *municipii fortunas omnes* (*Fam.* 13.7) and we have only to think of the serious difficulties suffered by the cities when this source was cut off.[67]

We must not forget, too, that the city *curiales* could and did transfer *munera* to the *vici* and *pagi*, such as the obligation to provide transport services (*vecturae*), supplies (*copiae*), wood (*ligna*) and straw (*stramenta*), although the references to these in the *agrimensores* (Thulin, 45; 129) make it clear that some of them were state services rather than for the benefit of the city.[68]

By far the largest part of a town's income, however, came indirectly from the land through *summa honoraria* and *munera* liturgies paid by the landowning classes, which was money that ultimately came from the rural workers and from the very considerable sums which the decurion class "siphoned off" in collecting state taxes from the countryside. The fact that such *munera* were also undertaken at a village and district level does not alter that fact.

So far this all looks like fairly straightforward urban exploitation in accord with the consumption model. But what are less clearly urban assets are many of the larger estates of the *territorium*. As a crude idea of the extent of land we are talking about, we can suggest that senatorial, equestrian and curial elites – that is, about 3 per cent of the population – earned something like 25 per cent of aggregate personal incomes, which is fairly well in line with other pre-industrial communities,[69] though we need to add in to this figure the quite considerable area of imperial property. Allowing for tenancies and agencies, that probably means that these urban elites owned about 50 per cent or more of the assets (mainly in land) and commanded far the greater part of disposable incomes. This gap between the rich and the poor only increased as the empire progressed.

The question is to what extent such an important slice of assets and incomes benefited the towns in whose territories they lay. In other words, how did their surplus produce pass through the urban market and what profits did they provide for the local town through payment of dues or by earning hard currency? The answer on many occasions, and particularly in the case of imperial, senatorial and equestrian property owners, seems to have been very little. It was this fact which led Andreau at the Paris *table ronde* to question the relevance of the town as a framework for the study of Roman economic life.[70] The massive export of wine in the late republic from the Ager Cosanus, for instance, developed at a time when the town itself was virtually abandoned, although the port and fisheries continued to be used.[71] By the end of the 1st century BC rich north Etruscan villas such as those which once belonged to the Sestii and the Ahenobarbi had their own private ports along the coastal lagoons or up the Albegna valley, and had no need to use the urban ports.[72]

Nor did the towns provide the market-place for transactions. Pliny's deal for his grape harvest with the *negotiatores* took place on his estate (*Ep.* 8.2) and was almost certainly bound up with his own personal patronage relations.[73] We know, of course, that Pliny also shipped his produce directly to Rome down the Tiber from one of his estates (*Ep.* 6.1). In Trimalchio's account of how he decided to build his own ships and sell his produce in Rome, no town comes into the narrative (Petronius, *Sat.* 76). From the provinces rich estate owners sold the produce of their estates through their own agents, as Libanius did from Antioch to Apamea (*Ep.* 133–6) or to Cilicia (*Ep.* 709), without recourse to the local urban market. Jongman's estimate that the estates of Pompeii produced only for the domestic market is, I think, mistaken not just because amphorae from Oplontis villa B have been discovered off the Porquerolles in southern France but also because estates such as those belonging to Agrippa Postumus (later imperial) or to Poppaea Sabina (*figlinae*) almost certainly lay outside the orbit of the local urban centre.[74]

The changes visible in the Ager Cosanus reflect a general detachment of the villas, at least the villas of the very rich, from the urban market economy – a fact which could be responsible for the difficulties archaeologists experience in predicting urban or village markets by central place theory, whether in Italy or in the provinces.[75] You can see the attitude in Palladius, when he says that the full range of craftsmen should be retained on the estate "so that the reason for desiring the city does not divert countrymen" (1.6.2). This is not just a late Roman development, since Varro, citing Saserna, says that rural workers were discouraged from using the urban market "for fear they walk around on working days as though on holidays" (*RR* 1.16.5).

Direct purchase from rich villa estates "from which you can buy cheaply all you need on the farm" (Varro, *RR* 1.16.3), or exchange between them, was apparently common in the late republic. And we all know Pliny's letter (*Ep.* 5.4) describing the opposition by the town of Vicetia to the rich senator, Bellicius Sollers (of Verona, note), holding a periodic market on his estate in its territory. Though the senate refused Sollers permission on this occasion, they did not always do so and the practice is thought to have become more common as the empire progressed, although this theory is not, as far as I can see, based on much hard evidence (e.g. Suet. *Claud.* 12 – Claudius, CIL VIII. 270 – saltus Beguensis).[76] It may well be correct, given what was probably a rather low level of market tax, that the main damage done to cities would have been to increase their difficulty in providing *annona*, rather than the loss of their revenue.[77] Two important functions of the estate *nundinae*, in the later empire, at least, were as labour exchanges and centres of tax collection, both of them usurping the rôle of the urban centre.[78]

It was, as we know, quite common for wealthy proprietors to own whole villages, including presumably the village market, even close to Rome (Strabo, 5.3.2). It was precisely this circumstance that led to the *controversiae agrorum* recorded by the *agrimensores* over the allocation of *munera* involving estates of both *privati* and the emperor (Thulin, 46). There seems little doubt that it was this that led to the phenomenon observed recently in eastern Spain, where the growth of luxury villas coincided with their withdrawal from the urban market.[79] These were the "alternative power-structures" that recent studies talk about, which underlay the formal urban–rural institutions of Italy.[80]

The paradox lies in the fact that the greater the surpluses of the villa economy, the greater the possibilities for the urban market; but also the greater the probabilities that the wealthy opted out of the urban framework. If the disposable cash income of the majority of *rustici* was minimal and the rich ceased to buy or sell in the urban market, the system could hold out only as long as the liturgies of the town were paid and the public rents were collected. But, as we all know, in the later empire that all came under strain. The *potentiores* usurped the public land from the town, while at the same time the emperors permitted a massive increase in immunities to *honorati* and clerics from urban *munera*. The "ruralization of the city" – to use Marx's phrase[81] – was complete.

This paper began by asking whether theories of the ancient city matter. The answer is, of course they do. Weber's model of the consumer city, for all its faults, is far more illuminating than any alternative economic theory. But there is a danger that familiarity with the debate leads to boredom, as though it did not matter any longer. And so, as we have seen, all sorts of misunderstandings and errors creep in about the fundamental nature of the ancient economy and unconsciously there is a drift back to the bad old ways when huge trade, industry and capital formations were discovered in every petty street-corner workshop of Roman towns.

So why then do I think urban economic theories unsatisfactory, including even Weber's consumer city? The reasons are the same as those which caused Weber himself to lose interest in the consumer city when he came to write *Die Stadt*: because of the ambiguity of spatial distinctions in the ancient city between the *pars urbana* and the *pars rustica*; because of the indifference of a specifically economic relationship between urban and rural; but above all because the study of cities is only an imperfect way of studying the operations of power in society.

Notes

1. R. J. Holton, *Cities, capitalism and civilization* (London, 1988), p. 14.
2. P. Rossi, *Modelli di città* (Turin, 1987), p. xix
3. Wallace-Hadrill's introduction to *City and country in the ancient world*, eds J. Rich & A. Wallace-Hadrill, (London, 1991), p. xii
4 G. Barker & J. Lloyd (eds), *Roman landscapes: archaeological survey in the Mediterranean region* (archaeological monograph of the British School at Rome) (London, 1991) p. 77.
5. T. E. Rihill & A. G. Wilson, Modelling settlement structures in ancient Greece: new approaches to the polis, in *City and country in the ancient world*, eds J. Rich & A. Wallace-Hadrill (London, 1991) pp. 59–95. In so far as I understand their mathematical modelling of the city "as a focus of social intervention", they reproduce

yet another version of central place theory which has often been declared unsatisfactory (cf. n. 75 below).

6. Cf. J. Lyotard, *The postmodern condition* (Minneapolis, 1990), pp. xxiv.

7. Holton, *Cities, capitalism and civilisation*, p. 19.

8. P. Abrams, Towns and economic growth: some theories and problems in *Towns in societies: essays in economic history and historical sociology* eds P. Abrams & E. A. Wrigley (Cambridge, 1978), p.10.

9. I. Wallerstein, Cities in socialist theory, *International Journal of Urban and Regional Research*, **8**, 1984, p. 71.

10. B. Elliott & D. MacCrone, *The city: patterns of domination and conflict* (London, 1982) p. 34.

11. H. Bruhns, La cité antique de Max Weber, in *La città antica? La cité antique*, eds J. Andreau & F. Hartog, *Opus*, **6–8** (1987–89), pp. 29–42.

12. M. Weber, *The city* (tr. of *Die Stadt*, eds D. Martindale & G. Neuwirth) (New York & London, 1958); Elliott & MacCrone, *The city: patterns of domination and conflict*, p. 33.

13 R. Osborne, Pride and prejudice, sense and subsistance: exchange and society in the Greek city, in *City and country in the ancient world*, eds Rich & Wallace-Hadrill, pp. 133–5.

14. P. Arthur, Territories, wine and wealth: Suessa Aurunca, Sinuessa, Minturnae and the ager Falernus, in *Roman landscapes*, eds Barker & Lloyd, p. 157.

15. M. I. Finley, *The ancient economy* (London, 1985), pp. 107, 109.

16. Finley, *The ancient economy*, pp. 188–9.

17. C. R. Whittaker, Late Roman trade and traders, in *Trade in the ancient economy*, eds P. Garnsey *et al.* (London, 1983), p. 173.

18. As Wallace-Hadrill claims in Rich & Wallace-Hadrill, *City and country in the ancient world*, p. xv.

19. *Ibid.*

20. Weber, *The city*, p. 155.

21. W. Jongman, *The economy and society of Pompeii* (Amsterdam, 1988).

22. D. W. Engels, *Roman Corinth* (Chicago, 1990).

23. E.g., P. D. A. Garnsey, *Famine and food supply in the Graeco-Roman world* (Cambridge, 1988), pp. 191–2.

24. See e.g. R. W. Goldsmith, An estimate of the size and structure of the national product of the early Roman empire, *Review of Income and Wealth* **30**, 1984, p. 275: my estimate is that rural workers had a per capita income of about HS 200 average p.a. of which, following Goldsmith, HS 130 was needed for food and the rest for rent/tax, clothes, durables, etc.

25. C. R. Whittaker, Inflation and the economy in the 4th century AD, in *Imperial revenue, expenditure and monetary policy in the 4th century AD* (BAR Int. Ser. 76), C. E. King, (Oxford, 1980), pp. 1–22.

26. I have assumed, in the absence of any discussion by Engels, that no such investigation was possible.

27. Bologna – R. Scagliarini, Bologna (Bononia) and its suburban territory, in *Roman landscapes*, eds Barker & Lloyd, pp. 88–95; Africa – R. Duncan-Jones, *The economy of the Roman empire* (Cambridge, 1974).

28. A. Tchernia, Italian wine in Gaul at the end of the republic, in *Trade in the ancient economy*, P. Garnsey *et al.* (London, 1983), pp. 87–104.

29. A. Tchernia, *Le vin de l'Italie romaine* (Rome, 1986), p. 36; Duncan-Jones, *The economy of the Roman empire*, p. 46.

30. M. I. Finley, The ancient city: from Fustel de Coulanges to Max Weber and beyond, in *Economy and society in ancient Greece,* eds B. D. Shaw & R. P. Saller (London, 1981), p. 18.

31 W. Liebeshuetz, *Antioch* (Oxford, 1972).

32. Engels, *Roman Corinth*, p. 33. E. might have cited London in his support. But London is complicated by the notorious problem of what territory, if any, it possessed, or whether it remained within the territory of the Cantii: R. Merrifield, *London: city of the Romans* (London, 1983), p. 133–5

33. R. MacMullen, *Roman social relations 50 BC to AD 284* (New Haven, Conn. & London, 1974), p. 20; Ph. Leveau, La ville antique et l'organisation de l'espace rurale: villa, ville, village, *Annales ESC* 4, 1983, 920–42.

34. J. Gascou, Y avait-il un pagus carthaginois à Thuburbo Maius? *Ant. Afr.* **24**, 1988, pp. 67–80.

35. B. D. Meritt, *Corinth vol. VIII, Part I, Greek inscriptions, 1896–1927* (Cambridge, Mass., 1931), nos. 80–83.

36. J. Wacher, *The towns of Roman Britain* (London, 1974), pp. 71–2; Ph. Leveau & Chr. Goudineau, La ville antique, ville de consomation, *Etudes rurales* **89–91**, 1983, 275–89.

37. From, amongst others, C. R. Whittaker, The consumer city revisited: the vicus and the city, *JRA* **3**, 1990, pp. 110–18, and Goudineau in Leaveau & Goudineau, La ville antique.

38. *Ibid.*

39. R. Hingley, *Rural settlement in Roman Britain* (London, 1989).

40. I. Hodder & M. Millett, Romano-British villas and towns: a systematic analysis, *World Archaeology* **12**, 1980, pp. 69–76; M. Millett, *The Romanization of Britain* (Cambridge, 1990), p. 192; contra B. C. Burnham & J. Wacher, *The "small towns" of Roman Britain* (London, 1990), p. 44. Hingley, *Rural settlement in Roman Britain*, pp. 118–20, is neutral.

41. Ph. Leveau, La ville romaine et son espace rural. Contribution de l'archéologie à la réflection sur la cité antique, in *La città antica? La cité antique*, eds Andreau & Hartog, p. 93.

42. M. Weber, *The agrarian sociology of ancient civilisations*, tr. R. I. Frank (London, 1976), pp. 359–60; cf. Finley, The ancient city, p. 17, which accepts and summarizes W.'s argument.

43. L. Cracco Ruggini, La città romana dell'età imperiale, in *Modelli di città*, ed Rossi, p. 147.

44. M. Millett, Romanization: historical issues and archaeological interpretations, in *The early Roman Empire in the West*, eds T. F. C. Blagg & M. Millett, (Oxford, 1990), 35–41, and Millett, *The Romanization of Britain*; G. Woolf (unpublished PhD thesis, Cambridge 1991).

45. P. Gros & M. Torelli, *Storia dell'urbanistica: il mondo romano.* (Bari, 1988), p. 59.

46. E. Gabba, La città italica, in *Modelli di città*, ed Rossi, p. 121, with references to earlier articles.

47. J. R. Patterson, Settlement, city and elite in Samnium and Lycia, in *City and country in the ancient world*, eds Rich & Wallace-Hadrill, pp. 147–68; J. Lloyd, Farming the highlands: Samnium and Arcadia in the Hellenistic and early Roman imperial peri-

ods, in *Roman landscapes*, eds Barker & Lloyd, pp. 180–93.

48. P. Arthur, Territories, wine and wealth: Suessa Aurunca, Sinuessa, Minturnae and the ager Falernus, in *Roman landscapes*, eds Barker & Lloyd.

49. Ager Tarraconensis – M. Millett, Roman towns and their territories: an archaeological perspective, in *City and country in the ancient world*, eds Rich & Wallace-Hadrill, p. 182; Italy – Lloyd's conclusions in Barker & Lloyd (eds), *Roman lanscapes*, p. 236.

50. M. Christol, Rome et les tribus indigènes en Mauretanie Tingitane, *L'Africa Romana* 5, 1988, 305–37; I have adopted this idea as a result of private correspondence with Ph. Leveau. But since I wrote this paper, Christol's interpretation of the term *provincia* has been challenged by J. Gascou, *Ant. Afr.* **28**, 1992, pp. 161–72.

51. Patterson, Settlement, city and elite in Samnium and Lycia; Lloyd, Farming the highlands.

52. E. R. Cregeen, The changing rôle of the House of Argyll in the Scottish Highlands, in *History and social anthropology*, ed. I. M. Lewis (ASA Monograph, 7) (London, 1968).

53. K. Hopkins, Taxes and trade in the Roman empire, *JRS* 70, 1980, pp. 101–25.

54. E. Gibbon, *The history of the decline and fall of the Roman Empire*, 12 vols (London, 1819) pp. 53–4; I am grateful to A. Avidov for drawing my attention to this passage.

55. E.g. Rich & Wallace-Hadrill, *City and country in the ancient world*, p. xv; Hingley, *Rural settlement in Roman Britain*, p. 9.

56. The consumer city revisited.

57. J. Remesal Rodriguez, *La annona militaris y la exportación de aceite bético a Germania* (Madrid, 1986).

58. A. Giardina & F. Grelle, La tavola di Trinitapoli: una nuova costituzione di Valentiniano I, *MEFR* **95**, 1983, 249–303; cf. M. Frederiksen, Changes in the patterns of settlements, in *Hellenismus in Mittelitalien*, ed P. Zanker (Kolloqium, 1974) (Göttingen, 1976), vol ii, p. 355, for other references to taxes and the late empire *pagus*.

59. Burnham & Wacher, *The "small towns" of Roman Britain*.

60. See e.g. G. M. Harper, Village administration in the Roman province of Syria, *YCS* 1, 1928, pp. 105–68; E. Frézouls (ed.), *Sociétés urbaines, sociétés rurales dans l'Asie mineure et la Syrie hellénistique et romaine* (Strasbourg, 1987).

61. Burnham & Wacher, *The "small towns" of Roman Britain*, pp. 5, 52.

62. Gaul – F. Laubenheimer, Les amphores gauloises sous l'empire: recherches nouvelles sur leur production et leur chronologie, in *Amphores romaines et histoire économique*, eds Lenoir *et al.* (EFR, 114; Rome, 1989) pp. 105–138; Campania – Arthur, Territories, wine and wealth; Tunisia – D. P. S. Peacock, F. Bejaoui, N. Belazreg, Roman amphora production in the Sahel (Tunisia), in *Amphores romaines et histoire économique*, eds Lenoir *et al.* (Rome, 1989), pp. 179–222.

63. Lloyd's conclusions in Barker & Lloyd, *Roman landscapes*, p. 236.

64. P. L. Dell'Aglio & G. Marchetti, Settlement patterns and agrarian structures of the Roman period in the territory of Piacenza, in *Roman landscapes*, eds G. Barker & J. Lloyd, pp. 160–68; Scagliarini, Bologna and its suburban territory.

65. A. Wallace-Hadrill, Houses and households: sampling Pompeii and Herculaneum, in *Marriage, divorce and children in ancient Rome*, ed. B. Rawson (Oxford, 1991), pp. 191–227.

66. M. Corbier, City, territory and taxation, in *City and country in the ancient world*,

eds Rich & Wallace-Hadrill, 211–39.

67. A. H. M. Jones, *The later Roman empire* (Oxford, 1964), pp. 131, 732–3, says officially by Constantine, but Millar, Italy and the Roman Empire: Augustus to Constantine, *Phoenix* 40, 1986, p. 305, shows that the usurpation by decurions was illegal until later in the 4th century.
68. Corbier, City, territory and taxation, p. 234.
69. Goldsmith, An estimate of the national product of the early Roman empire, p. 278.
70. J. Andreau, La cité antique et la vie économique, in *La città antica? La cité antique,* eds J. Andreau & F. Hartog (1987–89), pp. 175–85.
71. F. E. Brown, *Cosa: the making of a Roman town* (Ann Arbor, Mich, 1980), pp. 73–5; A. D. McCann, *The Roman port and fishery of Cosa* (Princeton, NJ, 1987), pp. 26–7, 32.
72. I. Attolini *et al*, Political geography and productive geography between the valleys of the Albegna and the Fiora in northern Etruria, in *Roman landscapes,* eds Barker & Lloyd, pp. 142–52.
73. A. Tchernia, Encore sur les modèles économiques et les amphores, in *Amphores romaines et histoire économique,* eds Lenoir *et al.*, pp. 529–36.
74. Jongman, *The economy and society of Pompeii*, p. 118; J. d'Arms, Rapporti socioeconomici fra città e territorio nella prima età imperiale, in *Il territorio di Aquileia nell' antichità* (Antichità Alto-Adriatice, 15; Udine, 1979), vol. ii, p. 78.
75. Lloyd, *Farming the highlands*, p. 234; Millett, Town and country, p. 428.
76. Ruggini, La città romana dell'età imperiale, p. 148.
77. E. Gabba, Mercati et fiere nell' Italia romana, *SCO* 24, 1975, p. 158.
78. B. D. Shaw, Rural periodic markets in Roman North Africa as mechanisms of social integration and control, *Research in Economic Anthropology* 2, 1979, 91–117.
79. S. Keay, The ager Tarraconensis in the late empire: a model for the economic relationship of town and country in eastern Spain, in *Roman landscapes*, eds Barker & Lloyd, p. 84.
80. Millar, Italy and the Roman empire.
81. K. Marx, *Grundrisse* (tr. M. Nicolaus) (London, 1973), p. 479.

2

The limits of the ancient city and the evolution of the medieval city in the thought of Max Weber

L. Capogrossi Colognesi

Credit should be given to two great scholars, Moses Finley and Arnaldo Momigliano, for having drawn our attention to the work of Max Weber specifically devoted to the history of the ancient world.[1] It is above all because of the influence of Momigliano that the first of Weber's essays, the *Roman agrarian history* (1891), is now generally regarded as less important than his later *Agrarian relations in antiquity*, published in the third edition of the *Handwörterbuch der Staatswissenschaften* (1909).[2]

With regard to this later work of 1909, Momigliano himself observed how Weber's vision expands and its focal point shifts: it is "the general knowledge of social evolution which guides us in our interpretation of documents specifically concerned with agricultural history". On the other hand, in the earlier *Roman agrarian history* Weber had used legal documents as evidence to determine the characteristic agricultural structures of ancient Rome.

Whereas the 1891 essay was focused on the history of ancient agriculture and the resulting socio-economic relations, in that of 1909 greater stress was laid on the history of the city-state and its subsequent evolution, above all in the case of Greece and Rome.[3] By 1909, Weber had arrived at an understanding of the institutional and economic forms on which he based his typology of the ancient city, in addition to the comparative analysis – *per differentiam* – of other models of cities, principally that of the medieval city.[4]

The starting point of Weber's 1909 essay would appear to support my statement. Here we should remember that from the end of the 1890s, and under the growing influence of Eduard Meyer, Weber's reflections on the origins of Greek and Roman political structures increasingly tended to replace the model of agrarian community, so important in his early work of 1891, with that of city feudalism.[5]

The *polis* had its origin in the emergence of a feudal aristocracy, which dominated the surrounding country from its new urban settlements, in contrast to the individualist and agricultural nature of medieval feudalism.

The medieval city also enjoyed a balanced, steady development of its own industry through its relationship with the outside environment in the form of economic activities and military–political rôles. These two types of relations are completely opposed to those which characterized the ancient city-state. The medieval city, in fact, developed in a political context which was more widely defined both in relation to larger – even if comparatively weak – territorial powers, and in relation to the military and political functions performed by the feudal lords in the country. Thus it can be defined as an essentially economic structure whose growth, according to Weber's proposed interpretation of 1909, appears to be intimately connected with "peace", unlike the ancient city-state. In fact, both the Greek cities and Rome are essentially political structures, and therefore have an underlying military connotation.[6] In the archaic phase of urban feudalism and a hoplite-based constitution, the *polis* takes over all political functions, and in the defence of its sovereignty becomes the most formidable war machine known to the ancient world.[7]

Later on, we have a particular flourishing of the economy in the capitalist sense, latent in the Greek city-states but evidently materializing in the late Roman republic. The strength and the foundations of ancient capitalism lie in war, partly because war provided the basic element, namely cheap slave labour,[8] and partly because the finance for military expansion, especially in Rome, was centred on the state's contracting policy which was geared towards war commitments[9]. In the case of Rome, the origins of the most advanced economic enterprise (in the capitalist sense), the slave villa which is described by all the Roman agricultural writers, are to be found in the great availability of public land and slaves resulting from Rome's military conquests.[10]

Weber's account of the subordination of the economic life of the *civitas* to politics enables him to clarify the particular weakness of ancient capitalism and its limited potential: this kind of capitalism was fated to operate in a world which knew no purely economic forecasts and calculations, but was conditioned instead by choices of a political–military nature, the results of which were bound to be unpredictable and beyond economic appraisal.[11]

However, the political rôle of the city-state, from its inception, ensured supremacy over the surrounding country. Unlike the more balanced relationship of the medieval town with its adjacent territory, it involved a transfer of products from the country to the town. This arose not on the basis of exchange of goods, but as a result of political sovereignty and of a system of landed property which tied the country to the town. These ties are of both a political and a legal nature.

In the medieval city, in contrast, the relationship is more balanced, with the country being subordinated to ancient feudal ties. This system of government in fact ensures relative well-being for the peasant population, as well as for their feudal lords; the peasants have enough purchasing power to gain access to town markets both as sellers of their products and as buyers. The city market serves its prime and most immediate function in this exchange between goods from the country and those from the city. It forms the basis for the subsequent development of the city within wider commercial networks.[12]

Another characteristic of the organization of the ancient city is that the members of the political community are qualified by their landholdings. In both Greece and Rome, the hoplite classes qualify by virtue of their estates. It follows that the system is not purely economic in nature, since its prime importance is political. Hoplites are landowners in so far as they are citizens and vice versa.

A remote consequence of this is that landed property long retained a quasi-economic character, at least in the case of Rome. Despite Rome's decidedly capitalist orientation, landed property continued to be associated with the political rôle of the aristocracy for the whole of the republican period, and helped to maintain its "lordly" connotations. This feature directed landowners towards safe monetary returns rather than exploitation based on a permanent commitment to business.[13]

Here we can see two distinct and somewhat contrasting threads in Weber's intepretation of the Roman economy (capitalistic and anti-capitalistic). We can understand the real meaning of this ambiguous attitude if we consider the peculiar reversibility of ancient capitalism.

In the case of artisan workshops in cities (especially in Greece), we very rarely come across more than a simple concentration of slaves, not necessarily organized into an *ergasterion*. In the case of the Catonian villa, its owner would have had no difficulty in breaking it up into separate tenancies, and letting it to a host of small cultivators.[14]

On the other hand, a great emphasis was placed in antiquity upon slave labour, which boomed in particular in the late Roman republic. This represents an additional limitation, ethical in nature, arising from the social debasement of work itself. It contributed to a shift in the focus of social conflict, which in the ancient world came to be centred on the ownership and control of land. In the medieval city, by contrast, conflict tended to arise between capitalist businessmen and workers, and was essentially about salaries.

If we consider the entire range of Weber's reflections on ancient societies, one point emerges with ever greater clarity: namely, the rôle of slavery as a factor limiting economic growth. Increasingly, Weber points to this factor to account for the persistence – or rather the re-emergence in Roman society during the late republic – of forms of the "*oikos* economy", with the re-emergence of areas of productive self-sufficiency and the consequent limitation of the spheres of the market and exchange.

The direct relationship between medieval capitalism and free labour is the reason for the far greater potential of the medieval city in comparison with the economies of ancient cities.

The differences between ancient *poleis* and medieval cities were discussed by Weber in his essay of 1909, but the peculiarities of the history of medieval cities had been an important theme in his intellectual work well before then. In part, his aim was to explore the limits and peculiarities of ancient capitalism, and to define the precise importance of the history of ancient societies, especially of Rome; but he also singled out the various preconditions and reasons for that historical trend which, for modern Western societies, began in the cities of medieval Europe and has continued until the present day.

My assertion presupposes two basic assumptions in Weber's work, which may not be easy to prove in an exhaustive manner, but which should none the less be emphasized. The first is perhaps the more straightforward of the two. It is that in Graeco-Roman antiquity, no less than in medieval Europe, significant economic phenomena – processes governing the entire economic order of such societies – are located in, and focus upon, the organization of the city. In both cases it is the cities which constitute the organizing force behind economic processes and the decisive factor in determining the form and the character of such processes. The second assumption on which Weber's analysis seems to be based is less clear but no less significant. In some way Weber's work presupposes a certain degree of homogeneity in the two systems under examination, such as to make a comparison between them both possible and significant. But there is also a certain heterogeneity, given Weber's tendency to go some way towards connecting medieval capitalism with the modern forms – a possibility which can, however, be categorically excluded for ancient societies.

I shall come back to this point in more detail presently. For the moment it is enough to note that this tendency permitted a certain streamlining of the history of the economic forms of medieval and modern Europe. It should be added, especially in connection with the essay of 1909, that this simplification in Weber's history of medieval cities constitutes only one particular aspect of a more general process, based on a stringent selection of facts under examination, designed to construct a series of ideal-typical models.

The point can be exemplified by the comparison, so central to this work, between ancient and medieval cities. For this purpose, Weber was forced to leave on one side a set of situations which were impossible to include in this comparison, but whose importance also detracted from the significance of the main issue.

I am referring above all to the presence, in the area central to the essay of 1909, of a set of urban models unrelated to the polarity Weber was attempting to delineate. These include the various types (at least two) found in the ancient Near East and Egypt. In fact, the ancient Egyptian city displays a series of features analogous to those that characterize the Greek *poleis* and Rome, but it assuredly did not possess any form of capitalist economy, although it did have a market. The Mesopotamian cities on the other hand seem to have permitted the limited development of a system of exchange and of a capitalist type of production; but the rise of the great bureaucratic monarchies seems to have crushed this network before it could grow.

Weber, however, abandons the idea of achieving a broader vision that might be more complete but would be too analytical, and basically weak. He prefers to identify the ideal types which are obviously more valuable as examples. Applying this framework to the subsequent handling of *The city* in 1920 helps us to grasp the basic approach which guided the process of simplification.

The radical change in the themes dealt with in this later work, as compared with the essay of 1909, is immediately reflected in the way in which it presents the typology of urban structures in various historical and social contexts. It could be said that by inverting the chronological order, the essay on *The city* arrives at the point where that on *Agrarian relations* leaves off. In *The city*, Weber engages in a systematic analysis of the multiplicity of forms of urban aggregation. His aim is to enquire into the character of the city and to define some variants. This close examination of the various types of city known in the history of human societies is conducted by assessing the greater or lesser distancing from the ideal type defined explicitly by Weber in its constituent elements. These elements, in synthesis, include the following: the presence of a defensive element consisting of fortifications; the rôle of the city market; and the tendency of the city members to form associations.

In this way "citizens" became a separate corporation distinguished from less differentiated territorial or peasant communities. Finally, the last aspect is connected with the two other requisites: a form of administrative autonomy and political government for the city community, and the establishment of the citizens' own "law" and, in time, of specific law courts.

Within this interpretative framework it can be seen how close medieval European cities were to their ancient classical counterparts and how isolated they were from the many variants attested in other ancient societies and in those of subsequent ages. This is the basis, amply demonstrated in 1920, for that brief comparison between medieval and ancient cities on which Weber had been working in 1909. With this perspective applied to the ideal type of the city, Weber was able to draw up a hierarchy of city models based on their greater or lesser resemblance to the *Idealtypus*, at the head of which is the medieval city of north-central Europe, with the ancient *poleis* and medieval Italian cities being grouped together lower down the list.

In the essay of 1909, the historical peculiarities of the cities of classical antiquity are treated in depth, and traced back to the time of their more remote origins, in that phase of "city feudalism" in which they were formed. The nature and history of the Greek and Italian cities thus distance them clearly from the cities of Egypt and the ancient Near East. From the economic point of view the split is even clearer. The early transformation of landed property and its mobility on an individual plane, and the subsequent flourishing of a capitalist economy in the optimum conditions of Rome, present a completely different picture from the conditions of ancient Near-eastern societies. In the latter we have the early emergence of a strong monarchical power based on a pervasive system of *corvées* and on a professional army financed out of the king's "treasure"; this corresponds to a series of closed economies, a system of *oikoi*, in the sense of the primitivist interpretation of Rodbertus & Bücher. Here the great productive systems are removed from the sphere of the market, increasing the weight of economic self-sufficiency. The bureaucratic nature of the great eastern monarchies allowed little room for the possible operation of a private financial capitalism that lacked most of the opportunities offered by the public contract system, a highly developed feature of the Greek cities and Rome.

In the later essay on *The city* Weber picked up this theme of the peculiarity of the ancient city as one thread among many, but now he extended the overall fabric of his analysis. The comparison is no longer only between the two great models of Mediterranean society – the empires of the Near East, with their anti-capitalist orientation, and the Graeco-Roman cities. Rather, the horizon is now extended to include examples drawn from the whole history of civilization.

The peculiarity of the cities of classical antiquity is thus made evident in relation to a broader spread of situations. In fact Weber extends his interest to cover all those societies which, despite reaching a high level of development, did not go beyond kinship and tribal systems, and where the forms of citizens' guilds within the city were either lacking or in their early stages[15]. Weber turns to the different historical contexts in which city structures, compared with their counterparts in classical antiquity and medieval Europe, either did not develop at all or else developed very little; he goes as far as the civilizations of the Far East, the Islamic world, the societies of India and Russia.[16]

The breadth of such comparisons tends to isolate the Graeco-Roman phenomenon, accentuating its historical peculiarity which, as I have mentioned, finds a counterpart only in medieval Europe. Inevitably, in this much broader survey compared with that of 1909, Weber underlines the aspects which these two city models have in common, rather than stressing their differences, as he had done in the earlier essay. In *The city*, the differences are between these western models and other social formations in recorded history. To return to a point which I briefly touched upon earlier, the qualifying criterion of an ideal model of a city in his later essay is identified in the grouping of its citizens into associations, rather than in its specifically economic function. In other words, the key element of the ideal type is the setting up of a compact social body through a process which frees the individual from his previous archaic ties and puts him on a new plane, secured by the presence of a "city" law.

Indeed it is through the emergence of this "law" that the Western city, both ancient and medieval, manages to play a decisive, and apparently unique, rôle: it helped to break those intermediate ties which absorbed the individual and located him within groups of differing types, all, however, decidedly static and archaic in character – from the tribal community to that of the village, from castes to forms of kinship and lineage.[17]

The affiliation of a number of individuals who had originally belonged to different structures, but were now united by the fact of belonging to a city and its law, therefore becomes a decisive factor for change in the history of human societies.

In this context the old medieval saying "the city air makes one free" takes on a new significance.[18] It refers not only to the freedom of the individual from the links of feudal society, but, above all, to his freedom from the afore-mentioned archaic ties which, with the emergence of the city, simply appeared unacceptable.

The whole architecture of the 1909 essay had led to a considerable thematic simplification, designed to underline the different economic perspectives of ancient and medieval cities, and to contrast the trajectory of ancient capitalism with the flourishing of the city economy in medieval Europe.

The broader outlook of *The city* necessarily entailed the examination of far more extensive and heterogeneous historical material. This was matched, in Weber's efforts to produce a set of interpretative models with which he could order this material and find a meaning for it, by the construction of a more complex typology than that encountered in *Agrarian relations*. There are as many types as there are concrete forms and historical contexts in which cities emerged and evolved.

These efforts can be noted above all in the second part of *The city*, where the generalizing schemata introduced in the early pages are contrasted with the reality of the historical situations and the conditions in which the various cities evolved. Above all, it was a question of filling out the classificatory system in the early chapters with concrete examples; in this essay, as we have seen, Weber placed the ancient city and the city of medieval southern Europe on a lower level than their north-central European counterpart. In the end, how-ever, the refinement and deepening of the analysis serve to highlight elements of weakness or, at the very least, of obscurity and uncertainty in this develop-mental schema.

For further clarification, it would be worth returning briefly to the typol-ogy of cities as depicted by Weber in relation to their history. The initial phase would seem to correspond roughly to the formation of an urban nucleus or-ganized or authorized by the lord of the land in order to boost his income.[19] Party to this scheme were the local aristocracy who, without severing their connections with their country estates, played a pre-eminent rôle in town life and in its government. The integration in the city of the ancient feudal nobil-ity seems particularly accentuated in medieval Italy, in the form defined by Weber of the "patrician city" ("*Geschlechterstadt*"). Although there are notable differences between northern European and Italian cities, the former in this phase still fall within the canons which were already laid down clearly in 1909. In Weber's later analysis we find confirmation in particular of the peaceful de-velopment of the northern European city, its integration within larger politi-cal units which ensured its "pacific" and essentially economic orientation, and lastly of the separation between the city order and feudal structures.

As I mentioned just now, Weber's characterization of the second phase in the evolution of the medieval city, the model of the "plebeian city", is more perplexing. This type of city, whether it be ancient classical or medieval Italian

(Weber yet again brings them close together), seems in fact to highlight those basic features which, in *The city*, Weber himself had identified as constituting the essence of the city in comparison with other traditional social structures.

Political independence and the subsequent capacity for autonomous legislation, self-government, taxation and economic policy – these are the characteristics which Weber explicitly attributes to Italian cities as peculiar to them.[20] We are therefore talking about structural characteristics which coincide with the constituent elements of Weber's ideal city. There is therefore a flaw in the very foundation of the general classification which is summarized above, which puts the city of northern and central Europe at the top of city types.

There is a key passage in *The city* which highlights this singular contradiction of Weber's:

> During the age of greater autonomy of the cities, their conquests tended confusedly and in rather varying ways towards the following ends: (1) towards political independence . . . (2) towards autonomous legislation . . . (3) towards autocephaly, or towards a completely independent legal and administrative authority . . . (4) towards fiscal power over the citizens and their exemption from taxation by the outside world . . . (5) towards a free market, a proper overseeing of industry and commerce and powers for the relevant monopolist regulation.[21]

These developments can be discerned, not in the medieval cities of central and northern Europe, but rather in the ancient *poleis* and the cities of medieval Italy, according to the evidence explicitly set out by Weber. It is symptomatic that he is repeatedly forced, in the schematization which I have just quoted, to define the exact limits within which it could be applied to northern European cities. In particular, it was difficult for cities flourishing under powerful unitary monarchies to achieve a strong politico-administrative and fiscal autonomy, as well as their own legislation and jurisdiction; I am referring first and foremost to the cities of England, which seem to have specifically attracted Weber's attention.

A clue to a better understanding of Weber's analysis can be found in his closing pages. Here we find expressed with greater clarity the old assessments of 1909, relating to the great distance between the ancient and the medieval city. This distance is marked by the clear economic orientation of the latter compared with the chiefly politico-military rôle of the former, within whose ambit a politically oriented capitalism flourished.[22]

Actually, there is almost a suspicion that in *The city* we have different lines of thought which impede the linear development of the discourse. Besides, it must not be forgotten that between the 1909 essay and that on *The city* there was a very significant shift in perspective. In the former, Weber had based his analysis essentially on the economic differences between classical and medieval

34

cities, in particular on the peculiarities of ancient capitalism *vis-à-vis* the medieval version. Moreover, such an orientation arose directly from the subject matter of that essay, which was dedicated to the agrarian history of antiquity. *The city* on the other hand seems to aim at an analysis of the politico-institutional aspects and the overall make-up of the various types of cities. We must remember how the essay, already published independently by the author in 1920, was to appear in the posthumous *Economy and society*, positioned right at the centre of the part devoted to the *sociology of power*.

Returning therefore to our problem, we could, then, suppose that the superiority of the northern European cities, already mentioned in 1909, is to be attributed primarily to economic aspects. That is to say, where the scale of appraisal adopted by Weber is primarily based on economic parameters, the superiority of northern and central European medieval cities relative to those of classical antiquity and medieval Italy seems certain. Where on the other hand those institutional and political elements, so highly valued in the essay on *The city*, take on a central function in the classification of the various types of city, ancient and medieval Italian cities re-emerge as pre-eminent, demonstrating that, in some ways, they were neither secondary nor inferior to the type of development of the northern European cities.

There is another passage in *The city* that brings us back to a problem merely touched upon in 1909, and which radically affects the understanding of it. In one of the many brief comparisons between classical and medieval cities that reappear in *The city* we encounter a passing reference to the various possible outcomes of the two types of city and society. Starting from the emphasis – itself of great interest for understanding Weber's particular method of using historical material – given to the cyclical nature of the evolution of cities in various contexts, he nevertheless underlined the importance of this with reference to medieval Italian cities.[23] In trying to uncover similar characteristics in classical antiquity, Weber hastened to make it clear that the ancient city did not give rise to spectacular phenomena such as "modern capitalism or the modern state". On the other hand this cannot be excluded in medieval cities: their development, "although by no means the only decisive precursor, and not itself their carrier, is inseparably linked as the crucial factor with the rise of these phenomena".[24]

Thus we have a perfect explanation for the ambiguous contrast in the essay of 1909 between the lack of outlets for ancient capitalism and the apparent absence of limits inherent in medieval capitalism. In truth, neither in 1909 nor subsequently in *The city* was Weber to make explicit a direct connection between the economy of the medieval city and the history of modern capitalism. But the stress placed by Weber on the greater growth potential of medieval capitalism leads one to think of uninterrupted development rather than of the disruption of medieval economic forms, an evolution directed towards the subsequent horizons of modern history.

Nevertheless, the issue at the centre of Weber's attention in 1909 only indirectly recalls these aspects. As has been said, it essentially concerns the possible reasons behind the different outcomes of two situations which developed in analogous conditions. Given the comparability of the medieval city to that of classical antiquity, why did the capitalist starting points in the former have such a radically different outcome from those we find in the latter? This is the central question posed by Weber, which would seem to allow for, but also to obscure, the aspects of continuity between medieval capitalism and that of modern Europe. In the same way, in 1909 Weber sidesteps the related problem concerning the unchanging significance of the notion of capitalism, whether applied to the medieval city or to the great nations of the modern era.

In conclusion, we can say that if the continued history of medieval capitalism, and its welding with subsequent events in modern European societies, is evoked by its supposed "unlimitedness", Weber has taken no further position which would warrant an independent historiographical hypothesis. This perspective does not appear to change substantially in his subsequent essay on *The city* either, where he goes no further than to raise a possibility; a possibility which, as is later pointed out in this last work, would be confirmed by the radical difference between ancient and medieval cities. This difference had already been extensively explored in the essay of 1909; it is now given a new and clearer significance than in the broad fabric of the earlier work. It is affirmed by Weber as the conclusion of an analysis which, unlike that of 1909, places more emphasis on structural similarities between ancient and medieval cities than on their differences.

Notes

1. See M. I. Finley, The ancient city: from Fustel de Coulanges to Max Weber and beyond, in *Economy and society in ancient Greece*, eds B. D. Shaw & R. P. Saller (London, 1981); M. I. Finley, Max Weber and the Greek State, in *Ancient history: evidence and models* (London, 1985); A. Momigliano, foreword to M. Weber, *Agrarverhältnisse im Altertum* (Ital. tr. *Storia economica e sociale dell' antichità*) (Rome, 1981); A. Momigliano, New paths of classicism in the nineteenth century (*History and Theory* 21, 1982), in Momigliano, *Studies in modern scholarship*, eds G. W. Bowersock & T. J. Cornell (Berkeley, 1994), pp. 236 ff.
2. A. Momigliano, Dopo Max Weber? (1978), in *Sesto contributo alla storia degli studi classici e del mondo antico* (Rome, 1984) p. 299.
3. L. Capogrossi Colognesi, *Economie antiche e capitalismo moderno* (Bari, 1990), pp. 139 ff.
4. See M. Weber, *Agrarverhältnisse im Altertum* (Tübingen, 1909) (Engl. tr. *The agrarian sociology of ancient civilizations* (London, 1976)), pp. 255 ff. (Eng. tr. pp. 358 ff.).
5. See Capogrossi, *Economie antiche e capitalismo moderno*, pp. 251 ff.; also pp. 137 ff., pp. 197 ff, pp. 223 ff.
6. *Ibid.*, pp. 265 f.

7. Weber, *Agrarverhältnisse im Altertum*, p. 261 f. (Engl. tr. p. 346 f.; Ital. tr. p. 333); see Capogrossi, *Economie antiche e capitalismo moderno*, p. 265.

8. *Ibid.*, pp. 266; 284.

9. See already M. Weber, *Die römische Agrargeschichte* (Stuttgart, 1891) (crit. edn J. Deininger, (ed.) (Tubingen, 1986)), p. 236; Weber, *Agrarverhältnisse im Altertum*, p. 14 f. On this point I will quote once again Capogrossi, *Economie antiche e capitalismo moderno*, pp. 269, 282 f.; but see also p. 257 and n. 92.

10. Weber, *Agrarverhältnisse im Altertum*, p. 236 (Eng. tr. pp. 315 f.; Ital. tr. pp. 301 f.).

11. Capogrossi, *Economie antiche e capitalismo moderno*, pp. 52, 54, 80–86, 150 f., 246 ff.

12. *Ibid.*, pp. 269 f. See also J. R. Love, *Antiquity and capitalism* (London, 1991), pp. 227 ff.

13. *Ibid.*, pp. 59 f., 62 f., 153.

14. *Ibid.*, pp. 216 ff., 281 ff.

15. M. Weber, *Die Stadt* (Tübingen, 1921), now in M. Weber, *Wirtschaft und Gesellschaft,* ed. J. Winckelmann (Tübingen, 1985) (tr. G. Roth & C. Wittich as *Economy and society* (Berkeley, Calif., 1978)), pp. 736: "Nicht jede 'Stadt' im ökonomischen und nicht jede, im politisch-administrativen Sinn einem Sonderrecht der Einwohner unterstellte, Festung war eine 'Gemeinde'. Eine Stadtgemeinde im vollen Sinn des wörtes hat als Massenerscheinung vielmehr nur der Okzident gekannt."

16. So Weber, *Die Stadt*, pp. 738 (1978, p. 1229).

17. Cf. *Ibid.*, pp. 741, 747 ff (1978, pp. 1236, 1247).

18. *Ibid.*, p. 742 (1978, p. 1239).

19. *Ibid.*, pp. 746, 763 (1978, pp. 1244, 1277).

20. *Ibid.*, p. 787 ff (1978, p. 1322).

21. *Ibid.*, pp. 788 ff (1978, p. 1322).

22. *Ibid.*, pp. 804 f., 809 (1978, pp. 1351, 1359).

23. *Ibid.*, pp. 787 f. (1978, p. 1322).

24. *Ibid.*, pp. 788 (1978, p. 1323).

3

Public honour and private shame: the urban texture of Pompeii

Andrew Wallace-Hadrill

Virtue is something lofty, elevated and regal, invincible and indefatigable; Pleasure is something lowly and servile, feeble and perishable, which has its base and residence in the brothels and drinking houses. Virtue you will meet in the temple, the forum and the senate house, standing before the walls, stained with dust, with callused hands; Pleasure you will find lurking and hanging around in the shadows, round the baths and saunas and places that fear the aedile, soft and gutless, soaked in liquor and perfume, pale and plastered with the make-up and medicaments of the funeral parlour.[1]

In the vision of the moral philosopher Seneca, the city had a moral geography. Different areas, different buildings and monuments, each carried their own charge, on a scale ranging from virtue to vice. Considerable progress has been made in recent years in learning to measure the emotive and ideological charge attached to imperial monuments.[2] Yet the investigation has been in a sense one-sided, as if only imperial monuments were ideologically charged, set against a neutral background of ordinary, uncharged, urban landscape. The aim of this paper is to use Pompeii to suggest that Roman urban landscape was differentially charged overall, so that for every area of positive charge there must be an area of negative charge set against it.

This paper serves a double purpose. Pompeii as a site offers the historian incomparable opportunities for engaging with central aspects of Roman social and cultural life. Yet, for a variety of reasons, historians are too inclined to write it off as a trite and unusable source of evidence. Before turning to the moral geography of Pompeii (p. 43), I wish to offer some observations about the difficulties and potential offered by the site.

Pompeii and the historian

In the first half of the 20th century, there was great optimism about the use of Pompeii to illustrate urban life. This was the period when the excavators, especially Maiuri, consciously set about their work with this end in view;[3] when Della Corte was using the graffiti to resuscitate the whole dramatis personae;[4] and when Tenney Frank and Rostovtzeff could confidently reconstruct an economy and society.[5] In the post-war period, that confidence evaporated. The rate of discovery slowed down; awareness grew of how outdated local archaeological method had become; and scepticism spread among historians about the reliability of the "facts" offered to them by Pompeian archaeology.

What for the historian has been the greatest obstacle is failure to publish. The last recognizable excavation reports, detailing both structures and finds, date from the 1930s.[6] It is ironical that one of the most important forthcoming studies of Pompeii, Roger Ling's detailed study of the Menander block, which for the first time will unite proper structural, art-historical and artefactual analysis of a whole insula, has chosen precisely the block which we know best from excavation reports.[7] Subsequent excavations have been at best partially and anecdotally recorded. The whole sequence of blocks to the south of the Via dell'Abbondanza excavated by Maiuri after the Second World War, seemingly in a hurry, and by no means to his own previous standards, was never reported; only now are scholars attempting to salvage what they can from the already tattered remains of the daybooks of the excavations.[8]

Excavations by Maiuri's successors were, by deliberate contrast, a model of slow and careful progress; yet by ill fortune we still await the results. Alfonso De Franciscis died before publishing the House of Julius Polybius, excavated between 1966 and 1978,[9] and the reporting of the large and important House of Fabius Rufus, showpiece excavation of the 1970s and early 1980s, still hangs fire. To some extent this situation is being salvaged by publications such as the new 10–volume series under the auspices of the *Enciclopedia Italiana*, the first two volumes of which offer valuable documentation of the houses of Regio I.[10] But these still fail to provide crucial archaeological material, and one must welcome the return in the new *Rivista di Studi Pompeiani* to the practice of publishing interim excavation reports year by year as work proceeds. It is essential that these should be followed up by full archaeological reports.

The excavation report is the instrument of the archaeologists' authority; without it, the historian ceases to respect their claims. I suspect this has been a prime reason for the outright scepticism expressed by historians such as Andreau, Castrén, and most recently Mouritsen.[11] But this has been compounded by another, scarcely less dangerous, tendency. Pompeii has become the victim of compartmentalization. Different specialists have divided the evidence into separate areas that no longer seem to communicate with each other. Art historians have long been the most active scholars on the site; but, though the emphasis is now changing, their work has continued to suffer from lack of archaeological contextualization. The impressive series of single-house studies produced by the prolific team of Michael Strocka has done much to re-integrate study of mural decoration within its domestic context; yet the very choice of the house (rather than the block) as the focus of study, and the concentration upon houses chosen for their paintings, means that the project is destined to illuminate the decoration, not the urban texture, of Pompeii.[12]

Historians have not been innocent either: they have managed to define epigraphy as the historian's proper source of information; the tablets of Caecilius and the electoral *programmata*, vital though these documents are, are in danger of becoming the sole sources of information.[13] What is absurd about this is that the archaeology of structures and finds must constitute the prime source of social and economic information. But we seem to have lost confidence in them. Jongman's study, to take one example, makes valuable contributions to discussion of the Pompeian economy on the theoretical front: yet the only chapter for which archaeology is the prime source of information is that on the textile industry, in which he, perfectly properly, demonstrates that the evidence is not sufficient to sustain the quaint theses of Moeller.[14] With Moeller gone, archaeology has no further contribution to make to his picture of the urban economy.

But lamentable and frustrating though the state of publication of the site may be, there is still a surprising amount that can be achieved with what stands on the ground, and the inadequate reports that do exist. I draw attention, for example, to Stefano De Caro's reinvestigation of Maiuri's excavations of the temple of Apollo.[15] By going through the *Giornali degli Scavi* of 50 years before, and chasing up the finds of pottery in the depositories, he was able to stand Maiuri's interpretation of the material on its head, and win a far more convincing picture of the early history of the settlement in the late 7th/early 6th century. Other studies which, however narrowly, make good use of structures and finds to illuminate aspects of the economy are Cerulli Irelli on a lamp workshop,[16] Verena Gassner on *tabernae*,[17] and Bettine Gralfs on metal workshops.[18]

What of new opportunities? Even within the last five years, the local situation of the archaeology of Pompeii has changed enormously. The really significant factor is the scale of financial resources now being pumped into the site; on the one hand for an ambitious programme of clearing up, restoration, and publication; and on the other, under the auspices of the Consorzio Neapolis, for the creation of an ambitious computer databank.

On the strictly archaeological front, I draw attention to the current excavation, under Antonio Varone, of the block on the north side of the Via dell' Abbondanza, I.12 (House of Chaste Lovers).[19] No less important is the programme of clearance, under the direction of Antonio De Simone, in the blocks behind the amphitheatre, which were left semi-excavated and ruinous by Maiuri in his last days.[20] Here, for instance, Salvatore Ciro Nappo has been able, by digging trenches designed to answer questions about the historical development of the block, to demonstrate the traces of a row of early 2nd century BC houses beneath what were in AD 79 vineyards and garden plots.[21] That single discovery has major implications for our interpretation of the urban development of the town. Rather than assuming a gradual expansion outwards from the inner core of the "Altstadt",[22] which only reached its full extent in the city's later stages, we may now think of shifting patterns of habitation within a circuit of walls already delineated in the 6th century BC.

Important opportunities likewise arise for the historian in the creation of a computer databank. This is described in two recent publications.[23] The first, a two-volume compilation issued by the Consorzio Neapolis,[24] represents only the earliest stages of the project, a point which must be borne in mind in considering its shortcomings; it offers new maps and listings of the complete site, together with computer based analyses of the distribution of various activities within the city. The second, *Rediscovering Pompeii*, is the catalogue of an exhibition currently on tour across the world.[25]

In brief, the program consists of a series of interlinked databases, which allow one to progress from the level of the region (the Vesuvius area, with information on each separate site), to the town, to the house, to the room. Information thus integrated includes the cartographic (plans of houses with dimensions, etc.), the bibliographical, the pictorial (select a room, choose a wall, and bring up an image of its decoration), and archaeological data (finds).

If this ambitious project had already achieved its goals, it would offer an analytical tool of extraordinary power and interest. In my own work on Pompeii over the last few years, I have found nothing so frustrating as the lack of reliable information in a form suitable for statistical manipulation.[26] Accurate plans and measurements of the structures exposed, visual recording of surfaces as a whole (not just mythological scenes snipped out to decorate art histories), but above all information on the finds, all interlinked in a computer program, are what is needed to conduct the sort of analysis of distributions and relationships that could illuminate the site as a whole.

But for the time being we must content ourselves with aspirations. The project has been running since only 1986, and it is no wonder that a mass of dependable and accurate information could not be accumulated at that speed. The mapping offered by the new publications is still a token. For good plans that reliably indicate the general contours of structures, the *Corpus topographicum Pompeianum* of Van der Poel is far preferable.[27] The listing of houses as now printed in *Pompei: l'informatica* is little advance on Eschebach,[28] merely registering, as he does, traditional attributions of names and activities to houses.

The worst gap is in the treatment of finds. The only source of information for most of the finds of the site remains the pages of the *Giornali degli Scavi*. These have until fairly recently been inaccessible to scholars. They take the form of a diary, recording (by hand) day by day where excavation has been done, and noting by category of material (metal, glass, pottery, bone, etc.) the

42

objects found. No plans are given. Deciphering this information requires a considerable degree of skill and patience, as the doctoral study of Penelope Allison has shown.[29] Interpretation requires great delicacy in making out which room in which house is under discussion; and then intimate knowledge of the quaint vocabulary used by the excavators to describe the dismaying variety of household fittings, attachments, utensils and furnishings which turn up, and which the excavators themselves often had the greatest difficulty in interpreting. To date, the computer database can offer no more than photographs of the pages themselves, cursorily indexed. The database is not house by house, but page by page, so that the computer cannot perform analyses of the distribution of artefacts (such as loom-weights, toilet articles, or writing implements) which might help us examine work within the household or gender-divisions, or study the linkages between luxurious articles (statues, silverware, furniture fittings) and size and decoration of houses.

It is only a matter of time until we can start asking such questions. At that moment at last it will be possible to start moving from Maiuri and Della Corte's all too anecdotal account of the economy and society of the city. Meantime I turn to my second section, which grows out of the first. I want to take an example of the preliminary analyses offered in *Pompei: l'informatica* of distribution of urban activity, and use it as basis for a counter-interpretation.

Honour and pleasure in the city

Forming a picture of the distribution of different types of use of space – residential, productive, commercial, horticultural and public – is basic for making sense of the urban texture of Pompeii. Eschebach made the first, and useful, attempt, though in a very general way.[30] Raper sophisticated the analysis.[31] I have looked briefly at the problem through sampling.[32] But it is the central purpose of *Pompei: l'informatica*. The database listing of houses enables the production of a variety of graphic analyses, whether of distribution of different activities within a given region, or of the distribution of a particular activity across different regions.

The data so assembled are then analyzed by La Torre in a chapter examining the distribution of certain visually obvious commercial or productive activities across the city: drinking places and inns, bakeries, textile establishments and the like.[33] All produce the familiar pattern of a seemingly random scatter of activity across the town, though there may be greater concentrations in one area than another. There is a clear pattern whereby shops of all sorts cluster on the main thoroughfares of the city (Fig. 3.1). In this there is little surprise.

However, La Torre goes on to make a striking observation about the distribution of bars and pubs: there are very few around public buildings, in the

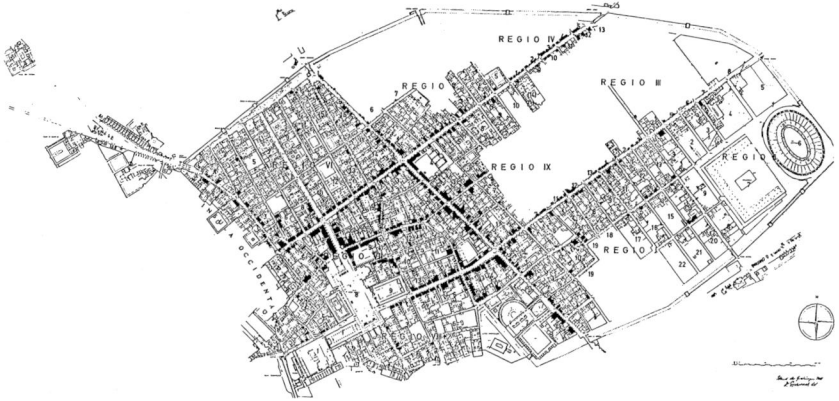

Figure 3.1   Distribution of shops in Pompeii (after Eschebach).

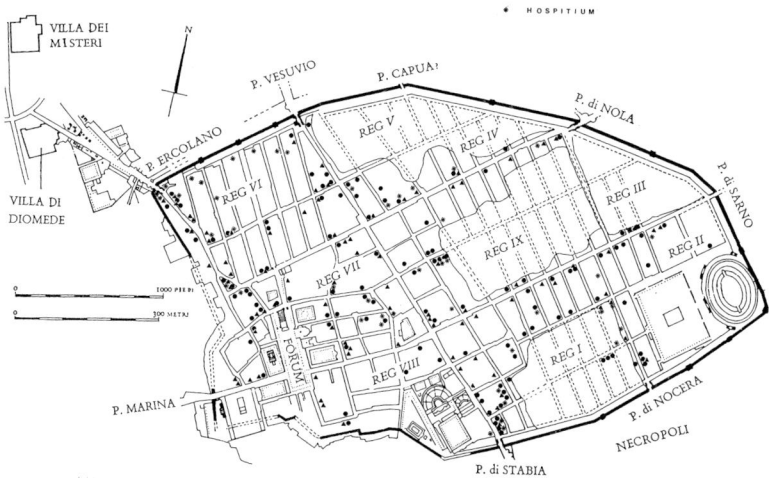

Figure 3.2   Distribution of bars, inns, etc. in Pompeii, according to La Torre (Pompeii: L'informatica al servizio di una città antica, *p. 77, Fig. 1).* ● caupona; ▲ thermopolium; * hospitium.

forum and elsewhere (Fig. 3.2). The observation is seen as surprising because of the expectation of a concentration of bars at the major focuses of public activity. La Torre links this pattern to the impact of earthquakes on the economy: most of the public buildings were badly damaged by the earthquake of AD 62, and had still not in 79 been repaired. Consequently there was little circulation in these areas, which he characterizes as building sites.[34] But this explanation implies that any bars that had been in the proximity of public buildings before the earthquake had not only fallen into disuse, but had suffered the complete removal of traces which indicate to archaeologists the presence of a bar, that is the characteristic L-shaped masonry counter with inset containers. These are substantial structures, and it strains credulity to suppose that effort was expended on systematically eliminating bars in neglected parts of town suffering from earthquake damage.

Kleberg, who had earlier noted the same phenomenon, implied a rather different explanation.[35] He noted an absence of bars in the proximity of temples and public buildings, and a rarity in the proximity of the grander houses in the northwestern part of the city (Regio VI). That would suggest a voluntary avoidance in the smarter areas of the low-life associations of taverns, which he well documented.

But the pattern, as we will see, is too marked to be satisfactorily explained by voluntary avoidance, and we should consider the hypothesis that bars and inns were deliberately excluded from certain areas by official action. A familiar string of passages in the sources for the early empire show emperors from Tiberius to Vespasian attempting to control and repress *popinae*.[36] Tiberius is reported as giving the aediles the job of controlling *popinae* and *ganeae* to the extent that they could not even sell bakery products.[37] Claudius is (inconsistently) reported as banning the sale of cooked meats and hot water, and removing the control of *popinae* from the aediles because one had earlier fined his tenants for selling cooked food.[38] Nero is said to have banned the sale in *popinae* of cooked foods apart from vegetables;[39] Vespasian all cooked foods except peas and beans.[40]

Despite some confusion evident in these passages, it is clear that *popinae* were a focus of public concern in the early empire, and that whatever edicts emperors issued, it was only to reinforce or modify the traditional control which the aediles exercised over all aspects of the markets. We could hypothesize that the same ideology that at Rome led to repeated attempts to control *popinae*, at Pompeii led to the deliberate exclusion of *popinae* from those areas most closely associated with public and official life. To test this suggestion it is necessary to take a closer look at their location.

One source of rich confusion is generated by the categorization and labelling of the establishments under discussion. The Consorzio Neapolis database follows Pompeian convention in distinguishing three categories of bar/restaurant/inn/hotel: the *caupona* (alternatively labelled the *taberna*); the *thermopolium*; and the *hospitium* (sometimes *stabulum*). Kleberg was able to show that these labels had only a partial grounding in the usage of the sources. In particular, *thermopolium* is a highly dubious usage: the word is attested only in Plautus, and may well be a transposition from the usage of Greek comedy (though it is not otherwise attested in Greek any more than in Latin).[41] In all three passages the sense of "hot drinking" is to the fore – so in the *Rudens*, Labrax jokes, emerging from a shipwreck, that Neptune is a cold bathman, and Charmides replies that he has provided no *thermopolium*, so salt and chill

45

is the drink he offers.[42] It is also represented as a place of dissipation, where those "Graeci palliati" are forever drinking.[43] But while *thermopolium* has no life outside these Plautine passages, Kleberg shows that though a whole range of vocabulary, none sharply distinct in application, is used of places for drinking, eating, entertainment and hospitality, *popina* is particularly prominent as a term for a drinking place where hot drinks and food may be served.[44]

While we may prefer to substitute *popina* for the odd Pompeian category of *thermopolium*, the distinction between this and the category labelled *caupona/taberna* has an inadequate archaeological basis.[45] There are several different varieties of masonry bar-counter, with or without inset *dolia*, or arrangements for heating and cooking; and there is a variety of spatial dispositions with or without additional space and provision for sitting or reclining. But no firm typology has been established, and the labels are applied with apparent indifference, sometimes to the same establishment (e.g. I.12.5, known indifferently as Caupona all'insegna d'Africa/d'Alessandria, Thermopolium e officina all' insegna d'Africa/d'Alessandria). To state that there were 120 *cauponae* and 89 *thermopolia* (27 of which also functioned as *cauponae*)[46] is to elevate these vagaries of modern usage into a fantasy statistic. Moreover, the absurdly elevated number of over 200 bars or inns in a city of this size (whether of 10,000 or 20,000 inhabitants),[47] must surely alert suspicion that a significant number of other types of shop, which also happened to use similar counter arrangements, have been swept up into the category.[48]

Given the surely excessive generosity with which drinking places have been identified, it is the more remarkable if central areas of the city emerge as without them. It is particularly striking how scarce they are in the long stretch of the Via dell'Abbondanza sloping down from the forum to the Stabian baths, onto which some 63 shop fronts open. The subsequent stretch of the same road is exceptionally well provided, and Kleberg characterized the Via dell'Abbondanza, with 20 bars in 600 metres, as the best-provided road in the city.[49]

On the whole stretch between the forum and the Stabian baths, La Torre registers only three *cauponae* or *thermopolia* (see Fig. 3.2). Yet two at least may be discounted. That marked on the corner of the forum, where stands a large public building, sometimes identified as the Comitium, is simply an error. A second (VIII.4.12) is the product of wishful thinking. It is a house with a number of *dolia* in its peristyle, which has nothing structurally in common with other alleged *cauponae*. It was identified by Fiorelli as a bar/gambling den/brothel on the grounds that it was a handy place for such an establishment just across the road from the main entrance to the Stabian baths. Even Della Corte comments that it was well disguised.[50] If such activities went on here (and there is no positive reason to suppose they did), it was officially invisible to the passers-by. There remains only one establishment (VII.1.62) plausibly identifiable by its counter and its place on the corner of the block containing the Stabian baths as a drinking place.

There are other indications that there was something special about this stretch of the Via dell'Abbondanza. At the forum end it is cut off by a pavement and kerbs to render it impassable to wheeled traffic. It has been assumed that the function of the barrier was to keep traffic out of the forum. But at the Stabian baths end too it is doubly cut off: by an upwards ramp to the west of the baths, then by a sharp drop in level of at least a foot to the east of the baths at the junction with the Via Stabiana. It is notable too how the road broadens outside the entrance to the Stabian baths in a wide triangle, effectively forming a small piazza[51] (see Figs 3.3–5).

This observation is further illuminated by an important recent study, by a Japanese group, of wheel-ruts in the paving of the city.[52] Their careful observations refute the general assumption that wheeled traffic ran freely round the whole city. They have demonstrated that careful placement of kerbs, stepping stones and road blocks not only cut off several stretches, but had the effect of imposing a traffic system, controlling the flow of traffic in certain directions, and limiting corners to turns in one or other direction. Study of the depth of the wheel-ruts produces a telling picture (Fig. 3.6): some streets carried heavy traffic, while others carried little or none. The stretch of the Via dell'Abbondanza in question is either very faintly rutted, or, in the piazza in front of the Stabian baths, not at all.

The absence of traffic from the road (or at least its severe restriction) might seem to offer in itself an explanation for the rarity of drinking establishments. Since it would be necessary to supply a bar by wagon, it would be impractical

Figure 3.3   Via dell'Abbondanza, viewed from the forum end. Note kerb stones.

Figure 3.4 Via dell'Abbondanza, viewed from the junction with the Stabiana, looking towards the forum. Note the sharp drop in road level.

Figure 3.5 Via dell'Abbondanza, looking towards the junction with the Strada Stabiana. To the left is the Insula of the Stabian baths, with a possible popina *on the corner.*

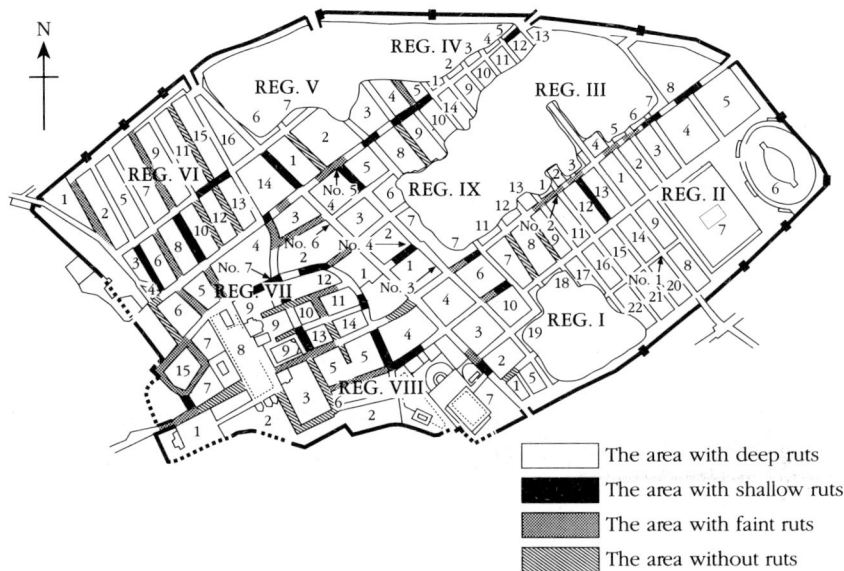

Figure 3.6 Distribution of wheel-ruts in the streets of Pompeii (Sumiyo Tsujimura, Opuscula Pompeiana, *1 (1990), Fig. 5).*

to maintain an establishment in this area. But this explanation is inadequate: access was at least physically possible, if necessary, from side streets. Moreover, lack of vehicular access cannot by itself explain absence of bars, since it is part of the same problem: why in the first place was traffic restricted at this end of the Via dell'Abbondanza, in sharp contrast to the following stretch to the east, which is one of the most heavily rutted roads in the city, as well as the best equipped with bars?

The answer must lie in the crucial link the street provides between the two main areas of public building in the city, both dating back to the 6th century BC.[53] To the west, the forum is focus both for the administrative buildings and a dense cluster of temples (Jupiter, Apollo, Venus, Genius Augusti, Fortuna Augusta); to the southeast, the area around the so-called Triangular forum houses three temples (the Doric temple of the Triangular forum itself, the so-called Jupiter Melichios and Isis) and the two theatres. With the exception of the amphitheatre and the Central baths, all the public buildings of Pompeii are contained in the southwestern sector, which coincides precisely with the area where wheel-ruts are most scarce. The western end of the Via dell'Abbondanza served as a vital link in this complex. It surely served as a processional route in public festivals, religious and civic ceremonies passing between forum and theatre, or from temple to temple.

There is nothing far-fetched in the suggestion that activities in the streets might be subject to official control. On the contrary, it is a defining feature of the Roman city that it was subject to a set of regulations modelled on those of the city of Rome and displayed city by city in bronze tablets such as the long familiar Tabula Heracleensis or the recently discovered Tabula Irnitana.[54] The Lex Julia Municipalis included detailed regulations on urban fabric and order, making it the responsibility of the aediles. If we consider the range of duties either imposed by this law on the aediles, or attested as actually carried out by them, the significance of the special treatment of the southwestern corner of Pompeii becomes more apparent.[55] In Mommsen's analysis, the aediles' duties fell into three areas: first, trade (shops, weights and measures, the market, specifically food supply and control of luxuries); second, the fabric of the city (streets, pavements and drains, their paving and cleaning, temples and public buildings); third, public games and festivals.[56] Restrictions on shops and taverns, control of traffic and state of paving, concern for areas containing public buildings and especially temples, and responsibility for processions (including funeral processions), festivals and the *ludi publici* of the theatres all put the areas of Pompeii linked by the Via dell'Abbondanza at the heart of the aedile's statutory concern.

One important feature of the aedile's rôle is its moral dimension. It is not conceived as purely practical (maintenance of public buildings, streets and services), and there is no sign that it is economic in the sense of regulating and promoting commerce. The aedile's job is to maintain Roman proprieties and decencies, to clear away filth, squalor and indecency, both literal and moral. Not only does the municipal aedile check weights and measures (Juvenal's vision of municipal pettiness is the patchy aedile in empty Ulubrae smashing undersize measures),[57] but he stops the sale of luxuries. Apuleius' *Metamorphoses* evokes a parodic image of the local aedile (albeit at Hypata in Thessaly), who, running into his friend Lucius, and hearing the high price he has paid for fish, storms up to the market vendor and proclaiming that he will make a display of his *morum severitas*, has his attendants throw the stock of fish over the ground and trample them underfoot.[58] Implicitly the aedile is not concerned simply with market prices, but with suppressing the immorality of excessive prices for luxury wares.

We have seen that *popinae* were subject to action by the aediles. The debate here is one about morality, with Tiberius responding to outrage in the senate over table luxury by referring action to the aediles, and Claudius later (and ridiculously) playing down the threat of the cookshop ("who can live without a little snack?").[59] Gambling is part of the same concern (so it is the aedile to whom Martial's gambler in a hidden *popina* is betrayed by the rattling of his dice-box).[60] Prostitution is under his supervision for similar reasons (it is with the aedile that the noble Vistilia registers as a prostitute when she wishes to evade the adultery laws).[61] It is more than public health that leads a Cato or a Fabius Maximus as aedile to regulate the public baths: "men of the noblest family performed this function too as aediles in entering places which were frequented by the people and exacting cleanliness and a useful and healthy control".[62] Even the purging of the streets and the sewers (done in spectacular and exemplary fashion by Agrippa, though sadly neglected by Vespasian, who had his lap filled with filth by Caligula)[63] has its symbolic aspect: the tide of ordure that laps at the feet of Roman civilization is simultaneously physical (house-holders had to be stopped from throwing excrement and dead animals out into the highway) and moral (the filth of drinking places, gambling dens, brothels and baths). The aediles maintained symbolic as well as literal purity: Augustus made them responsible for ensuring that togas were worn in the forum.[64]

Traffic control, such as we see at work in the Via dell'Abbondanza, was central to the symbolic cleanliness of the city. The traffic regulations of the Tabula Heracleensis are eloquent testimony of the self-image the Roman city aspired to hold up to the world.[65] Wagons (*plostra*) were banned from Rome during the hours of daylight; but then a long list of exceptions follows. Wagons might carry building or demolition material for sacred temples of the immortal gods or other public works. On days on which the Vestal Virgins, *rex sacrorum* or *flamines* should process in wagons for public sacrifice, or for triumphs, or for public festivals or where a procession was due for the *ludi circenses*, wagons might be driven for those purposes unaffected by the law. The wagons too that entered the city by night to remove nightsoil might leave, full or empty, after sunrise.

Whether or not the same law applied in Pompeii in exactly these terms (the loss of the bronze documents, and consequently the publicly displayed laws of the city is one of the major blanks of Pompeii), the principle of division fits the archaeological traces precisely. Traffic is divided into seen and unseen. By day wagons conduct ritual processions, or assist in the glorious construction of the buildings of the gods, or even complete their work of purifying the city of unsightly filth; by night the private business of trade or private building is conducted out of sight. The temporal division of the law is seen at Pompeii in a spatial division. On the conspicuous incline of the Via dell'Abbondanza between the temples of the immortal gods processions might roll, leaving only slight traces of rutting; the heavy traffic of commerce is kept out of the centre and sent around the winding streets at the back.

The counterpart to the purification of one area of the centre is the displacement and concentration of impure activities in another inconspicuous and hidden, but nevertheless central area. The irregularly shaped blocks of Regio VII, immediately to the east of the forum, approached by the narrow, dark, winding streets which follow the perimeter of the hypothetical "Altstadt", represent the polar opposite of the conspicuous, regular, symmetrical, open spaces of the forum or the upper Via dell'Abbondanza. It is precisely here in Regio VII that we find a concentration of those activities most strictly excluded from the parade centre: fulleries (with their offensive use of human urine) and other wool-working establishments, or bakeries as well as *popinae*.[66]

But perhaps the best illustration, because of its clear location in a system of moral categorization, is the distribution of brothels. A process of accretion of speculative identifications, never controlled by a systematic examination of criteria, has generated the extraordinary statistic of 34 brothels distributed across the city. There are, in my view, three reliable criteria, which all converge in

Figure 3.7   Vicolo del Lupanare, with Lupanare to the right.

the famous Lupanare at VIII.12.18–20 (Figs 3.7–9). The most reliable is the structural evidence of a masonry bed set in a small cell of ready access to the public (Fig. 3.9); the second is the presence of paintings of explicit sexual scenes; the third is the cluster of graffiti of the "hic bene futui" type (this site produced an unparalleled cluster of over 120). Questionable evidence is the occurrence of isolated pornographic paintings (private house-owners might reasonably be supposed to value these), or isolated graffiti of the "hic bene futui" type. A brothel is not any place where people occasionally had sex, but a space specifically dedicated to this purpose for profit.

Now of course there were grey areas. *Popinae, cauponae, deversoria* and the like were notoriously places where prostitution was common. This was part of the moral objection to such places, and the lawyers were prepared to treat serving girls at inns as tantamount to prostitutes for the purposes of the adultery laws. Ulpian also ruled that a legal arbitrator could not summon litigants to meet in a dishonourable place such as a *popina* or a *lupanarium*.[67] Brothels

Figure 3.8 Lupanare (VII.12.18); interior view with entrances to two
cellae, *and pornographic scenes above.*

and bars belonged to the same seamy world, marked by the indelible stain of
infamia,[68] populated by an underclass of actors and actresses, prostitutes and
pimps, gladiators, undertakers, and public executioners, people of "abject condition" who, together with their children, were formally excluded from
respectable life and any legal privileges that went with it. Even so, it is important to maintain the distinction between places specifically set up to offer
sexual services and places where those services might incidentally be pur-
chased, but which could present a slightly more respectable front.

By my criteria, 34 brothels reduce to one certain *lupanar*,[69] and some nine
distinctive *cellae meretriciae*, that is single room structures containing masonry
beds, which open directly on the streets, with no more than a wooden shutter
or a curtain to give privacy (Fig 3.9).[70] The rest are inns in which sexual activity may be posited as a sideline, sometimes on plausible grounds,[71] sometimes
on none at all,[72] or private houses which reveal some sign of sexual activity.[73]

Figure 3.9 Cella meretricia *(VII.11.12) with masonry bed.*

If we concentrate on the definite brothels, there is a clear pattern (Fig. 3.10). They are never on the wide main roads, but are hidden away on the narrow back streets. That is just where literary sources place them, in the dark places that fear the aedile, the *angiportus*. Consider the description at the start of the *Satyrica* of how Ascyltus, lost in a strange city, asks for directions home, and is led by a stranger (apparently a respectable *paterfamilias*) down a succession of winding streets ("per anfractus . . . obscurissimos") until suddenly he finds himself in a brothel.[74] That is precisely the feeling of the area where the certain brothels cluster (Fig. 3.10).[75]

Brothels lurk in the dark back streets, and in the blocks behind the public baths. The associations of *balnea, vina, Venus* are familiar;[76] but I draw attention to the ambivalence of the position of baths on the scale of public morality. On the one hand, they are major public buildings, and hence centres of respectability; on the other, centres of physical pleasure and luxury. I see that ambivalence reflected in the spatial organization: the façade of the Stabian

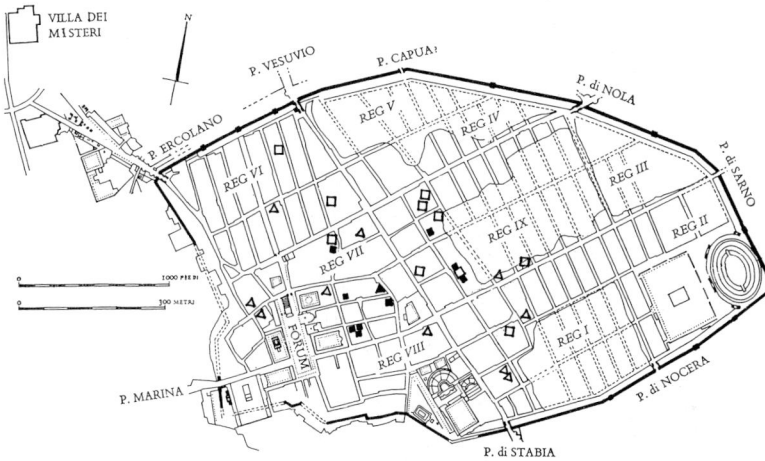

Figure 3.10 Distribution of brothels in Pompeii. ▲ lupanar; ■ cella meretricia; △ caupona, *supposedly* lupanar; □ *private house, supposedly* lupanar.

baths looks nobly onto that part of the Via dell'Abbondanza which seems to have a special status; the back entrance leads within a few yards to the largest brothel in town. A precisely analogous spatial disposition can be found in the grand houses such as the House of the Centenary (IX.8.6): the front door leads to the peristyle and fine reception rooms; the back door leads to an area hidden away which includes baths and a famous room with pornographic decoration.

Conclusion: ideology and urban economy

Pompeii offers us two contrasting yet interlocked worlds. One is of public life, of decurions and magistrates, of litigation and judgement, of religion and ceremonial, of public honours, statues and arches. These naturally focus on the forum, but extend also in the direction of a secondary forum. The contrary world is one of exchange, commerce and services, and is by the 1st century AD predominantly served by freedmen. A moral criterion defines a principle of pollution according to which some activities are more acceptable in proximity to public life. Those activities least appropriate for the forum are those which bring most intense physical satisfaction: drinking, eating and sex. The aedile has a particular function in policing this principle. The haunts of pleasure are places that, as Seneca puts it, "fear the aedile".

The morality that underlies this distinction is articulated in two passages of Seneca. In the first, quoted at the start of this paper, he contrasts the moral charges that attach to different buildings and areas in the city. In the second, he

55

gives a vivid picture of the motives that bring men to Rome.[77] It takes the form of a series of rhetorical antitheses, between virtue and vice. Some are attracted by political ambition, duties of office, or official missions; for others the draw is luxury in a place rich with opportunities for vice. Some have come for scholarly studies, others for the games. Some have come to sell their speaking talents, others their bodies. All possible types are attracted by a city which sets an equal premium on virtue and on vice.

It is this moral construction of the city as place of virtue and vice that creates the greatest problems for us in making sense of its economy. Moses Finley highlighted the passage of Cicero's *De officiis* (1.150 f.) that defines certain areas of trade as improper for a gentleman, and underlined its implications for the ideological location of trade.[78] Cicero's scale of values is very much that of Seneca later: all crafts are unworthy of the freeborn citizen, but especially those that serve pleasure, and he turns to the language of Roman comedy to evoke low life, "mongers, butchers, cooks, bird-stuffers, fishermen", as Terence says, "to which add, if you like, perfumers, dancers, and the whole school of dicing".

The evidence of Pompeii has been deployed against Finley, as if the vivid picture archaeology evokes of humble trades flourishing on the ground refuted the implications of the elitist theorizing of the sources.[79] My argument, on the contrary, is that archaeology confirms that such ideologies could indeed shape the life of a Roman city. But the effect of the erection of ideological barriers was not necessarily to inhibit trade, but to create a context within which it could be incorporated into the public façade of the city.

The process by which trade was separated out from a purified world of public life is already visible in the creation of a specialized *macellum* in 3rd century Rome.[80] The butchers and fishmongers whose presence had been a notable feature of the sights and smells of the early Forum Romanum were progressively extruded (and their stalls replaced by those of money-changers), a process which by the 1st century BC Varro could look back on as bringing *dignitas* to the forum.[81] But the same process that turns the forum more and more into the showplace of Roman might, creates a new and specialized setting for the fishmongers in the Macellum, an architectural form with its neat rectangular surround and elegant circular central *tholos* which was to become characteristic of Roman urban form.[82] In Pompeii as in Rome,[83] the Macellum left the forum free (and odourless) for the display of local civic pride. But of course, there is no reason to suppose that the effect was to inhibit the operation of trade. On the contrary, it is arguable that concentration and specialization promoted trade. Though the old integration of economic with religious and political civic activity may have suited the ideology of a "face-to-face" city-state, the separation of the market is linked historically to rising prosperity and luxury. Even prostitution might flourish better, to judge from the elaboration of Pompeii's Gran Lupanare, when concentrated in its own quarter.

A Roman could not have told us whether his was a consumer or a producer city. But he could say what attracted people to the city, whether as permanent residents or temporary visitors. They were attracted because, as Horace's bailiff knew, compared to the country, the town offered much better opportunities for conspicuous virtue and inconspicuous vice: "The brothel and greasy tavern fill you with longing for the city, I see . . . [in the country] there is no neighbouring bar to offer you wine, nor a flute-playing tart, whose rhythm can get your heavy feet dancing."[84] The bigger and more powerful the city, the better the opportunities for both virtue and vice. Compared to Pompeii, Rome was better both for public office and for brothels. A major conscious preoccupation of a city was to enhance the opportunities for both: that is, to make sure that virtue was rewarded with the finest public display, and that vice was kept inconspicuous.

If we wish to examine the ancient economy in the context of ancient ideology and culture, we should think further about the structures through which the city enabled two closely intermeshed worlds to flourish alongside each other, and yet symbolically to preserve their mutual distance and purity. Among these, one vital symbolic barrier was erected by the social and moral differentiation that separated freeborn and freed, respectable people in pursuit of honour from the *infames* ready to sacrifice their sense of shame for the gratification of others. The same barrier had its spatial dimension, between the wide open, well ordered, pure, shining and conspicuous places of honour, and the dark, dingy, narrow, windy, inconspicuous streets of ill repute. One of the benefits of Pompeii is to allow us to see Roman ideology inscribed on the ground, down to the wheel-ruts in the paving stones.

Notes

1. Seneca, *De vita beata* 7.3 "altum quidam est Virtus, excelsum et regale, invictum infatigabile: Voluptas humile servile, imbecillum caducum, cuius statio et domicilium *fornices et popinae* sunt. Virtutem *in templo* convenies, *in foro in curia*, pro muris stantem, pulverulentam coloratam, callosas habentem manus: Voluptatem latitantem saepius ac tenebras captantem circa *balinea ac sudatoria ac loca aedilem metuentia*, mollem enervem, mero atque unguento madentem, pallidam aut fucatam et medicamentis pollinctam." On the theme, see C. Edwards, *The politics of immorality in ancient Rome* (Cambridge, 1993), pp. 173 ff.
2. Most notably by P. Zanker, *The power of images in the age of Augustus* (Michigan, 1988). For discussion of the language of honour, see A. Wallace-Hadrill, Roman arches and Greek honours: the language of power at Rome, *PCPS* **37**, 1990, pp. 143–81.
3. A. Maiuri, *L'ultima fase edilizia di Pompei* (Rome, 1946) is the best statement of his views on the economic development of the city; Maiuri, *Pompeii* (Novara, 1960) for an accessible popular account.
4. M. Della Corte, *Case ed abitanti di Pompei* (2nd edn, 1954) originally appeared in

instalments between 1914 and 1925. Cited here from the third edition of 1965.

5. T. Frank, *An economic and social history of ancient Rome*, vol. V (Baltimore, 1940), pp. 252–66; M. Rostovtzeff, *The social and economic history of the Roman empire*, 2nd edn (Oxford, 1957), pp. 72 f. and *passim*.

6. O. Elia, Relazione sullo scavo dell'Insula X della Regio I (1), *NSc.*, 1934, pp. 264–344.

7. R. Ling, The insula of the Menander at Pompeii: interim report, *Antiquaries Journal* 63, 1983, pp. 34–57.

8. E.g. V. Castiglione Morelli del Franco & R. Vitale, *L'insula* 8 della *Regio* I: un campione d'indagine socio-economica, *Riv. Stud. Pomp.* 3, 1989 pp. 185–221.

9. A. De Franciscis, La casa di C. Iulius Polibius, *Riv. Stud. Pomp.* 2, 1988, pp. 15–36, is a brief posthumous summary.

10. G. L. Pugliese Carratelli (ed.), *Pompeii, pitture e mosaici*, vols I–II Regio I (Rome, 1990). The habit of entitling books with multiple authorship on Pompeii by the name of the site is a source of extreme bibliographical confusion.

11. H. Mouritsen, *Elections, magistrates and municipal elite: studies in Pompeian epigraphy* (Rome, 1988), p. 13, on historians' dissatisfaction with the Pompeian tradition.

12. Strocka (ed.), *Häuser in Pompeji*. For reports on progress of this ambitious project, cf. *Riv. Stud. Pomp.* 3, 1989, pp. 295–9. For criticism of the scope of the project, see R. Ling, German approaches to Pompeii *JRA* 6, 1993, p. 335.

13. J. Andreau, *Les affaires de Monsieur Jucundus* (CEFR; Rome, 1974); P. Castrén, *Ordo populusque Pompeianus: polity and society in Roman Pompeii* (Rome, 1975); J. L. Franklin, *Pompeii: the electoral programmata, campaigns and politics, AD 71–79* (*MAAR* vol. 28; Rome, 1980); H. Mouritsen, *Elections, magistrates and municipal elite: studies in Pompeian epigraphy* (Rome, 1988).

14. W. Jongman, *The economy and society of Pompeii* (Amsterdam, 1988), pp. 155–186, attacking W. O. Moeller, *The wool trade of ancient Pompeii* (Leiden, 1976).

15. S. de Caro, *Saggi nell'area del tempio di Apollo a Pompei* (Naples, 1986).

16. G. Cerulli Irelli, Officina di lucerne fittili a Pompei, in M. Annecchino *et al.*, *L'instrumentum domesticum di Ercolano e Pompei nella prima età imperiale* (Rome, 1977), pp. 53–72.

17. V. Gassner, *Die Kaufläden in Pompeii* (Diss. Wien, 1986).

18. B. Gralfs, *Metallverarbeitende Produktionsstätten in Pompeji* (BAR Int. Ser. 433; Oxford, 1988).

19. A. Varone, Attività dell'ufficio Scavi: 1987–1988 *Riv. Stud. Pomp.* 2, 1988, pp. 147–8; A. Varone, Attività dell'ufficio scavi: 1989 *Riv. Stud. Pomp.* 3, 1989, pp. 231–6; a fuller preliminary report is promised in the Atti del Convegno "Ercolano 1738–1988: 250 anni di ricerca archeologica".

20. Cf. A. De Simone, Le insulae su Via di Nocera. L'insula 8 della Regio II *Riv. Stud. Pomp.* 2, 1988, pp. 184–202.

21. S. C. Nappo, Regio I, insula 2, *Riv. Stud. Pomp.* 2, 1988, pp. 186–92.

22. The idea of the central core of old city, proposed by F. Haverfield, *Ancient town-planning* (Oxford, 1913), pp. 63–8, and taken up by H. Eschebach, *Die städtebauliche Entwicklung des antiken Pompeji*. MDAI (R) suppl. 17; Heidelberg & Rome, 1970), pp. 17–61, modified by J. B. Ward-Perkins, Note di topografia e urbanistica, in *Pompei 79: raccolta di studi per il decimonono centenario dell'eruzione vesuviana*, ed. F. Zevi (Naples, 1979), pp. 25–39, were thrown into question by P. Arthur, Problems of the urbanisation of Pompeii, *Antiquaries Journal* 66, 1986, pp.

29–44, and rejected by L. Richardson, *Pompeii: an architectural history* (Baltimore, 1988), pp. 36–43; against Richardson, see R. Ling, The architecture of Pompeii *JRA* 4, 1991, pp. 253–4.

23. See also the brief report in *Riv. Stud. Pomp.* 3, 1989, pp. 69–77.

24. De Simone *et al.* Le insulae su Via di Nocera.

25. B. Conticello *et al.*, *Rediscovering Pompeii* (New York, 1990), esp. pp. 104–15; reviewed by P. Allison, in *JRS* **82**, 1992, p. 274.

26. See esp. A. Wallace-Hadrill, *Houses and society in Pompeii and Herculaneum* (Princeton, 1994).

27. Van der Poel (ed.), *Corpus topographicum Pompeianum: pars 3A. The insulae of regions I–V* (Rome, 1981); *pars 5. Cartography* (Rome, 1987).

28. Eschebach, *Die städtebauliche Entwicklung des antiken Pompeji*, pp. 117–55.

29. P. Allison, *The distribution of Pompeian house content and its significance* (PhD Diss., Sydney, 1992); see also Allison, Artefact assemblages: not "the Pompeian premise", in *Papers of the Fourth Conference of Italian Archaeology. 3. New developments in Italian archaeology Part I*, eds E. Herring *et al.* (London, 1992) pp. 49–56.

30. Eschebach *Die städtebauliche Entwicklung des antiken Pompeji*, and in B. Andreae & H. Kyrieleis (eds), *Neue Forschungen in Pompeji* (Recklinghausen, 1975), p. 331.

31. R. A. Raper, The analysis of the urban structure of Pompeii: a sociological examination of land use (semi-micro), in *Spatial Archaeology*, ed. D. L. Clarke (London/New York, 1977), pp. 189–221; R. A. Raper, Pompeii: planning and social implications, in *Space, hierarchy and society: interdisciplinary studies in social area analysis*, eds B. C. Burnham & J. Kingsbury (BAR Int. Ser. vol. 59) (Oxford, 1979), pp. 137–48.

32. A. Wallace-Hadrill, *Houses and society*, pp. 65 ff.

33. G. F. La Torre, Gli impianti commerciali ed artigianali nel tessuto urbano di Pompei, in A. De Simone *et al.*, *Pompeii: l'informatica al servizio di una città antica*, 2 vols (Rome, 1988), pp. 75–102.

34. La Torre, Gli impianti commerciali ed artigianali, pp. 76–7.

35. T. Kleberg, *Hôtels, restaurants et cabarets dans l'antiquité romaine: études historiques et philologiques* (Uppsala, 1957), p. 52.

36. Collected by Kleberg *Hôtels, restaurants et cabarets*, pp. 101 ff., re-examined by G. Hermansen, *Ostia: aspects of Roman city life* (Alberta, 1982), pp. 196–203; see also O. F. Robinson, *Ancient Rome: city planning and administration* (London, 1992), pp. 135–7.

37. Suet. *Tib.* 34. The context is control of luxury, evidently the result of the debate of AD 22 reported in Tac. *Ann.* 3.52–5, in which Tiberius leaves responsibility with the aediles for control of the market.

38. Dio, 60.6.7, Suet. *Claud.* 38: these accounts have been made to square only by selective quotation.

39. Nero: Dio, 62.14.2, Suet. *Ner.* 16. Since Suetonius states that all types of cooked food were previously available, we must assume either that Claudius had in fact lifted the ban on cooked food, or that previous bans had been ineffective.

40. Dio, 65.10.3.

41. Kleberg, *Hôtels, restaurants et cabarets*, pp. 24–5.

42. Plaut. *Rudens* 527–30.

43. *Curculio* 292; cf. *Trinummus* 1013.

44. Kleberg, *Hôtels, restaurants et cabarets*, pp. 16–18.

45. Kleberg, *ibid.*, pp. 36–44 refuses to draw the distinction. Neither is it supported by J. E. Packer, Inns at Pompeii: a short survey, *Cronache Pompeiane* 4, 1978, pp. 5–51, nor by the parallel survey of Ostian taverns of Hermansen, *Ostia*, 1982, pp. 125–83.
46. So La Torre, Gli impianti commerciali ed artigianali, p. 78.
47. Observed by La Torre, Gli impianti commerciali ed artigianali, and implausibly explained by demand from the temporary influx of building labour after the earthquake.
48. Packer, Inns at Pompeii, p. 47, rightly notes that the *dolia* in the counters must have been for dry produce such as grain, not for wine as is assumed. In this case, why take counters with *dolia* as indicative of bars? Gassner, *Die Kaufläden in Pompeii*, pp. 78–81 emphasizes the difficulty of distinguishing bars and other shops.
49. Kleberg, *Hôtels, restaurants et cabarets*, p. 52.
50. M. della Corte, *Case ed abitanti di Pompei*, 3rd edn (Naples, 1965), p. 237.
51. Cf. H. Eschebach, *Die Stabianer Thermen in Pompeji* (Berlin, 1979), p. 6.
52. Sumiyo Tsujimura, Ruts in Pompeii: the traffic system in the Roman city, *Opuscula Pompeiana* 1, (1990), pp. 58–86. I am grateful to Dr Ray Laurence for this reference.
53. The best study of the public buildings of the city and its changing image over the years is P. Zanker, *Pompeji: Stadtbilder als Spiegel von Gesellschaft und Herrschaftsform* (Mainz, 1988).
54. J. Gonzalez, The lex Irnitana: a new copy of the Flavian municipal law, *JRS* **76**, 1986, pp. 147–243, for the composite text of the law from Irni, Salpensa and Malaca.
55. Still fullest on the functions of the aedile, in Rome and elsewhere, is T. Mommsen, *Römisches Staatsrecht*, 3rd edn (Berlin, 1887) ii.1, 480 ff.; more briefly, J. Marquardt, *Römische Staatsverwaltung* (Darmstadt, 1881), pp. 166 f.; W. Liebenam, *Städteverwaltung im römischen Kaiserreiche* (Leipzig, 1900), pp. 263 ff. Robinson, *Ancient Rome*, now offers thorough discussion of administration of the city of Rome. See also C. Nicolet, La table d'Héraclée et les origines du cadastre romain, in *L'Urbs: espace urbain et histoire* (CEFR 98), pp. 1–25, on aedilician responsibility for roads.
56. The Lex Irnitana XIX lists the aedile's duties as: "annonam, aedes sacras, loca sacra religiosa, oppidum, vias, vicos, cloacas, balinea, macella, pondera mensurasve exigendi aequandi, vigilias cum res desiderat exigendi".
57. Juvenal, 10.101 f.: "et de mensura ius dicere, vasa minora/frangere, pannosus vacuis aedilis Ulubris"; cf. Persius, 1.128.
58. Apuleius, *Metamorphoses* 1.24–5; cf. F. Millar, The world of the *Golden Ass*, *JRS* **71**, 1981, pp. 68ff.
59. Tacitus, *Ann.* 3.52 ff.; Suetonius, *Claud.* 40.
60. Martial, 5.84: "et blando male proditus fritillo/arcana modo raptus e popina/aedilem rogat udus aleator"; cf. 14.1.3 "nec timet aedilem moto spectare fritillo".
61. Tacitus, *Ann.* 2.85. Central control of brothels is also visible in the taxation of prostitutes (Suetonius, *Cal.* 41), and the ability of the regionaries of Rome to enumerate brothels region by region. Cf. Robinson, *Ancient Rome*, pp. 137–9.
62. Seneca, *Ep* 86.10; Robinson, *Ancient Rome*, pp. 113–16.
63. Dio, 49.43 on Agrippa; Suetonius, *Vesp.* 4. Robinson, *Ancient Rome*, pp. 69–73, 117–24.
64. Suetonius, *Aug.* 40.
65. Robinson, *Ancient Rome*, pp. 73–82, with a text of the Tabula Heracleensis.
66. See La Torre, Gli impianti commerciali ed artigianali, figs. 1–5.

67. *Dig.* 4.8.21.11.

68. The importance of the idea of *infamia* has been stressed recently by J. F. Gardner, *Being a Roman citizen* (London, 1993), ch 5.

69. VII.12.18–20, with its five *cellae*, paintings, and over 120 graffiti (CIL IV.2173–2296) is exceptional in all three respects. The graffiti include 27 instances of *futuo* and its forms; over half of all recorded occurrences in the city. Nowhere else has more than four. The collection of pornographic paintings is only paralleled by the newly discovered series in the Suburban baths outside the Porta Marina.

70. The *cellae meretriciae*, which are archaeologically distinctive, are: VII.4.42, VII.11.12, VII.12.33, VII.13.15 and 16 and 19, IX.6.2, IX.7.15 and 17.

71. The adjacent bars at I.2.19 and 20 have a small cluster of "hic futui" type graffiti: CIL IV.3929–3943. VII.3.28 has one isolated graffito (CIL IV.2310, cf. Della Corte, *Case ed abitanti di Pompei*, p. 149); VII.6.34 and 35/6 have various graffiti (CIL IV.1627–49, cf. *ibid.*, pp. 169–71), none pointing conclusively to sexual activity. IX.11.3 has suggestive graffiti outside (*ibid.*, pp. 307–8), but has not even been excavated.

72. Other "cauponae" also identified as *lupanaria* are: I.7.13/14 (*ibid.*, p. 319); VI.10.1/ 19 (*ibid.*, p. 55); VII.7.18; VIII.4.12–13 (see above, n. 50).

73. IX.5.19 has one room with pornographic decoration, but graffiti (CIL IV.5123 and 5127) advertise prices of girls (Della Corte, *Case ed abitanti di Pompei*, p. 162); but the same is true of VI.15.1 (House of the Vettii), never identified as a brothel. VI.14.43 (House of the Scientists) was identified as a brothel in the 19th century on the basis of graffiti outside its door (CIL IV.1516–7). The parodic verse form of these two graffiti sets them apart from standard "hic futui" declarations; nothing inside suggests a brothel. Other dubious identifications are: VI.10.2 (cf. Della Corte, *Case ed abitanti di Pompei*, p. 55); VI.11.16 (*ibid.*, p. 60–1; the graffiti at CIL IV.1379–91 and 4435–44 are inconclusive); VII.9.32; IX.2.8; IX.5.14; IX.6.8 (Della Corte, *Case ed abitanti di Pompei*, p. 163 on the basis of a single graffito, CIL IV.5187). Some are apparent errors: VII.4.44 (House of the Hunt) was not suspected even by Della Corte, *ibid.*, pp. 124f., and is presumably confused with the *cella* at VII.4.42.

74. Petronius, *Sat.* 8.

75. The liveliness of this area is brought out by J. R. Franklin, Games and a *lupanar*: prosopography of a neighborhood in ancient Pompeii, *CJ* 81, 1986, pp. 319–28.

76. Cf. F. Yegül, *Baths and bathing in classical antiquity* (Cambridge, Mass. & London 1992), pp. 40–42.

77. Seneca, *Cons. ad Helviam* 6.2: "alios adduxit ambitio, alios necessitas publici officii, alios inposita legatio, alios luxuria opportunum et opulentum vitiis locum quaerens; alios liberalium studiorum cupiditas, alios spectacula; quosdam traxit amicitia, quosdam industria laxam ostendendae virtuti nancta materiam; quidam venalem formam attulerunt, quidam venalem eloquentiam. nullum non hominum genus concucurrit in urbem et virtutibus et vitiis magna pretia ponentem."

78. M. I. Finley, *The ancient economy*, 2nd edn (London, 1985), ch.2.

79. Moeller, *The wool trade of ancient Pompeii*, for open attack on Finley, rebuffed by Jongman, *The economy and society of Pompeii*. See also M. Frederiksen, Theory, evidence and the ancient economy (Review of Finley *The ancient economy*), *JRS* 65, 1975, p. 170.

80. C. de Ruyt, *Macellum: marché alimentaire des romains* (Louvain-la Neuve, 1983), pp. 158ff.

81. Varro ap. Nonius, 532.

82. De Ruyt, *Macellum*, pp. 282 f. emphasizes the lack of Greek precedent for the form.
83. *Ibid.*, pp. 137–49.
84. Horace, *Epist.* 1.14.21–6: "fornix tibi et uncta popina/ incutiunt urbis desiderium, video . . . nec vicina subest vinum praebere taberna/ quae possit tibi, nec meretrix tibicina, cuius/ad strepitum salias terrae gravis". Similarly Columella, *RR* 1.8.2, urban slaves habituated to "otiis, campo, circo, theatris, aleae, popinae, lupanaribus"; cf. Edwards, *The politics of immorality in ancient Rome*, pp. 190 ff.

4

The organization of space in Pompeii[1]

Ray Laurence

Between the ancient and the new there is a distance, a fracture.[2]

Architects have looked back upon the Roman city as a city of precise planning and order.[3] For adherents to neoclassicism and to modernism, the ancient city and in particular Pompeii holds a strong position in histories of architecture. The archaeological remains of Pompeii directly or indirectly influence the form of the modern city. However, it would appear that the historian's and archaeologist's conceptions of the ancient city are in turn influenced by the modern city, in which they live or interact. This paper is about the search for a methodology for the interpretation of the urban landscape in Pompeii. It addresses the problem of how we interpret the built environment, and how this interpretation is influenced by present concerns: in other words, the dialogue between the architectural present and past. Finally, I will offer an interpretation of the organization of public space in Pompeii.

Pompeii as an artefact presents not only the past, but also the present. Pompeii is part of a heritage industry in which vast numbers – 4–5,000 daily[4] – visit the site, the appeal being the possibility of empathizing with the past, or of seeing daily life as it was! The appeal of Pompeii would not appear to permeate into present-day academic archaeology. Little analytical work has been attempted.[5] Why such a situation should arise is strange. The information-set available in Pompeii is large, although it has been recorded in a variety of manners. A reason for shying away from analytical work in Pompeii might be that there was a feeling that the destruction of Pompeii left a microcosm of Roman life, and was not really the concern of archaeologists. However, it is becoming increasingly clear, from Penelope Allison's work upon artefact assemblages in Pompeian houses, that the processes of deposition in Pompeii are as complicated as in any other archaeological site.

The questions and methods that we use in the analysis of Pompeii depend upon what we expect to find. These expectations can be divided into two types, both of which are culturally conditioned. The first set of expectations is that the excavated data from Pompeii should correspond to the written evidence of Vitruvius and other classical authors. Such a view could be justified on the grounds that both the archaeological and the written evidence come from the same historical and cultural context.[6] However, the classical authors wrote about Rome predominantly. In terms of population, area of the city and type of city, Rome and Pompeii in no way resemble each other. Another objection to the imposition of the classical authors as determinate in our interpretation of the archaeological evidence is that their writing is limited and may in no way correspond to any extant urban landscape.[7] In many ways the limited nature of analytical work in Pompeii reflects the limitations of Vitruvius' analysis of architecture. However, the Vitruvian evidence can contribute to our conception of urban society in Roman Italy. But this contribution should be controlled and should be seen as a guiding principle, rather than as the determining paradigm.

The second set of expectations would appear to be conditioned by present concerns about the city. This can be demonstrated from the debate concerned with the advent of town planning in England and Wales in the early 20th century. The Town Planning Act of 1909 formalized a movement for a change in the structure of cities, from being mere aggregations of people into consciously organized communities.[8] The act gave the local corporations the power of compulsory purchase and the ability consciously to organize space in cities. Reading the architectural literature of the time is instructive. Town planning was seen as the solution to urban socio-economic problems. Further, it gave the planner the power to organize what Adshead called the juxtaposition of the classes.[9] There would appear to have been a conscious decision to separate social groups into different areas. At the time, architects were most interested in the archaeological past and in particular in the classical city. At the fourth Conference on Town Planning held in London, in 1910, papers were read by three archaeologists. Gardner gave a paper upon the planned growth of the Greek city; Haverfield gave a paper upon planning in the Roman city; and Ashby gave a paper upon the irregular growth of Rome.[10] Both Gardner and Haverfield emphasized the straight streets and the right angles associated with these straight streets. Haverfield was later to write: "whenever ancient remains show a long straight line or several correctly drawn right angles, we may be sure that they date from a civilized age";[11] a civilized age presumably similar to that which was to be created by the 1909 Town Planning Act. It is interesting that Haverfield was incredulous to find that in Pompeii there was an appearance of symmetry, but that "there is hardly a right angle or even an approach to a right angle at any (street) corner".[12] His expectations of the ancient city were the straight streets and the right angles of an organized and planned urban environment.

What are our own expectations of the city? Geographers report that zones exist in cities in the western world. Indeed, it would appear that scholars expect there to be distinct zones in Pompeii, and these are loosely attributed. Two scholars can attribute the same area as a "plebeian stronghold" or an aristocratic centre in the course of their arguments.[13] The relevance of models of zoning to the study of the ancient city is limited. In the context of the pre-industrial city, the specialization of land use is not as great as that of the Western 20th century city. For example, the separation of work and residence does not occur.[14] Where zoning does appear in the preindustrial city, it is seldom due to economic rationality.[15] This might explain why Raper in his study of land use in Pompeii found little evidence of socio-economic zoning.[16] The attribution of a single function to land use in the context of Pompeii is to confine the ancient world to our conceptions of land use. For example, an atrium house could perform the function of a place of work, residence, entertainment, agriculture, etc. These activities were not neatly defined or separated. Therefore, to apply models of modern 20th century zoning directly to the context of Pompeii is anachronistic. We expect to find zoning in Pompeii, because we experience zoning in the modern city. However, we are not comparing like with like. Pompeii is not as big in either area or population as a modern city. In area, it is 167 acres inside the walls. Therefore, geographical models of zoning are of little help. Although some congregation of activities did occur, congregation is not the same as economic zoning.[17]

An alternative strategy for the evaluation of space is required. The work by Hillier & Hanson addresses the problem of space in the built environment, and the social logic of space in particular.[18] They question the three major facets of modern design: separation is good for the community, the hierarchization of space is good for relations between groups, and finally space works only if an area is defined as belonging to a group of individuals.[19] In other words they question the preconceptions of zoning, and the transformation of the organizing unit of the city from the street into the estate. In fact what they question is how we have been conditioned to think of space in the 20th century.

Hillier & Hanson had a fundamental problem, that is also common to both archaeology and ancient history: there was no discrete system from which they could build a theory of space.[20] In fact to build a theory of space, you need to understand the spatial entity, in this case society. To have such a conception is almost impossible if the theory is to be universal.[21] To overcome such problems they began to work upon the random patterns that can be observed and in particular the controls upon randomness that appear in the urban environment.[22] A glance at Pompeii reveals that there is a rather confusing pattern of settlement types. However, one of the controls upon this pattern would appear to be the street structure itself.[23]

The problem was then formulated as follows: what do we measure to understand the controls upon randomness in Pompeii? The street was selected as the public area of the city, in which public social interaction occurred.[24] The street was chosen because it is the organizing unit of public space in the pre-modern city. Our modern conception of the street has been adjusted to the conditions of 20th century transportation. A street was primarily an area of social interaction; now in the 20th century the street's primary rôle is that of a transport corridor.[25]

In Pompeii, there is obviously no direct evidence of street activity, for the simple reason that it is no longer occurring. However, there would appear to be a degree of evidence for the underlying structure of the street. The interaction and encounter patterns within the urban environment are directly affected by the nature and structure of space, as defined by the built environment.[26] In each street we know where doorways were that opened onto the street. These mark the interface between public and private space.[27] Also, we have information about where graffiti occur in the street. The position of the crossing stones in Pompeian streets is more related to poor drainage than to any form of social activity. How the streets link together is also important. Therefore, what we have in Pompeian streets is the syntax of street activity. This is rather like reading a sentence in which there is only punctuation. However, in the examination of space this syntax orders the arrangement of street activity.

To analyze the syntax of streets three basic methods were devised. The first was to measure the occurrence of doorways in a street. This was done by counting the number of doorways in a street and then dividing that figure by the length of the street. The result is a measure of the occurrence of doorways every x metres. The highest occurrence of doorways was every 2.5 m in Via dell'Abbondanza, and the lowest was every 86 m in the street between insulae II.4 and II.6. The median occurrence of doorways was every 7.3 m. Hence, the variation was high. These data are presented in a cartographic form in Figure 4.3. It should be stated that the median occurrence of doorways was taken to divide the data into two groups; subsequently each of these groups was divided into two, to form four groups of data.[28] Streets have a doorway occurring every 0–5 m in Figure 4.3a, and so on to streets which have doorways occurring less often than every 15 m in Figure 4.3d.

A pattern emerges. The highest occurrences of doorways were in those streets that formed through routes from the gates of the city. There are two exceptions: the streets leading from Porta di Sarno and the Porta Marina have lower occurrences. In the case of Porta Marina the figure is altered by the presence of public buildings which, although they are associated with high levels of social activity, do not have many doorways. The streets to the east of the forum were also found to have high occurrences of doorways. Interestingly, this area does not conform to a grid pattern, and less attention has been paid to it by Pompeianists. The lower occurrences of doorways tended to be in streets that had a grid pattern. Via di Mercurio, with high doorway occurrences, was an exception.

The second method was to measure the occurrence of street messages or graffiti. Rightly or wrongly, it was assumed that these street messages were set

Figure 4.1   Pompeii, Via degli Augustali: high occurrence of doorways.

Figure 4.2   Pompeii, Vicolo di Mercurico: low occurrence of doorways.

(a)

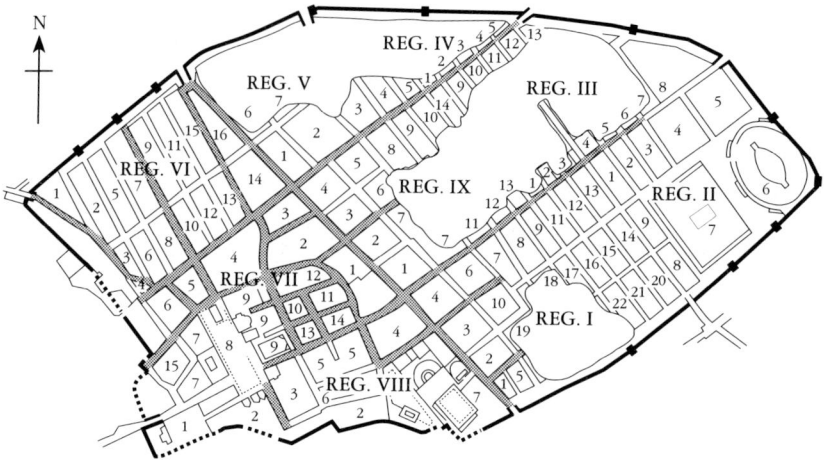

(b)

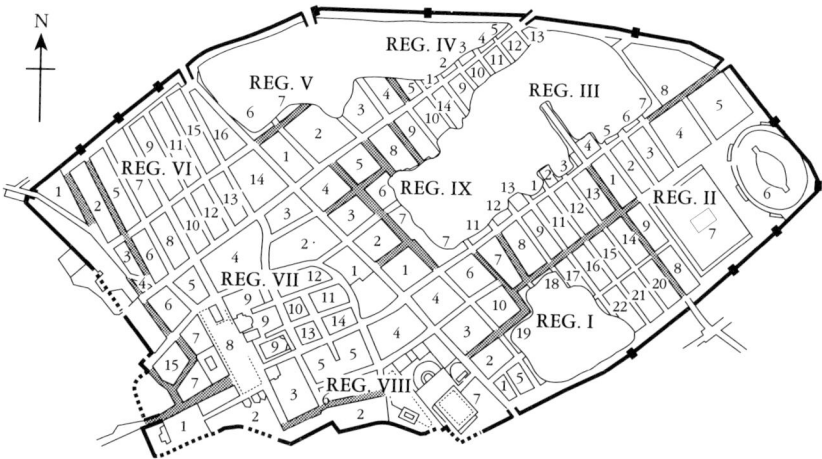

Figure 4.3   Occurrence of doorways in Pompeii: (a) 0–5 m; (b) 6–10 m.

up for maximum viewing figures. Therefore, the messages would reflect the occurrence of activity in a street. The problem with these two assumptions is that they give the human subject a rationality that may not exist. In any case, there is some discrepancy in the recording of graffiti in Pompeii between the earliest and the 20th century excavations.[29] However, from Figure 4.4 it would

(c)

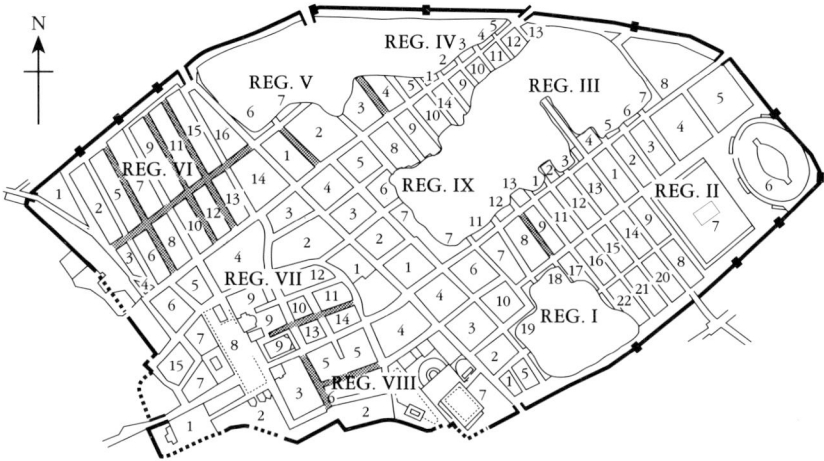

(d)

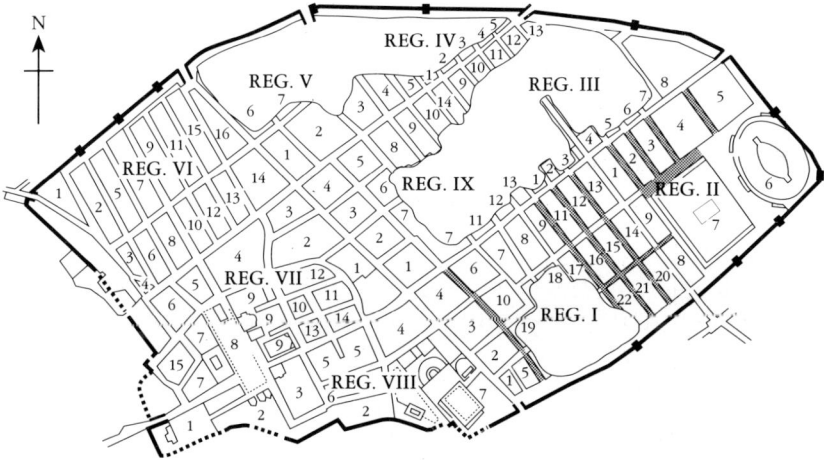

Figure 4.3   Occurrence of doorways in Pompeii: (c) 11–15 m; (d) 16+ m.

appear that the greatest occurrence of street messages was on the through routes. This method also identified some streets with few doorways occurring in them, that had high frequencies of message occurrence. Initially, this appears hard to explain. However, in a street that has significantly fewer doorways occurring in it, there is a greater extant area in which to write graffiti. To

(a)

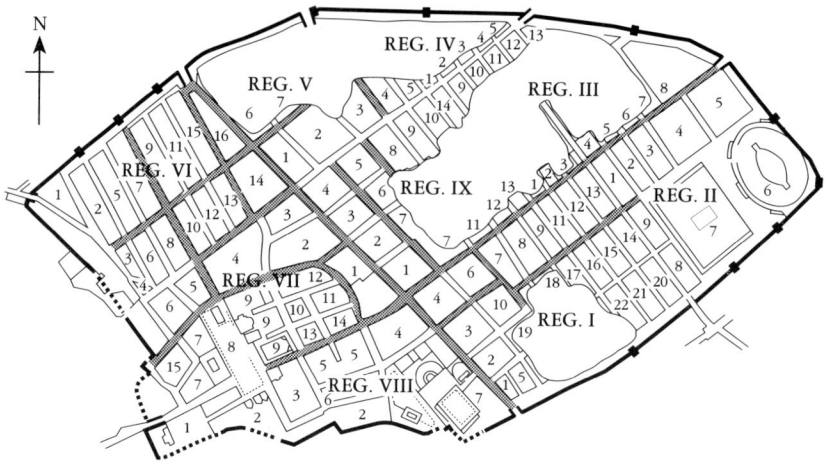

(b)

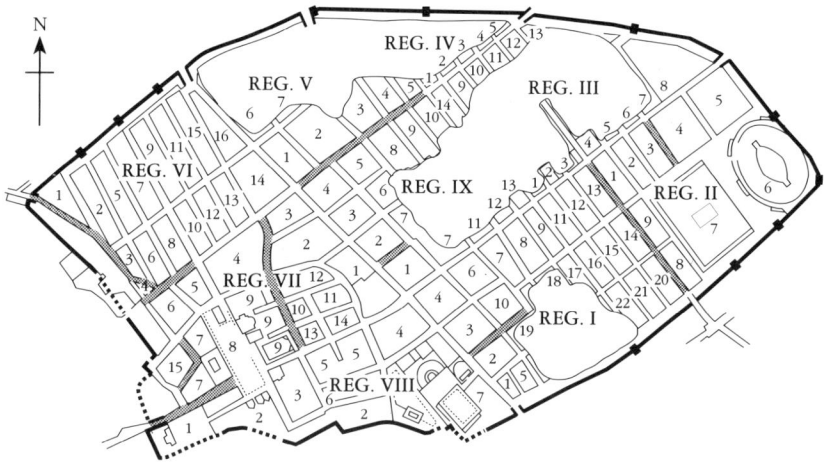

Figure 4.4   Occurrence of messages in Pompeii: (a) 0–4 m; (b) 5–8 m.

account for this it would be necessary to set a further control upon the data that reflected the amount of wall space available for graffiti. Such a reconstruction of extant wall space at the time of recording the graffiti is now impossible.

The third method was developed to reflect the different types of doorways in Pompeii. There are two types of doorway in Pompeii. Type 1 forms a corri-

(c)

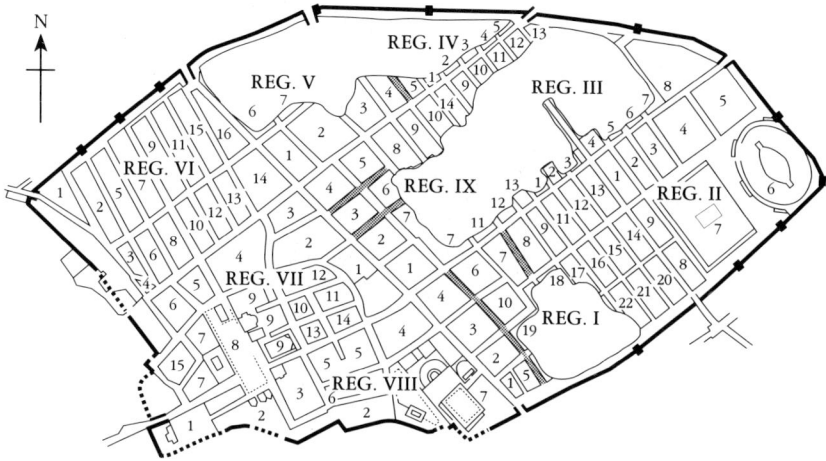

(d)

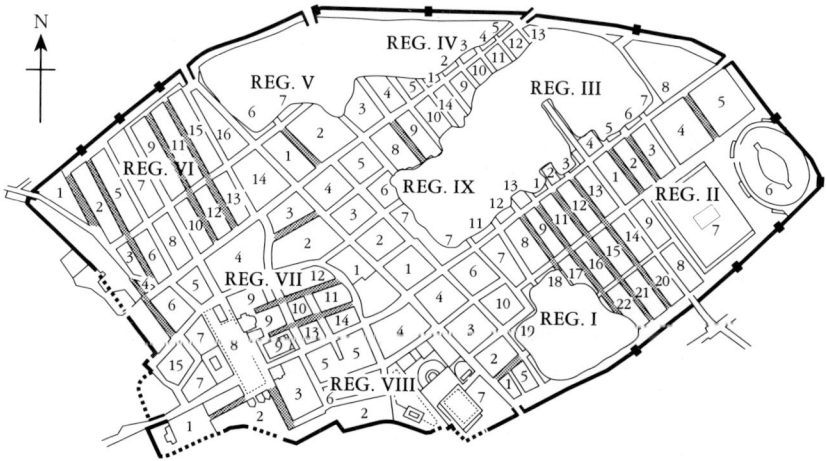

Figure 4.4   Occurrence of messages in Pompeii: (c) 9–12 m; (d) 13 + m.

dor distancing inhabitants from the street, normally referred to as a *fauces*.[30] Type 2 opens directly into the street, emphasizing contact between the property and the street. The two types of doorway in a street are compared as a ratio of type 1:type 2 (corridor:open). Again, plotted as a map the pattern is interesting (Fig. 4.7). The area with the highest ratio is in those streets to the

Figure 4.5   Pompeii, doorway (type 1).

east of the forum. It is noticeable that in Via di Mercurio there are fewer type 2 doorways, although there was a high occurrence of doorways in this street. In combination, these two aspects suggest that in Via di Mercurio there was competition for street frontage, but at the same time the occupants of the street wanted to emphasize their distance from the street.

How do we interpret this information? What does it all mean? The highest occurrences of doorways and street messages were found to be along the through routes from the city gates into the centre of the city.[31] This implies that the social relationship between the inhabitant and visitor was strong in Pompeii. In other words interaction with the city's rural hinterland or even other cities is stressed in the spatial structure of Pompeii. This emphasis upon these through routes also stresses the importance of movement from the city gate to the forum. Movement to the amphitheatre is not stressed, perhaps because it was not in use every day. Given this stress upon movement from city gate to forum, it is unusual that the area to the east of the forum is highlighted.

The visual narrative, as described by MacDonald, leads the stranger to the forum.[32] The stranger tends not to deviate from a wide linear route into a narrow street which is not straight. If this is the case, the social relationship between inhabitant and inhabitant is more usual in this area. If I wanted to attribute a zonal model for Pompeii, I might describe this as a lower-class zone. As I am no longer obsessed with finding zones in Pompeii, I would stress that the spatial configuration of these streets causes the pattern of doorway occurrences. In fact, this area forms the integrating core of the city. The streets join together the through routes from the gates to the forum. It is centrally placed between Via dell'Abbondanza, Via della Fortuna, Via Stabiana, and the forum. The irregular street pattern would also appear to facilitate the rôle as an integrating core. Regio VI in contrast is not an area of distributive streets, partly because of its position and street structure. There would be little reason to enter this area, unless there was a specific purpose and destination in it.

The pattern of doorway occurrences also reflects the internal structure of the buildings adjoined to the street. There appears to be a direct relationship between the frequency of doorway occurrences in a street and the number of spaces and the depth of the internal spaces within a building. The number of spaces corresponds to the number of rooms and corridors contained within a building. The depth of these spaces is measured from outside the building. When doorway occurrences are frequent, the mean number of spaces within the adjacent buildings was low. When doorway occurrences were less frequent, the mean number of spaces within adjacent buildings was higher. When door-

Figure 4.6 Pompeii, shop front (type 2).

73

(a)

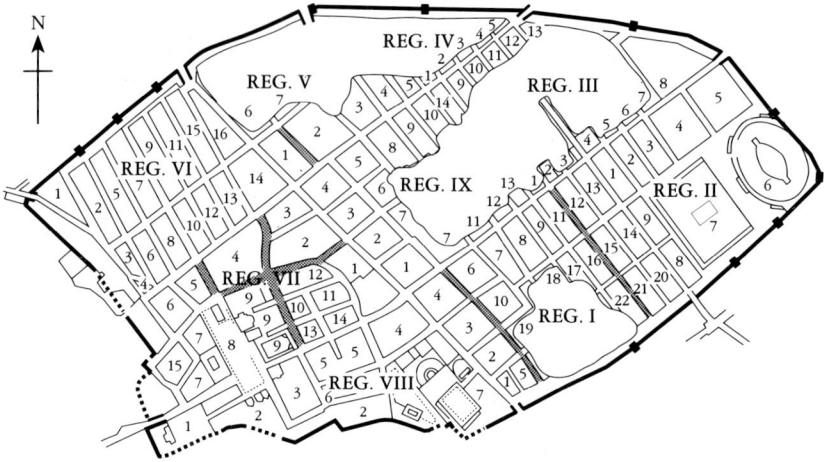

(b)

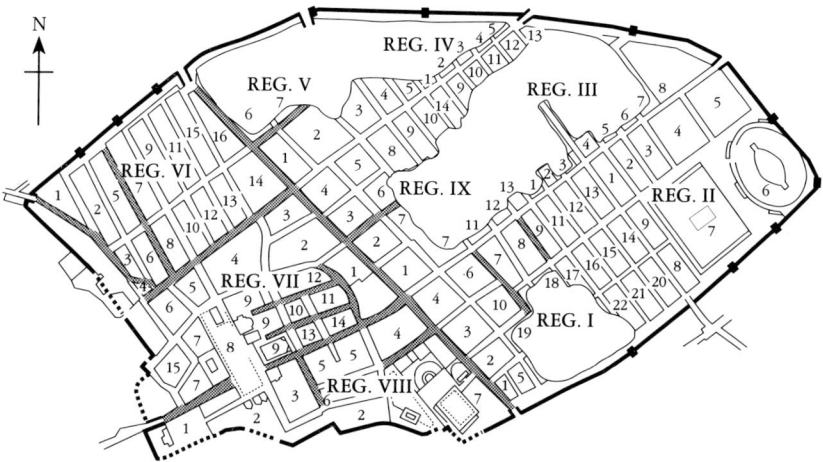

Figure 4.7   Ratio of type 1:type 2 doorways: (a) 1:6; (b) 1:4–6.

way occurrences were frequent, buildings tended to be shallow. When doorway occurrences were less frequent, the buildings tended to be deeper. Therefore, it seems that there was a relationship between the nature of the internal
and external space in Pompeii.[33]

   To conclude, it would appear from the Pompeian evidence that the arrangement of public space, streets, had a certain logic to it. This logic caused the

(c)

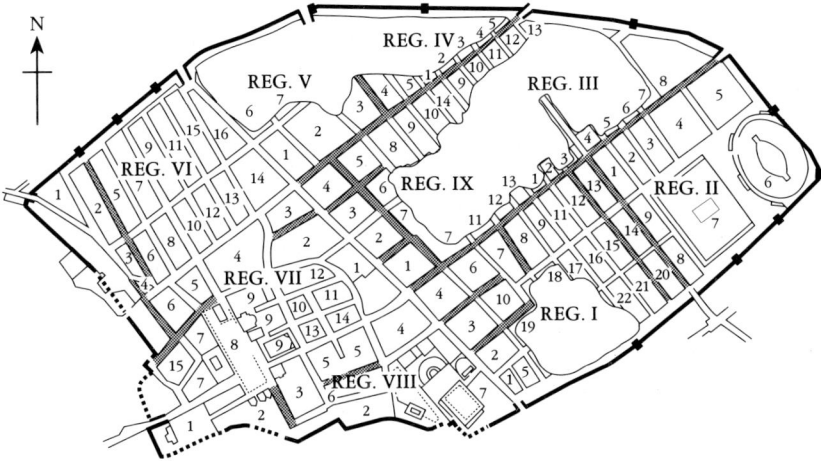

(d)

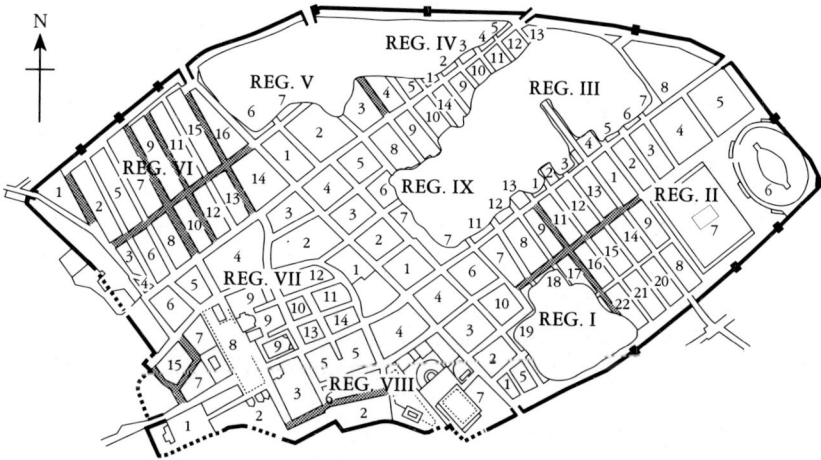

Figure 4.7 Ratio of type 1:type 2 doorways: (c) 1:2–4; (d) 1:1–2.

variation in the number of doorway occurrences, message occurrences and the ratio of type 1:type 2 doorways. Emphasis was laid upon the through routes as the streets with the greatest competition for street frontage. This suggests that the relationship between inhabitants and visitors was more dominant than the inhabitant–inhabitant relationship. Further, it suggests a high frequency of visitors to the site who did not live there. Another observation is that these through routes were integrated at the core of the city, by an area of irregular streets. The grid pattern may not be a system that promotes the integration of streets; rather it would appear that the irregular pattern of streets had a greater integrating rôle between streets. The separation of properties from the street was most pronounced in areas that were the least integrated within the street system. This would appear to be related to the amount of control a property has over its internal, rather than external, space.

This paper has been greatly influenced by Hillier & Hanson's work upon the social logic of space, which is a product of the recent architecture debates. In applying their methods I am only too conscious that I might be seeing the present in the past as much as Haverfield saw the expectations of the Town Planning Act realized in the Roman city. Questions of methodology still remain to be answered. How do we generalize from one site with a unique set of data, particularly, as this data set does not offer a diachronic view of space?[34] Further, to generalize about urban society in Roman Italy from the evidence of Pompeii may be to reduce regional variation to a version of Pompeii.

Notes

1. I would like to thank the British School at Rome for the support of this project. Whilst at the British School at Rome, I benefited from discussion of space with two architects, Jane Burnside and Hugh Petter. The present paper has evolved from earlier versions given at the British School at Rome, at the Theoretical Archaeology Group's 1990 Conference in Lampeter, for the Inter-Academy Seminar at the Canadian Academic Centre in Italy and the London conference. Finally, I would like to thank Jerry Paterson for his patient encouragement and advice. Upon all occasions the discussion was productive, but any present errors are my own.
2. Le Corbusier interviewed in Rome 1936. For full interview, A. Munoz, Le Courbusier parla di urbanistica Romana, in *L'urbe* 1, 1936, pp. 28–39.
3. For example Le Corbusier, *Towards a new architecture* (London, 1927), p. 156, with reference to Pompeii, in contrast to his views of ancient Rome: "Old Rome as regards architecture had nothing to show" (p. 154). See also C. Sitte, *The art of building cities* (tr. C. T. Stewart) (New York, 1945), p. 1, on Pompeii as an ideal type of urbanism.
4. Figures from J. P. Adam, *Degradation et restauration de l'architecture Pompeienne* (Paris, 1983), pp. 26–8
5. R. A. Raper, The analysis of the urban structure of Pompeii: a sociological examination of land use (semi-micro), in *Spatial archaeology*, ed. D. L. Clarke (London, 1977); C. M. Watts, *A pattern language for houses at Pompeii, Herculaneum and Ostia* (PhD thesis for The University of Texas at Austin, 1987). For a study of functional space see W. F. Jashemski, *The gardens of Pompeii* (New York, 1979), A. Wallace-Hadrill, *Houses and households in Pompeii* (Princeton, 1994) and R. Laurence, *Roman Pompeii: space and society* (London, 1994).

6. A. F. Wallace-Hadrill, The social structure of the Roman house, *PBSR* **56**, 1988, p. 48.

7. W. C. MacDonald, *The architecture of the Roman empire II: an urban appraisal* (New Haven, Conn., 1986), p. 3, stresses that Vitruvius (1.4.9) was mainly concerned with the need to return to the old methods in architecture.

8. R. Unwin, *Town planning in practice* (London, 1909), p. 10.

9. S. D. Adshead & H. C. Dowdall, The Town Planning Act [1909], *Town Planning Review* 1, 1910, p. 50.

10. Papers are recorded in full in *Transactions of the Town Planning Conference,* London, 10–15 October 1910. The discussion includes important contributions by Lanciani. See also The Town Planning Conference of the Royal Institute of British Architects, in *Town Planning Review* 1, 1911, 177–91. On the historiography of this period, see R. Laurence, Modern ideology and the creation of ancient town planning, *European Review of History* 1, 9–18.

11. F. Haverfield, *Ancient town planning* (Oxford, 1913). Haverfield (1913), p. 14.

12. *Ibid.*, pp. 64–5.

13. Watts, *A pattern language for houses at Pompeii, Herculaneum and Ostia*, p. 22 n. 19, makes this comparison between J. Packer, Middle and lower class housing in Pompeii and Herculaneum: a preliminary study, in *Neue Forschungen in Pompei*, eds B. Andreae & H. Kyrielies (Rome, 1975), pp. 133–42, and M. & A. de Vos, Scavi nuovii sconosciuti (I.9.13) pitture e pavimenti della casa di carere a Pompei, *Mededelingen van het Nederlands Instituit te Rome* **37**, 1975, pp. 47–85.

14. J. E. Vance, *This scene of man: the rôle and structure of the city in the geography of Western civilization* (1977), p. 37, states that industrialization led to the most dramatic morphogenesis that congregated classes and separated the workplace from the residence.

15. B. Ayeni, *Concepts and techniques in urban analysis* (London, 1979), p. 16. For reasons for location in the Roman city, see J. Rykwert, *The idea of a town: the anthropology of urban form in Rome, Italy and the ancient world* (London, 1976).

16. Raper, *The analysis of the urban structure of Pompeii.*

17. Vance, *This scene of man*, p. 35.

18. B. Hillier, & J. E. Hanson, *The social logic of space.* (Cambridge, 1984).

19. *Ibid.*, p. 28

20. The adoption of their theory and methods in archaeology is becoming more common. e.g. J. Foster, Analysis of spatial patterns in buildings (access analysis) as an insight into social structure: examples from the Scottish Atlantic Iron Age, *Antiquity* **63**, 1989, pp. 40–50. G. Erdosy, Social ranking and spatial structure: examples from India, *Archaeological Review from Cambridge* **5**, 1986, pp. 154–66. E. Yiannouli & S. J. Mithen, The real and random architecture of Siphnos: analyzing house plans using simulation, *Archaeological Review from Cambridge* **5**, 1986, pp. 167–80.

21. Hillier & Hanson, *The social logic of space*, p. 33. See C. Renfrew, Space, time and polity, in *The evolution of social systems*, eds J. Friedman & M. J. Rowlands (London, 1977), pp. 89–112.

22. There is not space to summarize their experiments upon randomness here. For full explanation see Hillier & Hanson, *The social logic of space*, pp. 33–53.

23. L. Martin, The grid as generator, in *Urban space and structure,* eds L. Martin & L. Marsh (Cambridge, 1972), pp. 6–27.

24. Rykwert, Streets in the past, pp. 15–28; Ellis, The spatial structure of streets, pp.

115–33.

25. R. Krier,*Urban space* (London, 1979), p. 17. Ellis The spatial structure of streets, p. 117. For an alternative conception of space in Japan see S. Lash, Postmodernism as humanism? Urban space and social theory, in *Theories of modernity and postmodernity*, ed. B. S. Turner (London, 1990), p. 69.

26. O. Newman, *Defensible space: people and design in the violent city* (London, 1972), p. 12; D. J. Walmsley, *Urban living: the individual in the city* (Harlow, 1988), p. 6; S. Anderson, Studies towards an ecological model of the urban environment, in *On Streets,* ed. S. Anderson, p. 267.

27. Wallace-Hadrill, The social structure of the Roman house, pp. 43–97. See also Y. Thébert, Life and domestic architecture in Roman Africa, in *The history of private life: from pagan Rome to Byzantium,* ed P. Veyne (London, 1987), p. 353.

28. This applies to all cartographic representation of data in this paper.

29. H. Mouritsen, *Elections, magistrates and municipal elite: studies in Pompeian epigraphy* (Rome, 1988).

30. Le Corbusier, *Towards a new architecture*, p. 183, observed that the *fauces* "frees your mind from the street".

31. Raper, *The analysis of the urban structure of Pompeii*, p. 208, observed that the distribution of shops was upon an optimizing basis along the major arteries.

32. MacDonald, *The architecture of the Roman empire*, pp. 5, 30–31.

33. R. Laurence, *Roman Pompeii: space and society* (London, 1994), pp. 88–120.

34. D. Perring, Spatial organisation and social change in roman towns, in *City and country in the ancient world,* eds J. Rich & A. Wallace-Hadrill (London, 1991), p. 284.

The Insula of the Paintings at Ostia I.4.2–4

Paradigm for a city in flux[1]

Janet DeLaine

Introduction

The life of a city is complex and ever changing, but archaeological and particularly structural evidence by its nature often tends to represent urban development as a series of static tableaux. Ostia is a case in point, despite the fact that here, as at Pompeii, we are dealing with a city more than two-thirds laid bare by excavation. Although the city existed for some 13 centuries, the fabric is predominantly that of the 2nd century AD, with some 3rd and 4th century buildings of note and pockets of construction going back to the original castrum walls of the 4th century BC; as a result we tend to assign all aspects of its development into a very few broad phases – five or six at the most – lasting several generations, while forgetting the dynamics of change which conspired to bring it about. Thanks to Russell Meiggs's heroic work of synthesis, the overall picture is familiar;[2] what eludes us are the nuances of the changing city, the city in flux. Meiggs himself was aware that the picture he presented was painted with a broad brush on a coarse canvas; when discussing the changes in the 4th century AD, his comment that "if we were better informed we should see a more complex picture" (p. 96) could be applied to almost any aspect and almost any period of Ostian life.

My intention here is to trace the changing nature of one structure, the Insula of the Paintings (I.4.2–4, Fig. 5.1), against the accepted outline of Ostian history from its earliest days into the 4th century AD. Built as a single unit in the 130s AD at the height of Ostia's expansion, the complex consists of three self-contained apartments – the twin Houses of the Paintings and of the Infant Bacchus, and the House of Jove and Ganymede – and a large garden; the joint and several lives of these apartments can be traced right through to the 4th century and beyond. In addition, thanks mainly to limited excavation below the floor of the imperial building, it is possible to trace the history of the site back at least to the 1st century BC, and beyond that to the 4th century since the

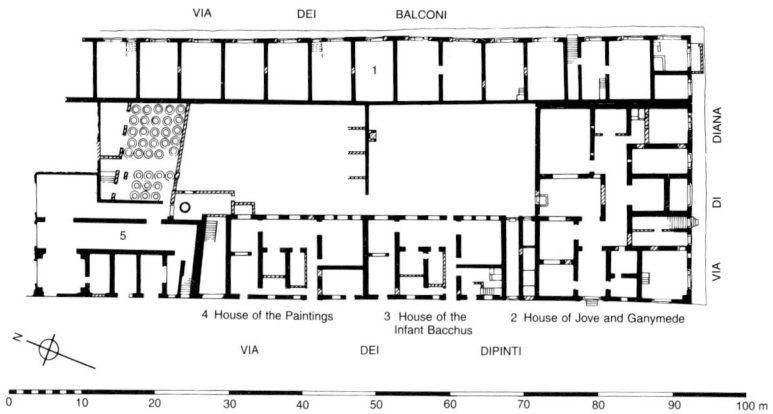

Figure 5.1 Insula 1.4, ground plan, final state.

House of Jove and Ganymede lies over the line of the old castrum wall. Here then is an opportunity, rare enough in Ostia, to trace the development of a single site over some 700 to 800 years. A small number of studies, notably the excavation of the Baths of the Swimmer and the Dutch programme of documentation and analysis of the House of the Porch and the rest of Insula V.2, have shown the potential gains from such an exercise.[3] By concentrating on the multiplicity of minor changes, rarely in themselves datable with any kind of accuracy, within a framework of a few major building phases, it is possible to highlight the rôle of the incidental and individual elements within the more sedate sweep of the city's changing fortunes. Often the small changes – the blocking of a door here, the opening of a door there – are our only guide to changes in property usage and property boundaries, and this is particularly important in the context of private building. Indeed, such signs of frequent alterations and adaptations of pre-existing buildings often provide the major evidence for the continued vitality of the urban environment in periods not distinguished by extensive new constructions.

The location of the Insula of the Paintings is an added attraction. Lying between the north wall of the castrum and the Tiber just east of the Cardo Maximus, close to the later forum and within a stone's throw of the Hadrianic *capitolium*, the site in question must have partaken fully of the active life of the city, and shared some at least of its changing fortunes. At the same time, as we shall see, its story can hardly be considered typical for Ostia in all its details, and the accidental and idiosyncratic will serve to remind us of the non-uniform nature of the urban pattern.

From the point of view of documentation – always a problem at Ostia – the insula is also an excellent subject for such an analysis. While a great deal of what follows is based on a new and detailed survey of the existing remains, much detail has been lost through decay since the original excavations and all evidence for the earlier and later phases can of course come only from excavation reports. In this we are relatively fortunate. Although the excavations conducted in the north and the southwest corner of the site between 1878 and 1905 were at best haphazard and poorly recorded, the major campaign carried out under the direction of Guido Calza between 1915 and 1919 was a vast improvement. An account of the excavations was published in some detail, including the late phase when the ground floor of the block was deliberately filled in and the ground level raised by several metres, and the excavation daybook (the *Giornale degli Scavi*) provides invaluable supplementary material.[4] Because of the height of the surviving structure (to the start of the third-floor level in the south part of the site) the Insula of the Paintings was much studied as an exemplar of the Roman insula and its place in the development of domestic architecture in Italy.[5] The well preserved wall-paintings, one of them bearing a convenient graffito giving a *terminus ante quem* in the reign of Commodus, ensured a continuing scholarly interest in the complex and in dating the paintings it contained.[6] If the excavations of the 1960s, carried out when some of the mosaics in the House of Jove and Ganymede were lifted for repair, still await formal publication, enough information has emerged to show phases going back at least to the early 1st century BC.[7] Needless to say, gaps do remain in the record, especially for the early and late phases, and there are problems in interpretation. Nevertheless there is sufficient material to make a reassessment worthwhile.

Prehistory

As we have already noted, the earliest activity which can be assumed on the site of the later insula is the building of the castrum wall. The line of this runs just south of the north wall of Rm 29 in the House of Jove and Ganymede (Fig. 5.1), while the Via di Diana which forms the southern boundary of the block is a survival of the inner pomerial road. Although the outer pomerial road on the north side of the castrum does not survive, a reflection of it may possibly be seen in the north boundary of the House of Jove and Ganymede and the passage (Rm 22) into the communal garden.[8] Thus the whole of the area on which the House of Jove and Ganymede was later built would have been free from any structures except the wall (and just possibly an *agger*[9]) until its defensive rôle was no longer required, according to Meiggs not earlier than the early 2nd century BC, although the excavations in the *taberna* of the invidiosus (V.5.1) may allow this date to be pushed back into the second half of the 3rd century.[10] No trace of the castrum wall is mentioned in the brief account of the excavations carried out in the House of Jove and Ganymede (Rms 24, 25, 29) during the 1960s published by Squarciapino.[11] The earliest identified structure consists of a couple of walls in *opus quasi-reticulatum*, dated vaguely to the 1st century BC, although the construction technique would fit better in the earlier part of the century, if not the late 2nd.[12] Squarciapino suggested that the structure may have been related to the corn supply; certainly a building of commercial character would suit both what little of the structure was uncovered and the location between the river harbour and the town. The north wall of this structure seems to respect the boundary of the presumed outer pomerial road, but there is simply no evidence to indicate whether there were other buildings between here and the Tiber at this date. On the other hand, the diagonal north boundary of the whole block (north wall of I.4.4, Rm 1; south wall of I.4.5) appears to run parallel to a much earlier road leading to the Tiber mouth and bypassing the castrum.[13] The continuation of this alignment strongly suggests that property boundaries at least had been fixed long before the early Hadrianic reorganization of the area, quite probably by the 1st century BC.

The next event in the structural development of the site was the demolition of the quasi-reticulate building and its replacement by a court, identified by paving and a surface gutter in tufa leading into a drain, with associated traces of minor walls. To this was later added what may have been a perimeter wall in brick-faced concrete, perhaps already fixing the west boundary of the insula, while it is clear that the court now extended further north than the House of Jove and Ganymede. The construction of this wall should be no earlier than the late Augustan period,[14] giving a maximum chronological range for the phase from Sulla to the Julio-Claudians. This was a period of great transformation for the old castrum and its associated settlement. Not only new temples were built, but also spacious atrium–peristyle houses. By 49 BC Ostia had its own local magistrates; by the reign of Tiberius if not earlier a new forum and *capitolium* had been laid out, and Ostia had gained a permanent theatre. The new construction on the site of the Insula of the Paintings fits comfortably into this picture. While there is insufficient evidence to determine the function of the building in this phase, it does seem to represent a change in boundaries and in architectural nature as well as possibly a more formal architectural style.

The brick perimeter wall remained in use during the next main phase, which saw the raising of the floor level by half a metre and the building of a complex structure in *opus reticulatum* with tufa quoins and including a black and white mosaic floor of simple geometric design. The level combined with the type of construction suggests a Domitianic or early Trajanic date.[15] Later a broad bench was added on three sides of one room, for a *triclinium* or a small shrine of some sort according to Squarciapino.[16] Either way, the commercial or public nature of the space indicated in the earlier phases seems to have been superseded by something of a more private and possibly domestic nature, even though the retention of the perimeter wall suggests that the boundaries of the property had not changed. This is the earliest candidate for a predominantly residential building north of the old castrum, although it must be admitted that the available evidence for pre-Hadrianic construction in this area is slight. Such a shift would, however, make sense in the context of the very real changes brought to the city by the building of the Claudian and Trajanic harbours, whereby the old river harbour became less important and the demands for purely commercial space on the river side of the city presumably less intense.

Perhaps the most unexpected result of the excavations is the identification of a separate phase preliminary to the actual construction of the insula in the 130s.[17] Once more all the structures within the perimeter wall were demolished but there was no further construction, although the floor level was raised on three separate occasions. In each case there was a simple beaten earth floor incorporating a certain amount of building rubble. To the south of the perimeter wall, however, another wall was built together with a floor of *opus spicatum* and these remained until demolished to make way for the present insula. The level of the *opus spicatum* floor allows us to associate it with a number of shop thresholds still preserved in the Via di Diana just in front of the south façade of the Hadrianic insula.[18] Into this picture we also have to fit the building of the long row of *tabernae* which forms the east side of the block fronting the Via dei Balconi (I.4.1), dated by brickstamps to AD 127–8. Slight as the evidence for this phase is, it is suggestive. It is clear from the dates given by the brickstamps that the great Hadrianic rebuilding of Ostia began before AD 120 in the area between the Decumanus and the Tiber north of the old castrum, with the *capitolium* as the focal point of the development.[19] The demolition of the reticulate building should belong to the general razing of this part of Ostia. Since the Via di Diana was an essential route for anyone trying to avoid the forum to the north, the building of a row of shops along it as part of the development of the area had much to recommend it, both economically and aesthetically, as did the construction of the *tabernae* on the Via dei Balconi. Leaving the remaining area vacant of construction for perhaps another ten years is another matter. Construction continued all over Ostia, buildings grew up on all sides, but the area remained empty. It was not, however, simply abandoned and unused; the maintenance of the boundary wall and the apparently deliberate raising of the ground level twice, as discrete events rather than as a continuous fill, preclude this.

The simplest explanation is that this area functioned as some kind of yard, and given the location of the site near the Tiber and in the heart of the initial reconstruction zone, it is tempting to see it as a builder's yard where bulky building supplies could be stored and possibly further worked, for example tufa into reticulate blocks. There may be a further indication from the garden area of the insula itself. At the time of the original excavations a large pit for slaking lime was found in the northern half, and there is some evidence that Calza had dug below the Hadrianic level in search of paving for the garden.[20] One further small piece of evidence may be significant here. A terracotta plaque representing builder's tools is built into one of the piers of the *tabernae* at the north end of the Via dei Balconi, and it has been suggested that this takes the place of a shop sign.[21] Given the well known tendency in the ancient world for businesses to group together in streets or districts, and given the presence of the seat of the *fabri tignuarii* not far away, the identification of a builder's yard in these surroundings may not be too fanciful. Building yards there certainly must have been. All of the building materials for Ostia – lime and pozzolana for mortar, brick and tufa for walls, travertine for thresholds and corbels, timber for roofs and ceilings – had to be brought from elsewhere, either by road or more likely by river to the Tiber wharves. Major developments such as the Garden Houses complex (mid 120s) and the area east of the theatre including the Baths of Neptune and the barracks of the Vigiles (early 130s) demanded very large amounts of building supplies, and there were many minor projects in hand as well.[22] In order for the work to progress at the rate it quite clearly did, supplies must have been ready to hand when required, which presupposes some reserves at Ostia itself.

The building of the insula

When the time came to demolish the shops on the Via di Diana and build the new insula (Fig. 5.2), even this was not all done in a single campaign but as three separate units, beginning with the House of Jove and Ganymede. There are clear construction breaks in the fabric on the garden façade corresponding with the north face of the north wall of the passage Rm 22 and the north face of the wall between Rms 9/10 and 11/12 (Fig. 5.3). In addition the brick cornice which supports the mezzanine floors of the insula was carried across the south wall of Rm 20 in the House of the Infant Bacchus despite the fact that this was intended to be a double-height room – a mistake much easier to make if the rest of the room was added only later. A stair (Rms 22/23) was included in the first unit since it served the mezzanine apartment over the western part of the House of Jove and Ganymede (Rms 124, 128, 134–6) as well as the second storey over the House of the Infant Bacchus. Although the brick-faced wall which divides the garden area in two between the House of the Infant Bacchus and the House of the Paintings cannot be securely dated on construction alone and has been thought to be later, it would make good logical sense to imagine it being built on the completion of the House of the Infant Bacchus in order to separate the construction site (??? and the remains of the builder's yard) from the new residential area. Once the House of the Paintings was complete, a fourth but separate unit (the Caseggiato dei Doli) with *tabernae* on the Via dei Dipinti was added to the north – not long after, to judge from the construction. Although the original arrangement is not clear, it may be that what now forms the north wall of the Severan room containing the *dolia defossa* was once the north boundary of the garden belonging to the Insula of the Paintings (cf. Fig. 5.1).

Figure 5.2   Original plan of I.4.2–4, ground and mezzanine floors.

In its original form the Insula of the Paintings (Fig. 5.2) provided a remarkably high standard of accommodation close to the political and commercial heart of the city.[23] The L-shaped insula consisted of two virtually identical *medianum* apartments – the House of the Infant Bacchus and the House of the Paintings – looking out onto a long garden, and a third much larger house (the House of Jove and Ganymede). The first two houses have their major reception room (*exhedra*, Rms 10 and 20) at one end of the *medianum* (Rms 6, 16) and a suite of *cubiculum/zotheca* connected by a door and a wide internal window at the other (Rms 2/3, 12/13).[24] The two main rooms (Rms 3 and 10, 13 and 20) had high ceilings, and these and the *medianum* were lit by large windows looking out over the garden. Included in each apartment were five rooms on a mezzanine floor inserted at half the height of Rms 3/13 and Rms 10/20. There were clearly at least one and possibly two independent apartments on the floor(s) above these two, but no details survive. The House of Jove and Ganymede, although sharing many elements in common with the other two, is organized on different principles. The focal point is an open court (Rm 26) with a broad corridor (Rm 29) and two main rooms (Rms 25, 27) opening off three sides only, and there is no *medianum*. The *exhedra* (Rm 27) opens widely to the court and is flanked by an *ala* (Rm 30) which gives access to a pair of

Figure 5.3 I.4.2–4, construction joint between the House of Jove and
Ganymede and the House of the Infant Bacchus.

service rooms (Rms 41 and 40), while a major *cubiculum* or minor reception
room faces axially onto the court across the corridor. As in the House of the
Paintings and the House of the Infant Bacchus there was a *cubiculum/zotheca*
suite, and a part of the mezzanine floor was probably included in the house;[25]
the original house would thus have had some 16 main rooms. The remaining
mezzanine rooms (Rms 124, 128, 134–6) formed a separate apartment reached
from the staircase on the Via dei Dipinti. There were certainly one and probably two or even three floors of apartments above, reached from exterior stair-
cases, but virtually nothing of this survives. The ground floor was completed
by two shops (Rms 36 and 39), the larger one of which was dependent on the
house, while the other probably included the room above it at mezzanine level.

The nearest parallel for the complex is the famous Garden Houses development at the western edge of the town. The Garden Houses themselves

(III.9.13–20) along with the other minor apartments on the periphery of the development (especially III.9.3 and the House of the Yellow Walls, III.9.12)[26] provide the closest architectural parallels for the two *medianum* apartments, and their relation to the enclosed garden space is similar. The only unusual feature in our building seems to be the narrow corridor running the length of each house on the west, presumably to give direct access to the main *cubicula* from the service area Rm 9/19, which also housed the stair to the mezzanine floor. The relationship between the House of Jove and Ganymede and the House of the Muses, however, is not as immediately obvious. The most striking feature of the House of the Muses, the central court surrounded by arcades on all four sides, is replaced by the three-sided court (Rm 26).[27] Nevertheless, the presence of the *cubiculum/zotheca* suite, the presence of the *alae*, the size and arrangement of the *exhedra*, are only the most important features the two houses have in common. The similarities between these particular houses and between the two developments in general are in fact sufficiently close to imagine them the work of the same architect.

If the House of the Muses can be seen as "the best dwelling constructed at the time",[28] and the Garden Houses complex as a whole "the most attractive for men of means",[29] the Insula of the Paintings must have been no less attractive, and in its way is even more remarkable. Quite how remarkable has never, I believe, been fully appreciated. In an area where every street façade was occupied by public or commercial buildings, a mere 18 m of the 94 m long façade of the insula was occupied by *tabernae*, and most of that by two sides of a single *taberna* (Rm 36) dependent on the main residence; in an area where the only open spaces belong to public or commercial buildings, as much as 900 m² – some 40 per cent of the insula – was apparently laid out as a private garden. The Garden Houses development, it should be remembered, arose at the western end of the town in a predominantly residential area where space was not so obviously at a premium. In addition, the House of Jove and Ganymede was clearly a house of considerable distinction. The geometric mosaics in Rms 24, 25, 27 and 28 which are the only part of the original decoration to survive in any reasonable condition, are of high quality.[30] The main reception room (Rm 27) is larger than any other in Ostia and the entrance vestibule is correspondingly grand. According to the Roman concept of *decor*, as enunciated by Vitruvius (VI.v.1–2), the house would have provided accommodation for someone of reasonably elevated rank and it is not surprising that scholars have identified it as the residence of the owner of the whole apartment block.[31] Certainly the large attached shop and the spacious vestibule suggest a considerable body of dependants and clients. If this identification is correct, then the owner must have been a person of wealth and consequence in Ostia. Indeed, the very location of this predominantly residential development in a commercial and public quarter at the heart of the city and the lavish use of open space also invite such a supposition.

The changing face of the insula

The insula flourished for roughly 150 years, during which it underwent a series of alterations to its structure, its decoration, the arrangement of its apartments, and its use. The dating of these phases is difficult, and it is often not possible to assign a particular change to any definite phase. The traditional method of dating by construction techniques proves even less certain than usual, since many of the openings appear to have been blocked with whatever rubbish was lying to hand. The difficulties are further accentuated by the aim of the excavators to return the building as nearly as possible to its original state, which included removing some doorway blockings and late walls as well as filling in later doorways. Construction techniques can, however, sometimes help to group some alterations together even when their absolute dating is not clear, and the relationship between structural change and decoration is often decisive.

The first phase of alterations took place sometime in the second half of the 2nd century, and before the end of the reign of Commodus (Fig. 5.4).

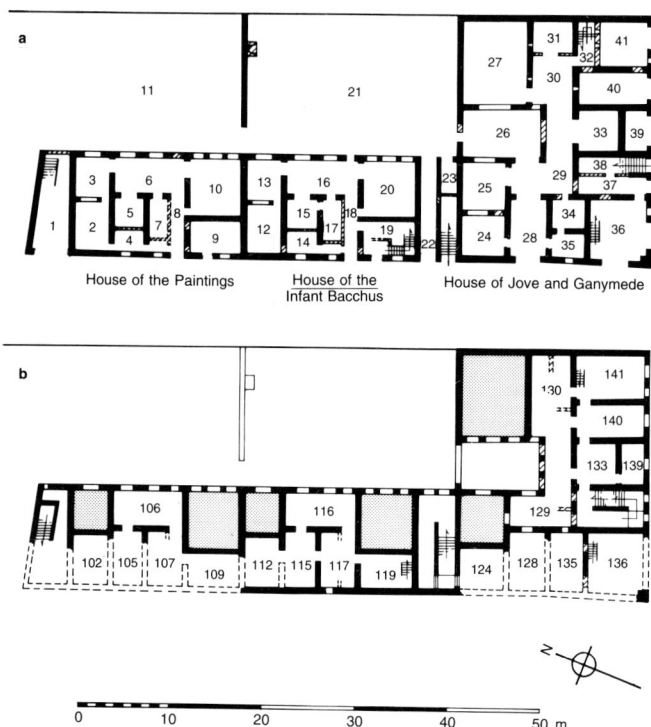

Figure 5.4 Plan at the end of the 2nd century, ground and mezzanine floors.

Figure 5.5   Rms 24/25, blocked doorway.

Although Calza recognized this phase only in the House of Jove and Ganymede,[32] in fact alterations were made in all three houses requiring an almost total redecoration of the insula. In the House of Jove and Ganymede the most important alterations were the blocking of the entrance from the Via di Diana into the corridor Rm 29, the dividing of the *cubiculum/zotheca* suite (Rms 24 and 25) into two separate rooms, and the creation of a separate room (Rm 31) at the east end of the *ala* (Rm 30). All of these can be related by the redecoration, and by the extremely poor nature of the construction, comprising a rough rubble of tufa and/or building rubbish in a white friable mortar apparently without pozzolana, and in the case of the blocked doors with only one built face in a rough approximation to block and brick (Fig. 5.5). The same kind of rough construction, but with one face of bricks set in a hard, greyish mortar, associated with the same kind of wall-painting, is found in the House of the Paintings and the House of the Infant Bacchus. The main changes indicated here are the insertion of the walls dividing Rms 4 and 5 and Rms 14 and 15, the blocking of the west doors between the service areas and entrance passages (Rms 8/9 and 18/19), and the wall dividing Rms 17 and 18.

One further alteration must belong to this phase, although the construction technique is different and no wall-painting survives actually over the new construction to link it directly to the others. This is the blocking of the opening between the court and the south branch of the corridor Rm 29 in the House of Jove and Ganymede, where the fill is brick-faced both sides and uses a much stronger mortar (Fig. 5.6). This is not simply the result of a change in function as the other alterations might have been. The arched lintel of the original doorway had cracked and begun to collapse, and the blocking was clearly intended to shore up this important wall which had to support the courtyard face of the apartments three or four floors above; for extra strength the windows on the mezzanine floor above were also blocked.[33] Since the collapse would have necessitated major repairs, it is reasonable to assume that it was this – one of

Figure 5.6 Blocking of opening Rms 26/29.

90

the incidentals of the city's history – which led to the restructuring of the insula. The immediate effect on the House of Jove and Ganymede was to reduce the amount of light in the corridor around the court, and particularly to block out the only source of light to Rm 33. In the original plan this was clearly an important space and, if the parallel with the House of the Muses is any indication, would have demanded a higher standard of decoration than the simple yellow-ground architectural scheme given it in the redecoration. Perhaps in recompense for the demoting of this room the *cubiculum* was given a wider opening and cut off from its *zotheca*, which was given a separate entrance from the vestibule; both appear to have had the more lavish red and yellow panelled style of decoration also found in the *exhedra*.

None of the other alterations, however, can be linked so directly to the effects of this loss of light. Rather, they are functional changes, and an analysis of their results allows us tentatively to include other alterations which cannot be independently dated to this phase. First, the closing of the access to the House of Jove and Ganymede from the Via di Diana may reflect the dissociation of the corner shop from the main residence. The passage itself, and the under-stair space which was closed off to make a separate room, were then presumably attached to the shop. The shop may also have acquired its own living quarters above, with the addition of an internal staircase and the blocking of the doors to Rms 134 and (probably) 135. This in turn affected the small mezzanine level apartment reached from the Via dei Dipinti, where two small rooms (Rms 134 and 135) were knocked together, presumably to make up for the loss of the original main living-room now dedicated to the shop. There were other alterations and additions to the mezzanine floor which may belong to this phase but are more difficult to interpret. Marks in the wall plaster in Rms 129 and 130 (Fig. 5.7) indicate the use of slender curtain walls to divide the space into a number of cells, but the arrangement of these and most importantly the connections between them are no longer recoverable.[34] The door and window from the stairwell into Rm 129 were blocked, presumably in relation to this subdivision of the space. It is not impossible, however, that this area had already been subdivided even before the threatened collapse.

A further set of interconnected changes to the House of Jove and Ganymede need to be discussed. At some time the two service rooms 40 and 41 were turned into independent shops by turning the exterior windows into doors opening onto the Via di Diana (Fig. 5.8) and blocking off the communicating doors. At the same time a stairwell (Rm 32) was carved out of Rm 41, which served the main residence. Perhaps also at this time in compensation for the loss of the service rooms below, the room above the small shop (Rm 139) was connected with the rest of the mezzanine floor and turned into a kitchen and lavatory.[35] Although Calza put these changes into the late Antonine period along with the major restructuring of the house, there is some evidence to suggest a Severan date. Several Severan brickstamps were found in this area during the excavations,[36] and this would be in keeping with the nature of the

Figure 5.7   Marks of curtain wall in Rm 129.

construction, which is brick-faced throughout. A substantial Severan phase can also be recognized in the rest of the insula. The shrine to Jove built against the south face of the garden wall is generally assumed to be Severan (on analogy with the similar construction in the Insula of Serapis), as is the installation of the *dolia defossa* in the northern part of the garden and its associated structures.[37] This latter has implications for the House of the Paintings since it assumes the blocking of the garden door to the external staircase, and the construction technique used for this is in fact similar to the sides of the shrine. It is also the best context for the blocking of the garden door of the house itself.[38] More tentatively, we may assign the changes in Rms 9 and 19, the service rooms of the House of the Paintings and the House of the Infant Bacchus respectively, to the same phase. In both cases a door was opened into the room from the street by adapting a pre-existing window, the same technique used in the creation of the shops from Rms 40 and 41. In Rm 19 the door led to a new staircase to the mezzanine floor, the older one going out of use. Traces of a partition wall survive which may have separated the stairwell from the rest of the house, thus creating an independent apartment on the mezzanine floor. No staircase remains from either phase in Rm 9, but it is worth noting that at the time of excavation, the second door from the room into the house was also blocked.[39]

A reasonably consistent picture emerges. Sometime in the Antonine period, and probably later rather than earlier, the threatened collapse of part of the

Figure 5.8 Door to shop, Rm 41, showing widening of window under the original lintel.

House of Jove and Ganymede led to modifications of the original plan. The house retained its original elegance and roughly its original size, although there seems to have been some subdivision of the mezzanine floor which may or may not have removed part of it from the main residence. At the same time, the large shop was detached from the house and rented separately with its own living quarters above. The other two houses also saw slight alterations, identical in their most significant details although perhaps not in all.[40] The uniformity of the modifications and the wall-painting which covered them strongly suggests that the whole block was still part of the same property, although when taken with the separation of the shop we may have evidence here for a change of ownership following the structural damage. No more than a generation later, parts of the insula had taken on a more commercial aspect. Two new shops had been opened on the Via di Diana, the House of the Paintings had been cut off from its part of the garden where a storeroom for bulk foodstuffs (oil or corn?) had been built, and two new separate apartments had been created from the mezzanine floors of the original *medianum* apartments. All this fits in well with Pavolini's overall picture of expanding commercial and artisan activity in late 2nd and early 3rd century Ostia, with a concomitant move to create more residential accommodation.[41] At the same time, the main residence remained a substantial one, the small shrine in the southern garden add-

93

ing a further note of distinction to the insula, and this despite the threat of collapse and the substantial alterations which this necessitated.[42]

The insula in the late empire

The next distinct phase which can be identified belongs to some time later in the 3rd century. At the time of excavation many if not most of the Antonine wall-paintings in all three houses, plus the garden shrine, were covered with a thin coat of whitewash which served as the basis for a new phase of decoration.[43] None of these paintings survived for long beyond the period of excavation, but there are other examples in the same technique elsewhere in Ostia; the dating has ranged variously from the 2nd quarter to the end of the 3rd century.[44] Some of the mosaic floors were repaired in a random fashion that paid no attention to the original pattern, a common phenomenon at Ostia although impossible to date except as post-Severan.[45] A small number of structural changes possibly belong to this general period as well (Fig. 5.1). Doors were opened from the Via dei Dipinti into Rms 2 and 12 respectively, perhaps indicating a further subdivision of these houses into smaller apartments, while the door from the court of the House of Jove and Ganymede into the main garden was blocked and a basin built in front of it in the court.[46] There is also evidence for substantial changes during the second half of the 3rd century or later in the garden area and in the Caseggiato dei Doli, although nothing can be seen on the ground today. The *dolia defossa* were discovered immediately under a coarse marble mosaic floor (believed by the excavators to be medieval); the rims had been deliberately cut down and the *dolia* filled with rubble that included a variety of unusual moulds which can be dated to the mid 3rd century and a series of terracotta theatrical masks.[47] Immediately to the south of the *dolia* was an area of basalt paving. A similar combination of coarse mosaic and basalt paving was found in the south garden associated with a number of rooms built in the garden space; other rooms exited against both sides of the dividing wall and against the north wall of the House of Jove and Ganymede.[48] A basin was also found in the south garden and some of the walls retained traces of painted wall plaster. The coarse marble mosaics are typical of Ostia in the late 3rd and 4th centuries, although Guidobaldi has argued that they go back to the middle of the 3rd at least.[49] At any rate these alterations must be earlier than the middle of the 4th century, by which time, as we shall see, the insula had been abandoned.

Irrespective of whether these alterations represent one, two, or more separate phases, the overall impression is of a positive attempt to maintain the insula with, if anything, an increasingly intensive use of the available space, even if the precise nature of that use cannot be identified. It seems likely that during this period the alienation of the garden area from the three original residential units, assumed to have begun with the insertion of the *dolia*, was complete. On the other hand, the uniformity of the redecoration of the insula may once again point to a single ownership, and may even indicate once more a change in that ownership. Compared with the earlier standards of construction, alteration and decoration we may detect a decline, but there is no decline in vitality. Yet this was clearly a period of great change for Ostia, and abandonment is as common as adaptation even within the same small area. If the later 3rd century saw the development of the well known *thermopolium* just across the road from the House of Jove and Ganymede on the Via di Diana, the blocks to the east were less fortunate. Sometime in the later 3rd century, the bakery on the Via dei Molini (I.3.1) was destroyed by fire and not repaired, and signs of intense fire damage were also found in the Via dei Balconi coming from the House of the Mithraeum of Lucretius Menander (I.3.5).[50] The adjacent House of Diana also suffered. While the latest wall-paintings there have been dated to the mid 3rd century, one of the main ground-floor rooms had already been turned into a stable before the house was abandoned in the late 3rd century, possibly at the same time as the bakery.[51] Such uneven development is characteristic of Ostia in this period. A phase of intense building activity has been shown by Boersma in Insula V.2, lasting through the 3rd and well into the 4th century,[52] while the nearby Baths of the Swimmer (V.10.iii) were abandoned in the middle of the 3rd century.[53] Within the Garden Houses complex, the Insula of the Ierodule (III.9.6) was abandoned early in the last quarter of the 3rd century, while the House of the Muses and the House of the Yellow Walls show signs of decoration which could be as late as the 4th.[54]

By the middle of the 4th century, the picture had changed dramatically. Over all the area of the Insula excavated by Calza including the garden, and over the Via dei Balconi and the *tabernae* flanking it (I.4.1), the ground level was found to have been raised between 2 and 5 m, firstly by building rubble from which all re-usable brick had been removed and above that by a layer of broken amphorae mixed with other general rubbish, in places some 2 m thick.[55] Calza dated the fill to roughly the end of the 3rd century, the latest find being a coin of Maxentius, although a recent reassessment of the amphorae from the Via dei Balconi suggests a mid 4th century context.[56] In Calza's view the building rubble resulted from the deliberate dismantling of the upper parts of the building in search of re-usable materials, after which the area was turned into a rubbish dump. Finally, at some later but unspecified date there was a period of rehabitation, indicated by a number of walls in rough *opus vittatum* and a pavement of beaten earth. The fill in the House of Jove and Ganymede extended to just above the original mezzanine floor level, from where it sloped down towards the north until in the House of the Paintings it was apparently barely 3 m deep. Only three late walls associated with this level were recorded at the time of excavation, but there are a number of alterations to the actual fabric which should belong to the same phase of reuse. The most easily identified are those which relate to the rooms which were not originally

*Figure 5.9 House of the Paintings (I.iv.4), late door at upper level be-
tween Rms 2 and 3.*

divided into two by a mezzanine floor: Rms 3 (Fig. 5.9), 13, 20, 25 and 27. A
wall divided Rms 129 and 130, and a window was made in the east wall of Rm
130, showing incidentally that by this stage the shops on the Via dei Balconi
were reduced to below this height.[57] The two other walls appear to have repeated two of the original boundaries between the houses, one along the line
of the garden wall and the other just one side of the north wall of the House of
Jove and Ganymede.[58]

To some extent, then, the Insula of the Paintings can be thought to have at
last shared in the general pattern of decay and abandonment already begun in
the middle of the 3rd century with the bakery on the Via dei Molini and continued towards the end of the century with the House of Diana. But there are
differences. Certainly there was a period of simple abandonment while the
structure of the building remained at least partially intact.[59] Given the earlier
instability in this part of the block, it is tempting to suspect a re-occurrence of

the old problem, threatening a collapse of the upper floors. Perhaps the blocking of the stair from the Via dei Dipinti and the removal of its lower steps, not otherwise datable, is to be associated with this phase.[60] On the other hand, the House of the Infant Bacchus seems to have had at least one intermediate phase before the final interment, involving a new level roughly a metre above the original.[61] At the same time, the actual demolition of the House of Jove and Ganymede – down to the first-floor vaults perhaps but no further – appears to have been systematic and deliberate, as could have been the fill of amphorae and general rubbish used to create a new floor level in the shell of the building.[62] Sadly, there is no evidence at all for the dating of the new walls (as opposed to the fill), although the apparent maintenance of some of the old property divisions may signify a shorter rather than a longer break. In other words, the raising of the level of the insula may represent a short period of intense activity intended to bring the abandoned building back into use, rather than a long slow period of decay.

The re-use of abandoned buildings and the creation of new areas of occupation at much higher levels are phenomena which recur elsewhere in the east part of Ostia during the 4th century (Fig. 5.10), although much of the evidence has been removed in the process of excavation. Calza mentions later walls inserted in the abandoned and partly filled House of Diana, and there must have been other examples.[63] More importantly, two new buildings facing the Decumanus just a block to the south of the Insula of the Paintings (a large semicircular *exhedra* and the forum of the Heroic Statue, I.12.2–3) were built at a much higher level than the 2nd century road by incorporating earlier structures in their platforms; there can be little doubt that these were deliberate rather than incidental events.[64] At the same time, the Forum Baths a little further south continued to operate at the 2nd century level, undergoing a number of restorations during the 4th century. Indeed, given all the changes in level it is hard to reconstruct the operational street pattern in this part of Ostia during this period. Unfortunately there is no evidence for any late levels on the Via dei Dipinti, but the absence of any basalt paving and of any record of blocked doorways (with the exception of that to the stairwell Rm 23) on this side at the time of the excavations strongly suggests that the high level extended across this as well, to be retained presumably by the rear wall of the *tabernae* facing the Cardo Maximus. Since the depth of fill in the Insula of the Paintings decreased towards the north, it is possible that it petered out before reaching the river bank. We have already seen that the Via dei Balconi was obliterated by the same fill which raised the level of the Insula of the Paintings, and this higher level appears also to have extended over part of the Via di Diana.[65] The Via dei Molini to the east, however, was apparently raised by little more than half a metre, and this difference in level was mediated by a late structure blocking the east end of the Via di Diana where it met the Via dei Molini.[66] To the south the Via dei Lari was blocked at the Decumanus and a late *nymphaeum* inserted next to it, opposite the new forum of the Heroic Statue. The continu-

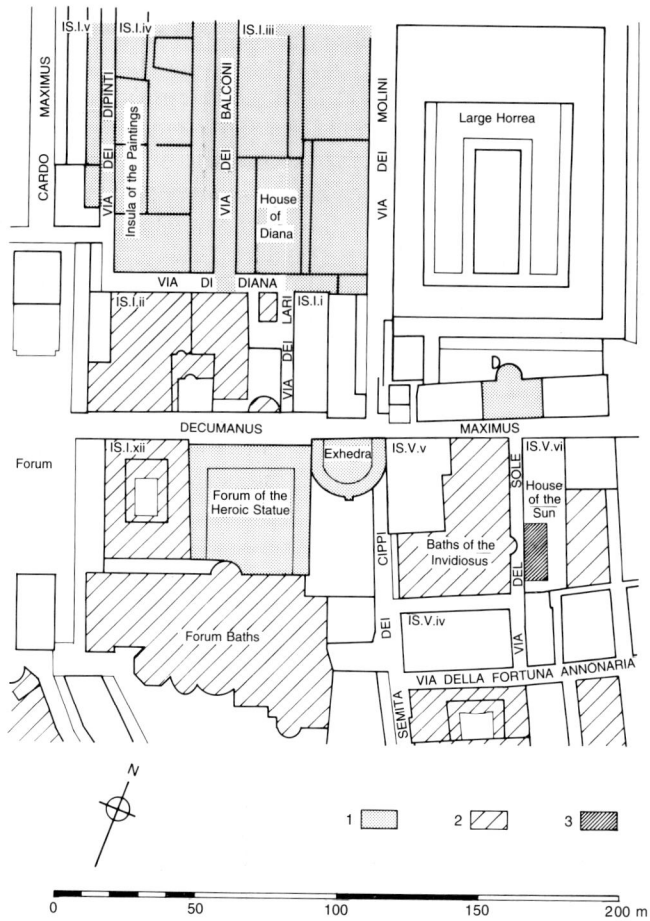

Figure 5.10   Area east of the forum in the 4th century ad, schematic plan. (1) New structures or re-use at higher level; (2) structures in use at the 3rd centruy level with the 4th century alterations; (3) structures abandoned by 4th century.

ation of the Via dei Molini (the Semita dei Cippi), however, was blocked by the new *exhedra*, while the Via del Sole shows several signs of being abandoned as a thoroughfare: part of the House of the Sun (V.6.1) was walled up after a fire and abandoned, a new apse added to the Baths of the Invidiosus (V.5.2) invaded the street, and the exit onto the Via della Fortuna Annonaria was blocked.

In the 4th century, therefore, as in the later part of the 3rd, the picture of life at Ostia presented by the Insula of the Paintings and the area around it is one of contrasts, of pockets of active reorganization amid zones of passive decay. As far as private buildings are concerned, within the general pattern of movement away from the river area towards the sea and the Via Severiana coming in from the coast, any sense of overall planning is absent, and the fate of each insula and even of each unit within an insula seems to depend very much on individual and local circumstances.[67] It can be no mere coincidence, as Pavolini has pointed out,[68] that the great changes in the nature of Ostia and the fabric of the city, the rise of the *domus* and the decline of the insula, are concurrent with the disappearance of the local magistrates from the epigraphic record and the subsequent passing of control over the city to Rome. A strong local magistracy presupposes considerable local landownership within as well as without the city, and thus strong economic incentives for maintaining both the urban fabric and its infrastructures. With the decline in Ostia's economic position, the fall in returns from privately owned commercial and residential property must have had their effect, particularly on those without other substantial sources of wealth. The abandonment of the insula, the disintegration of the city, and the decline of the local aristocracy would appear to go hand-in-hand.

The city in flux

By examining the insula in detail we have in fact been able to reconstruct a far more complex history than has hitherto been recognized. Two contrasting trends are apparent. On the one hand, predictably, the changing pattern of use of the land reflects the wider pattern of urban growth and change long recognized at Ostia. Thus the growth of the settlement beyond the walls of the castrum towards the all-important river harbour, the 1st century expansion marked by an increased architectural sophistication, the wealth of the Hadrianic city allowing for the complete renewal of the urban fabric, the flourishing commercial activity of the later 2nd century, the drastic changes of the 3rd and 4th centuries where decay is as common as renewal, are all reflected, however dimly, in the life of the insula. Overlying and at times interrupting this clear pattern are elements of the accidental and unforeseen which serve to highlight the variety and complexity of urban life. The long break between demolition and final construction in the Hadrianic phase and the piecemeal nature of the construction itself do not conform to the generally accepted pattern of development, the high status of the finished building is unexpected in its location, the threatened collapse and subsequent reconstruction are the result of pure accident.

Lack of evidence prevents us at present from knowing to what extent this complexity was usual or not. Certainly the location of the insula close to the heart of the city meant that it was developed sooner and maintained longer than some buildings in outlying parts of the town. Even within its immediate environs the Insula of the Paintings was a building of exceptional distinction, and the evidence seems to suggest that it continued to have a life somewhat apart from its neighbours even into the 4th century. However, where detailed analysis has been made of other buildings in other parts of the city, as with the insula containing the House of the Porch, the events in the structural history may be different but the nature of it is much the same.[69] The more this complexity becomes apparent, the more impressive is the sheer quantity of human effort it represents. Construction is a labour-intensive activity, and there can hardly have been a time, at least from the 1st century BC onwards, when Ostia was free from the sounds and sights of builders at work. Nor should we forget the demolition works and landfill which are the necessary concomitants of construction in an urban environment. Both building materials and fill had to be brought to the site through the streets of the city; the builders' carts which feature in the literary sources were not confined to the city of Rome.[70] At the peak of its expansion between the late 1st and the mid 2nd century a large part of Ostia must always have actually been under construction. The House of Jove and Ganymede provides an example. In a period lasting at the very most 40 years, the site saw the demolition of two structures and the building of three, while the ground level was raised on five different occasions by a total of over 1.5 m. At a rough estimate, there would have been builders at work on the site for at least a fifth of that period. This is the reality of the great rebuilding of Ostia. In relation to the presumably much reduced population of the city, the large landfill schemes and the building of the new *domus* of the 4th century must have appeared as another such period of intense activity. If we look just at the Insula of the Paintings, allowing for a 2 m depth of amphorae being brought into the site, roughly 300,000 basketfuls would have been needed just for the area between the Via dei Dipinti and the Via dei Balconi, and we have seen that the fill probably extended even further than that.

Superimposed on these periods of exceptional activity was a constant stream of minor building works – alterations, additions, redecorations, salvage works – and with it a demand for labour and materials. Because of the difficulty of dating many of these works and, for the late phases, the loss of much of the evidence, it is all too easy to overlook their importance. Up to the end of the 4th century at least, even when no major public works or large private schemes were in hand, there is ample evidence from studies of individual structures such as the Insula of the Paintings that the building trade, and therefore urban life, continued apace. The large size of the city of Ostia, its great wealth, and the long life of the *collegium* of the *fabri tignuarii* are at the same time symbols and results of a persistent vitality.

Notes

1. This paper arises from a survey of the Insula of the Paintings carried out by the author in the spring of 1991. The detailed evidence on which the following analysis is based will be published in the near future. I am extremely grateful to the Soprintendente of Ostia, Dott.ssa Anna Gallina Zevi, for permission to work on the insula and access to unpublished archival material, and to Dott.ssa Guiseppina Lauro for her kind offices in facilitating the project. The British School provided a base in Rome, and I would like to thank all its staff and particularly the Assistant Director Amanda Claridge for their help and encouragement. The fieldwork would not have been possible without generous grants from the Craven Committee, the Meyerstein Foundation, and St John's College, Oxford. My thanks are also due to the following people who gave practical help with the survey: Jean Keith Bennett, Jane Burnside, David Elkington, Clayton Fant, Sheila Gibson, Lynne Lancaster, Ray Laurence, David Leverett, Kathryn Lomas, Alison MacDonald, Bill Packer, Hugh Petter, and David Wilkinson. Finally I am grateful to John Lloyd and David Wilkinson for their helpful comments on earlier drafts of the paper. All drawings and photographs are by the author.

2. The debt to R. Meiggs, *Roman Ostia*, 2nd rev. edn (Oxford, 1973), of the most recent general accounts of Ostia by C. Pavolini, *La vita quotidiana a Ostia* (Bari, 1986), and R. Chevallier, *Ostie antique: ville et port* (Paris, 1986), is patent.

3. For the Baths of the Swimmer see Carandini *et al.*, Ostia I, *Studi Miscellenei*, **13**, 1968; Ostia II, *Studi Miscellenei*, **16**, 1970; Ostia III, *Studi Miscellenei*, **21**, 1973; Ostia IV, *Studi Miscellenei*, **23**, 1977 and the summary in C. Panella, Le Terme del Nuotatore ad Ostia Antica: scavo e pubblicazione, in *Un decennio di ricerche archeologiche* (Rome, 1978) pp. 477–85; for the House of the Porch, J. S. Boersma, T. L. Heres, H. A. G. Brijder, J. J. Feye, M. Gnade, S. L. Wynia *Amoenissima civitas. Block V.ii at Ostia: description and analysis of its visible remains* (Assen, 1985).

4. For the early excavations covering the Caseggiato dei Doli, the Via dei Balconi, the House of the Paintings, Rms 12 and 13 of the House of the Infant Bacchus, and Rms 22–24, 28, and 34–36 of the House of Jove and Ganymede, see G. Gatti, Ostia: rinvenimento di dolii frumentarii, *Notizie degli scavi*, 1903, pp. 201–202; A. Pasqui, Ostia: nuove scoperte presso il Casone, *Notizie degli Scavi*, 1906, pp. 357–73; D. Vaglieri, Ostia: scoperte varie di antichità, *Notizie degli Scavi*, 1908, pp. 329–36; J. Carcopino, Ostiensia: le quartier des docks, *Mélanges d'Archéologie et d'Histoire* 30, 1910, pp. 407–12; and L. Paschetto, *Ostia colonia romana, storia e monumenti* (Rome, 1912), pp. 323–24, 423–27. For the rest, see G. Calza, Gli scavi recenti nell'abitato di Ostia, *Monumenti Antichi* **26**, 1920, 321–430.

5. G. Calza, La preminenza dell' "insula" nella edilizia romana, *Monumenti Antichi* **23**, 1914, pp. 543–608; Le origini latine dell'abitazione moderna, *Architettura e Arti Decorative* 3, 1923–24, pp. 3–18, 49–63; Contributi alla storia della edilizia imperiale romana: le case ostiensi a cortile porticato, *Palladio* 5, 1941, pp. 1–33.

6. For the paintings, see Carcopino, Ostiensia, pp. 409–12 (House of the Paintings); Calza, Gli scavi recenti nell'abitato di Ostia, pp. 375–410; F. Wirth, *Römische Wandmalerei vom Untergang Pompejis bis am Ende des dritten Jahrhunderts* (Berlin, 1934), pp. 109–16; C. C. Van Essen, Studio cronologico sulle pitture parietali di Ostia, *Bullettino Comunale* **76**, 1956–58, pp. 155–78, *passim*; H. Joyce, *The decora-*

tion of walls, ceilings and floors in Italy in the second and third centuries AD (Rome, 1981), pp. 30–33, 51–2; J. R. Clarke, *The houses of Roman Italy, 100 BC–AD 250: ritual, space and decoration* (Berkeley, Calif. & Los Angeles, 1991), pp. 327–39. The graffito, on the south wall of Rm 29, refers to the month of Commodas and thus must be dated to that emperor's reign (AD 180–192) and most likely to the last few years of it (A. W. Van Buren, Graffiti at Ostia, *Classical Review* **37**, 1923, pp. 163–4).

7. For a recent discussion of the evidence for the pomerium and associated rods, see J. Brandt, Ostia, Minturno, Pyrgi: the planning of three Roman colonies, *Acta ad Archaeologiam et Artium Historiam Pertinentia* **5**, 1985, pp. 38–48. Brandt (pp. 44–6) places the outer edge of the outer pomerial road roughly 19 m from the castrum wall and assumes that it was equidistant on all sides, whereas R. Mar, La formazione dello spazio urbano nella città di Ostia, *MDAI(R)* **98**, 1991, p. 87 gives the (centre?) line of the roads as 15 m from the wall, based on existing streets. Gismondi's plan in Calza *et al.*, *Scavi di Ostia i* shows the western outer pomerium as narrower than the southern and eastern ones at 12 m to the centre of the Via del Pomerio. The distance from the castrum wall to that between Rms 22 and 23 of Insula I.4.2–4 is 11.8 m.

8. Described briefly by M. Floriani Squarciapino, Saggi di scavo nella Casa di Giove e Ganimede, *Fasti Archaeologici* **21**, 1966, n. 4479, but otherwise unpublished.

9. P. Cicerchia, Ostia: considerazioni ed ipotesi sul primo pianto urbano, *Xenia* **6**, 1983, pp. 45–62.

10. Meiggs, *Roman Ostia*, p. 120; M. Corta, I. Phl and F. Zevi, Ostia. La taberna della invidioso, *NSc* **32**, 1978, suppl. pp. 12–13, 19–29, 46–50.

11. The following brief account is based on Floriani Squarciapino, Saggi di scavo nella Casa di Giove e Ganimede, supplemented in places by information from the archives of the Soprintendenza di Ostia. The details must await the full publication of the excavations.

12. F. Coarelli, Public building in Rome between the Second Punic War and Sulla, *PBSR* **32**, 1977, pp. 1–23, dates the introduction of *opus reticulatum* into Rome to the 2nd century, and there is no real reason to imagine that its use at Ostia necessarily began much later.

13. C. C. Van Essen, A propos du plan de la ville d'Ostie, in *Hommages à Waldemar deonna,* Collection Latomus 28 (Brussels 1857), pp. 509–13, taken up by G. Hermansen, *Ostia: aspects of Roman city life* (Edmonton, 1981), pp. 2–4. For a general picture of the early road system and its relation to the castrum see R. Mar, La formazione dello spazio urbano nella città di Ostia, *MDAI (R)* **98**, 1991, pp. 86–7.

14. See M. E. Blake, *Ancient Roman construction in Italy from the prehistoric period to Augustus* (Washington, 1947), pp. 292–8 and M. E. Blake, *Roman construction in Italy from Tiberius through the Flavians* (Washington, 1959), p. 11 for the introduction of brick-faced concrete on a large scale.

15. For the level, cf. the first phase of the Caserma dei Vigili, begun after AD 82 and completed by 102 (F. Zevi & I. Pohl, Ostia. Caserma dei Vigili: scavo sotto il mosaico del vano antistante il "Cesareo", *Notizie degli Scavi*, 1970, Suppl. 1, p. 24). For the continuation of reticulate and block construction into the reign of Trajan see M. E. Blake & D. T. Bishop, *Roman construction in Italy from Nerva through the Antonines* (Philadelphia, 1973), pp. 150–51.

16. See above, n. 8.

17. M. Steinby, La cronologia delle *figlinae* doliari urbane dalla fine dell'età repubblicana fino all'inizio del III secolo, *Bullettino Comunale,* **84,** 1974–75, p. 28, cf. H. Bloch, I bolli laterizi nella storia edilizia di Ostia, in *Scavi di Ostia I. Topografia generale,* G. Calza *et al.* (Rome, 1953) p. 216 (*c.* AD 128–38). The majority of brickstamps are examples of CIL XV, 41, found also at Ostia in the portico of the Baths of Neptune where they are associated with stamps of AD 127 and 129 (*ibid.,* p. 220), and in I.16.2 with stamps of AD 134 and 135 (*ibid.,* p. 219).

18. For the excavation of these see *GdS* 1919, pp. 209–10.

19. For this construction, see G.Calza, G. Becatti, I. Gismondi, G. de Angelis D'Ossat, H. Bloch, *Scavi di Ostia I: topografia generale* (Rome, 1953), pp. 129–32, 167; Steinby, La cronologia delle *figlinae* doliari urbane, pp. 393–401.

20. *GdS* 1919, pp. 263–5, and see Calza's statement in Gli scavi recenti nell'abitato di Ostia, p. 328.

21. Pavolini, *La vita quotidiana a Ostia,* p. 65, Fig. 23. The combination of a street plaque showing mason's tools and a large open area suitable for a builder's yard is found at Pompeii, IX.1.5 (R. Ling, Street plaques at Pompeii, in *Architecture and architectural sculpture in the Roman empire,* ed. M. Henig (Oxford University Committee for Archaeology Monograph No. 29; Oxford, 1990) p. 62).

22. See Calza *et al.,* Scavi di Ostia I, pp. 129–39 and Fig. 32 for the chronology and extent of Hadrianic building at Ostia.

23. The reconstruction of this phase, based on my own recent survey of the building, differs slightly from that in Calza, Gli scavi recenti nell'abitato di Ostia, tav. 1. In agreement with J. E. Packer (The insulae of imperial Ostia, *MAAR* **31,** 1971, plan 6) I do not believe that the walls between Rms 4 and 5, and between Rms 14 and 15, formed part of the original plan. Rm 25 in the House of Jove and Ganymede was originally double height as were the corresponding rooms (Rms 7 and 17) in the other two houses, while Rms 2, 12 and 24 were all single storey in height. The door between Rms 133 and 139 on the mezzanine floor is also later and the floor above Rm 39 presumably formed a unit with the shop.

24. For the *medianum* apartment and its terminology, see G. Hermansen, *Ostia: aspects of Roman city life* (Edmonton, 1981), pp. 17–33.

25. This is contrary to the usual interpretation, and requires a few words of explanation. The clue lies in the paired doors between Rms 40 and 41 and the unnecessary second small window in the south wall of Rm 41, which are most easily explained by restoring a wooden stair in Rm 41 rising from just inside the northern door to Rm 40, with the second door and the window serving the under-stair space (cf. the arrangement in Rm 19 of the House of the Infant Bacchus). The fact that the main staircase (Rm 38) for the whole apartment block from the Via di Diana also serves this upper floor does not detract from this argument, since it would act as a service entrance from the street just as there is a secondary entrance to the ground floor of the house (Rm 37) alongside the stair.

26. See Packer, The insulae of imperial Ostia, pp. 172–3; Hermansen, *Ostia: aspects of Roman city life,* pp. 39–41, 49.

27. For the House of the Muses see Packer, The insulae of imperial Ostia, pp. 173–7; B. M. Felletti Maj & P. Moreno, *La pittura della Casa delle Muse* (Monumenti della pittura antica scoperti in Italia, III, Ostia III) (Rome, 1967).

28. Clarke, *The houses of Roman Italy,* p. 270.

29. Meiggs, *Roman Ostia,* p. 139.

30. M. E. Blake, Roman mosaics of the 2nd century in Italy, *MAAR* **13**, 1936, pp. 90–91, Pl. 15.1–2; G. Becatti, *Scavi di Ostia IV: i mosaici e i pavimenti marmorei.* (Rome, 1961), pp. 14–16.

31. E.g. C. Pavolini, L'edilizia commerciale e l'edilizia abitativa nel contesto di Ostia tardoantica, in *Società romana e impero tardoantico, vol. ii. Roma – politica, economia, paesaggio urbano*, ed. A. Giardina (Bari, 1986), p. 268, n. 114; J. R. Clarke, The decor of the House of Jupiter and Ganymede at Ostia Antica: private residence turned gay hotel? in *Roman art in the private sphere*, ed. E. K. Gadza (Ann Arbor, Mich., 1991), p. 91.

32. Calza, Gli scavi recenti nell'abitato di Ostia, pp. 360–62, tav. I, reiterated recently by Clarke, The decor of the House of Jupiter and Ganymede, pp. 90–92.

33. This remains in only part of the central window, but at the time of excavation all three were blocked (Calza, Gli scavi recenti nell'abitato di Ostia, p. 362).

34. Cf. *GdS* 1917, p. 32.

35. This door is clearly a later insertion as the jamb is rebuilt and there is no lintel arch. The identification of the kitchen and latrine has not previously been made. It is based on the *opus signinum* lining to the floor and part of the walls, the inserted drain in the northeast corner, and the remains of an upright support for a permanent bench. For the identification of other kitchens in private houses in Ostia see E. Salza Prina Ricotti, Cucine e quartieri servili in epoca romana, *Rendiconti della Pontificia Accademia di Archeologia* **51–2**, 1978–80, pp. 273–82, and 241–2 for the type of bench.

36. Examples of CIL XV 629 (AD 198–211) and 155 (AD 211–16), see *GdS* 1917, pp. 88–90 and 1916, p. 200 respectively.

37. Calza *et al.*, *Scavi di Ostia I*, p. 153.

38. Since removed. See Paschetto, *Ostia colonia romana*, p. 426.

39. *Ibid.*, p. 425. Unfortunately he gives no description of the nature of the blocking, but indicates that it is of a much later date. However, the rough construction used for blocking doorways in the Antonine period, if not covered by any wall-painting, could easily have been assigned a late date.

40. The House of the Paintings was the earliest part of the insula to be excavated and is the worst preserved. It is perfectly possible that the door between Rms 2 and 4 was once blocked. Part of the wall between Rms 7 and 8 is shown on Gismondi's plan (in Calza *et al.*, *Scavi di Ostia I*), but no longer exists. The poor quality of the construction in this phase has already been noted and would easily have led to the disappearance of these features.

41. Pavolini, L'edilizia commerciale e l'edilizia abitativa, pp. 241–5.

42. There is to my mind no indication that the House of Jove and Ganymede had by this time become a high class hotel with rooms set aside for homosexual encounters on the side as Calza (Gli scavi recenti nell'abitato di Ostia, pp. 370–75) originally argued. This was based on the existence of a small number (five in all) of homo-erotic graffiti on the walls of Rms 31 and 32, and the inclusion of the mezzanine floor as part of the main house making even larger a house already, in Calza's estimation, "piuttosto grande per una sola famiglia". Clarke (The decor of the House of Jupiter and Ganymede, cf. *The houses of Roman Italy*, pp. 320–36) has taken the argument a step further by reading explicit homo-erotic references in the iconography of the painting from the *exhedra* which gives the house its name, and makes his hotel definitely for a refined and specifically gay clientele. This is to take the evi-

dence too far. I have already suggested that the house always had included part of the mezzanine floor, and that it was intended for a resident of relatively high status whose needs for living space were rather different from those of the nuclear family apparently envisaged by Calza. The graffiti are only part of the total found in this house, which include all the other most common types: drawings of ships, animals, gladiators and huntsmen, plus dates and numbers. They come from predictable areas such as the corridor, the room at the end of it (Rm 31) and the yellow room off it (Rm 33), the stairwell and the mezzanine above, most of which were likely lingering areas for household slaves, visiting clients or the slaves of visitors, not to mention older children or other members of the family. The whole tenor of Calza's theory smacks of a 19th century puritanical prurience which completely misunderstands the nature of graffiti and ancient attitudes to sex in general and homosexuality in particular.

43. Calza, Gli scavi recenti nell'abitato di Ostia, pp. 376–84, 402; *GdS* 1917, pp. 71–4 (House of the Infant Bacchus), 1919, pp. 251–3 (garden shrine).

44. Calza, Gli scavi recenti nell'abitato di Ostia, p. 384 (late third); C. C. Van Essen, Studio cronologico sulle pitture parietali di Ostia, *Bullettino Comunale* **76**, 1956–58, pp. 172, 178 (garden shrine – Gordians; House of the Infant Bacchus – Gallienus); B. M. Felletti Maj, *Le pitture delle Case delle Volte Dipinti e delle Pareti Gialle* (Monumenti della pittura antica scoperti in Italia, III, Ostia I/II) (Rome, 1961), p. 37 (post-Severan); Joyce, *The decoration of walls, ceiling and floors*, pp. 32–3 (second quarter).

45. The repairs were removed during restoration (Calza, Gli scavi recenti nell'abitato di Ostia, p. 363).

46. It is impossible to know whether this door was completely blocked or not. Today only the eastern half is blocked, but even that is almost entirely restoration. The photograph in Calza (*ibid.*, Fig. 5), taken when only partly excavated, shows it in the same condition, but on completion of the excavation *GdS* 1917, pp. 64–9 records it as having been completely blocked and a basin built against it. This suggests two phases, the first perhaps during the late Antonine reconstruction, the second in a more fragile fabric in the later 3rd century.

47. Gatti, Ostia: rinvenimento di dolii frumentarii, pp. 201–202; Pasqui, Ostia: nuove scoperte presso il Casone, pp. 359, 371–2. For a discussion of the moulds, see M. Floriani Squarciapino, Forme ostiensi, *AC* 6, 1954, pp. 83–99.

48. *GdS* 1917, pp. 58, 60–63, 69–70; 1919, pp. 227–8, 255, 263–4.

49. Becatti, Scavi di Ostia IV, pp. 358–9; F. & A. G. Guidobaldi, *Pavimenti marmorei di Roma del IV al IX secolo*, Studi di Antichità Cristiana, **36** (Vatican, 1983), pp. 242–52.

50. G. Calza, Ostia: sterri nell'edificio detto delle pistrine, e presso la casa di Diana., *Notizie degli Scavi*, 1915, p. 249; Vaglieri, Ostia: scoperte varie di antichità, p. 330. A group of coins found in the bakery were largely 3rd century, the latest dating to the reign of Gallienus. For a recent survey of this building, see T. L. Heres, The building history of the Caseggiato dei Molini (Reg. I.iii.1) at Ostia: a preliminary study, *Mededelingen van het Nederlands Instituut te Rome* **48**, 1989, 37–74.

51. G. Calza, Ostia: la casa detta di Diana, *Notizie degli Scavi*, 1917, p. 323 (abandonment); Joyce, *The decoration of walls, ceilings and floors*, p. 32 (wall-paintings). See Pavolini, L'edilizia commerciale e l'edilizia abitativa, p. 253 for a summary of the evidence.

52. Boersma *et al.*, *Amoenissima civitas*, p. 230.

53. See the summary in Panella, Le Terme del Nuotatore ad Ostia Antica.

54. M. L. Veloccia Rinaldi, Nuove pitture ostiensi: la Casa delle Ierodule, *Rendiconti della Pontificia Accademia Romana di Archeologia* 43, 1970, p. 169; Felletti Maj, *Le pitture delle Case delle Volte Dipinti e delle Pareti Gialle*, pp. 32–3, *La pittura della Casa delle Muse*, pp. 43, 63–4.

55. Vaglieri, Ostia: scoperte varie di antichità; Calza, Gli scavi recenti nell'abitato di Ostia, pp. 337–8, 410–15. Important details not published by Calza are recorded in *GdS* for 1916, 1917 and 1919, *passim*. Paschetto, *Ostia colonia romana*, p. 427 records that the fill from the House of the Paintings contained a large quantity of domestic pottery, confirming that this too suffered the same fate as the rest of the insula. Sadly, there are no records from the late 19th century excavations of the Via dei Dipinti to indicate whether the fill extended over this street also.

56. Calza, Gli scavi recenti nell'abitato di Ostia, p. 425; Pavolini, L'edilizia commerciale e l'edilizia abitativa, p. 253, n. 72. Pavolini considers it only likely rather than proven that the fill in the Insula of the Paintings dates to the same period as that in the Via dei Balconi, but many of the amphora stamps recorded from the excavations of the House of the Infant Bacchus but not published by Calza do in fact also appear in the list of stamps definitely from the Via dei Balconi.

57. For the wall see Calza, Gli scavi recenti nell'abitato di Ostia, Fig. 4 and *GdS* 1917, pp. 1–4.

58. *GdS* 1917, pp. 1–4, 10–12.

59. Fragments of ceiling stucco were found on the floor of the *exhedra* (Rm 27) of the House of Jove and Ganymede mixed with a light layer of earth, while further fragments, albeit not necessarily of the same ceiling, were found mixed in with the fill (*GdS* 1917, pp. 64–9).

60. The blocking has since been removed. See Calza, Gli scavi recenti nell'abitato di Ostia, p. 346.

61. *GdS* 1917, pp. 75–8.

62. The use of amphorae and other rubbish as hardcore for fill has, to my knowledge, never been studied as a separate phenomenon, but examples are not hard to find, e.g. the platform of the Baths of Caracalla (L. Petrassi, Terme di Caracalla: indagini geotecniche, in *Roma: archeologia nel centro. Lavori e studi archeologici* 6.2 (Rome, 1985), pp. 601–4, and M. G. Cecchini, Terme di Caracalla. Campagna di scavo 1982–83 lungo il lato orientale, *ibid*, p. 587).

63. G. Calza, Ostia: scavo presso l'edificio delle pistrine, *Notizie degli Scavi*, 1914, p. 248.

64. Calza *et al.*, *Scavi di Ostia I*, p. 159.

65. *GdS* 1917, pp. 1–4.

66. Calza, Ostia: scavo presso l'edificio delle pistrine, pp. 245–8.

67. Calza *et al.*, *Scavi di Ostia I*, pp. 155–62 and Fig. 35; Meiggs, *Roman Ostia*, pp. 146–8; Pavolini, L'edilizia commerciale e l'edilizia abitativa, pp. 269–73 and tav. I–III.

68. *Ibid.*, 273–5.

69. Boersma *et al.*, *Amoenissima civitas*.

70. E.g. Tibullus 2.3.43–44; Horace, *Ep.* 2.2.72–4; Juvenal, *Sat.* 3.254–261; Digest 9.2.52.2.

6

Urban elites and cultural definition: Romanization in southern Italy[1]

Kathryn Lomas

Two of the key themes explored in the history of the Roman world in recent years are the social and economic rôle of the urban elite in the cities of the empire, and the problematic question of acculturation – what Romanization was, how it was expressed and how it was disseminated. Much valuable work has been done to clarify the processes of urban social interaction and those of acculturation, but with one major drawback – a surprisingly small amount of it has focused on Italy. Despite the wealth of research on the epigraphy and archaeology of Roman Italy which has been undertaken in recent years, comparatively few attempts have been made to synthesize this into a full-length study of Italian urbanism, and studies of a very limited number of individual cities – notably Pompeii, Ostia and Rome itself – have dominated the field.

To some extent, this pattern has been generated by the evidence. The epigraphic record left by the urban elites of the eastern empire is far more abundant than that of most Italian cities, and has provided the basis for illuminating studies of euergetism, elite self-definition, and urban social structures.[2] Similarly, processes of acculturation are more clearly identifiable in regions where contacts with Rome developed at a later date and where the indigenous and Roman cultures can be clearly distinguished – for instance, Britain, the Danube provinces, and Africa.[3] In Italy, the inadequate evidence for the history of the Roman conquest and the similarities between Roman and many other Italic cultures make the processes of Romanization very difficult to trace. There is, however, one region of Italy of distinctly non-Italic culture, for which it is possible to make some assessment of acculturation and of the central rôle of the urban elite in disseminating cultural influences and manipulating cultural rôles. The title of this paper, perhaps misleadingly, refers to southern Italy as a whole; the area on which I intend to focus is Magna Graecia, or rather on those cities of Magna Graecia which retained a distinctively urban identity after the social war. The Greek background of these cities makes them an interesting case-study in acculturation and particularly in the integration of Italy after the Social war, partly because of their non-Italic culture, but also because of the increasingly privileged status accorded to Greek culture by the Roman elite of the late republic and early empire.[4]

That major changes had taken place in these cities in the last two centuries BC was a fact recognized even in antiquity. Strabo comments, significantly, that of all the Greeks in Italy, the Neapolitans, the Rhegines and the Tarentines were the only ones to retain their Greek identity. The rest had become barbarized (i.e. Italicized), which is to say that they had become Romans, since all south Italians had subsequently become Roman.

> Now, apart from the Tarentines, Rhegines and Neapolitans, they [the Greeks] have become barbarians, and some have been captured and held by the Lucanians and Bruttians, and by the Campanians – in name, that is, but in reality by the Romans. For they themselves have become Romans.[5]

This phenomenon, as observed here, was clearly more than just political integration. It also had a cultural dimension. There are, however, some chronological problems. Doubt has been cast on whether Strabo was genuinely recording contemporary circumstances or was quoting from a 4th century source. Whether or not this statement is derived from an earlier author, it reflects some important considerations, and is also substantially supported by the epigraphic evidence from the region. Assuming, for the purposes of this paper, that Strabo is accurately reflecting the contemporary state of Magna Graecia,[6] his comment raises a number of very important questions about the processes of acculturation in Italy. To what extent, and in what forms, did Hellenism persist in southern Italy? To what extent were these cities Romanized? Were the elements of Romanization and local, or more specifically, Greek, identity mutually exclusive? I hope to demonstrate, through examination of the epigraphic records left by the elite of these cities, that a number of the Greek colonies in southern Italy retained a specifically Greek identity until the 2nd century AD; that Greek elements in civic life were consciously and deliberately cultivated by the elite, irrespective of the actual ethnic nature of the city; that this process was an important part of the language and ideology of power in these cities; and that such elements of civic life performed an important function in mediating the relationship between the municipal elite of southern Italy and that of Rome.

One problem which must be confronted in any discussion of cultural history and identity is that of terminology. Terms such as "Romanization" and "Hellenization" are rightly regarded as unsatisfactory in their implication that cultural influences are always transmitted in one direction only, from a dominant to a subordinate culture.[7] This is a clear oversimplification and distortion of the processes of cultural change and interaction, since it is very rare that these are simple one-way processes. In the case of interactions between Greek and Roman culture, the processes are very complex and far from being one-directional.[8] In southern Italy, there is the additional complication that there was already a considerable degree of interaction between Oscan and Greek culture before the region ever came under Roman control. This factor poses a terminological restriction in that "acculturation" cannot be used to describe these processes as it is sometimes necessary to differentiate between the different elements involved. For the purposes of this paper, I intend to continue to use the terms "Hellenism" and "Romanization". Bowersock, in a recent work, has made a powerful case for the use of "Hellenism" rather than "Hellenization" in that the former preserves the concept of a set of cultural ideas and artefacts which can be transmitted as a whole or in part and adapted in various ways, without the implication of dominance or cultural imperialism.[9] Romanization is a rather more problematic term to define, since Rome was in fact politically dominant and this undoubtedly affected the process of cultural transmission. What is certain, is that Romanization cannot be regarded as a simple linear process operating at the same rate and in the same manner at all levels of society.[10] Perhaps it could be defined as: The transmission of a characteristically Roman set of cultural attributes and assumptions, assuming that the speed and mode of transmission and the nature of their reception vary according to the nature of the recipient and the social and economic level at which the transmission operates at any given moment.

Even with a workable definition, the means by which such cultural changes can be recognized and studied remain problematic, particularly where written records are scarce. The problems of interpreting archaeological evidence for acculturation are legion. Diffusion of artefacts, or of technologies and stylistic features associated with them, is not a reliable indicator of the dissemination of cultural influences on a wider scale within society. Anthropological studies show that the significance and uses of artefacts can change dramatically in the process of transmission, making it difficult to assess the true extent and nature of the process of acculturation.[11] For the Roman period, however, some light can be shed on the question by the use of literary sources and inscriptions which give some insight into reactions to external cultural influences and the uses to which they were put. Inscriptions are, in themselves, a problematic category of evidence, since the significance of why they were used, the motivations and social assumptions behind them, the interpretation of the forms and language used, and the social signals they were intended to send, are only imperfectly understood.[12] However, some of the cities of Magna Graecia show some interesting epigraphic peculiarities which may cast light on both acculturation in southern Italy and on the behaviour of local and Roman elites.

As a means of elucidating these matters, a group of the Greek colonies in southern Italy can be treated as a case-study. Effectively, this is limited to those cities which continued to flourish under Roman rule and for which there is a reasonable amount of literary and epigraphic evidence. Those which failed to recover, as cities, from the wars of the 4th and 3rd centuries BC, or which are known mainly from archaeological evidence, will be omitted. Paestum and Cumae, already considerably Oscanized by the time of the Roman conquest, both have considerable quantities of epigraphic source material,[13] as do Tarentum, Naples and Rhegium, the cities mentioned by Strabo, and Locri, Vibo and Velia.[14] The fact that most of the evidence is epigraphic means that it is inevitably affected by patterns of excavation, and of recovery and survival of inscriptions, but examination of this evidence shows enough consistency in the cultural development of these cities to suggest that important trends can be recognized. Although the vast majority of the inscriptions are epitaphs, the texts which are of greatest interest from the point of view of acculturation are those which record the activities of the civic elites, for instance, *cursus* inscriptions with details of political careers, decrees of the local senate, records of religious festivals, and commemorations of individual acts of patronage and civic euergetism. By examining these, it is possible to gain some insight into how the municipal elites operated, and how they exploited their cultural background to establish higher status for their cities and to generate patronage from Rome.

At first sight, the epigraphic evidence for Magna Graecia presents a profile typical of many other Italian cities, with a large number of epitaphs, and most of the epigraphy concentrated in a narrow chronological period, from the 1st to the 3rd centuries AD.[15] Because of the relatively late date of most of the evidence, the survival of the pre-Roman languages in the epigraphy of the region is very uneven. Oscan inscriptions occur at Paestum and Cumae but die out during the 1st century BC.[16] Greek is rather more enduring as an epigraphic language, and there are substantial numbers of Greek epitaphs, as well as other types of inscription, at Naples and Velia, with lesser concentrations at Tarentum, Cumae and Rhegium. In some cases, the Greek epitaphs are of the Latin D(is) M(anibus) type translated literally into Greek, a graphic example of the way in which cultural forms can overlap.[17] Curiously, there is often an inconsistency between the choice of language for an inscription, funerary or otherwise, and the ethnic background implied by the names of individuals concerned. It is not at all uncommon to find individuals with Oscan names commemorating themselves in Greek, as in the case of the Neapolitan chamber-tomb containing the epitaphs of Epilytos Epilytou, Trebios Epilytou, Vibios Epilytou, and other members of the same family.[18] This may be an indication that Greek was regarded as a higher status language, even in cities such as Cumae which had ceased to be Greek-speaking, at least at an official level.[19] Language choice and its manipulation to signal status, ethnic origin or cultural identity is notoriously difficult to evaluate on the slight data available from the ancient world, but the persistence (or re-adoption) of Greek in essentially Oscan-speaking communities certainly seems to be indicative of a wish to underline status and identity.

The language choice of municipal elites of the early empire reveals a complex set of cultural values. While most high-status epitaphs use Latin, a large number of the public documents which record the individual or collective actions of the elite use Greek. These, however, have a very specific geographical distribution. The Oscanized cities of Cumae and Paestum, together with Locri and Vibo, have little evidence of public activity by their respective senates or magistrates. The elites were clearly engaged in municipal euergetism in much the same way as elites elsewhere in Italy. There were repairs and extensions to the temple of Demeter at Cumae,[20] a bath-house at Paestum,[21] and a number of payments for games and wild-beast shows, to name only a small number of examples.[22] As is the case elsewhere, civic amenities and entertainments were provided by a mixture of euergetism by office-holders or prominent families such as the Lucceii at Cumae, the Digitii and Tullii Cicerones at Paestum and the Muticilii at Vibo, and by patronage from outside the city, by Roman officials and notables or by the emperor.[23] The inscriptions recording these acts of patronage and euergetism are all in Latin, and their language and mode of presentation is very similar to examples found throughout Italy.

Another group of cities, namely Naples, Velia and Rhegium, show a very different pattern. Here, there continues to be a very noticeable bias towards Greek forms in civic life and in the ways of recording euergetism which persists until at least the middle of the 2nd century AD, if not longer. At Naples, the substantial minority of Greek epitaphs[24] argues that Greek language and culture survived to a considerable degree among ordinary citizens, but given the cosmopolitan nature of this particular city this may in part be the result of immigration from the East.[25] The number of Graeco-Oscan names appearing on epitaphs does, however, suggest that there was a Neapolitan element of the population which retained its non-Latin culture into the 1st century AD.[26] The more informative inscriptions, though, are the euergetic and commemorative texts set up by the ruling elite. These present a complex set of problems and are not all entirely explicable, but the key to the puzzle seems to be a conscious attempt by the elite to retain and manipulate the Greek identity of the city.

The most baffling aspect is the continuation of Greek magistracies – notable the offices of *archon*, *demarchos*, *gymnasiarchos* and *laukelarchos* – until the 3rd century AD.[27] In addition, the surviving examples of decrees of the local assembly are all presented in Greek, as decrees of the Boule. The appearance of Greek magisterial titles in official decrees and other inscriptions has prompted speculation that Naples never fully adopted a Roman municipal constitution. This is unlikely, and in any case, individual epitaphs show that Romanized magistracies – *quattuorvir*, *duumvir* and aedile – also existed during the first two centuries AD.[28] By the 2nd century AD, and possibly as early as the 1st century, the offices of *demarchos* and *laukelarchos* may have become honorific rather than administrative in function. They were held by a number of non-Neapolitans, mostly high-status Romans, of whom the most notable was the emperor Hadrian.[29] The offices of *archon* and *antarchon* seem to have retained a more directly administrative function, since they appear in decrees of the Boule and were clearly integral to these. Sartori's suggestion that the Greek titles mask the Romanized offices of *duumvir* or *quattuorvir* is plausible, although *archon* is not the usual translation of either of these offices.[30] Whether this was in fact a Hellenization of a Roman magistracy or the survival of a Greek office supplementary to the Roman ones, the fact remains that Greek forms, language and terminology were being deliberately and consciously employed.

The content and context of this group of decrees is, in itself, significant. All are honorific in nature, and are not in any way connected with the actual administration of the city. The majority concern commemoration of eminent citizens, and include declarations of public mourning, and funerals, tombs, and commemorative statues voted at public expense.[31] This specific genre of inscription, a statement of public mourning and condolence, is rarely found elsewhere in Italy, but is known from the Greek world, most notably from examples at Athens, Aphrodisias and Amorgos.[32] Both these and the Neapolitan examples are very closely related to the less specific form of honorific proxeny decree found in the Greek East throughout the Hellenistic and Roman period.[33] In this context, the use of Greek language and terminology, together with the adoption of a Greek form of honour, seems to point to a very powerful Hellenizing trend in those aspects of civic life connected with honours, patronage and euergetism, which is divergent from the Romanized administration and magistracies which appear in inscriptions of other sorts.

This pattern of prominence given to Greek institutions in public life is further reflected in the rôle of the phratries at Naples. As the name suggests, they probably originated as kinship groups, of which there were 12 in all: the Onioneioi, Artemisioi, Eumelidai, Eumeidai, Antinoitai, Eunostidai, Kretondai, Kumaioi, Euboiai, Pankleidai, Hermaioi and Artistaioi.[34] They almost certainly originated very early in the history of Naples, since many of the names are archaic in character, with the exception of the Antinoitai, who must have been created or renamed during the reign of Hadrian, but there is no evidence for them prior to the 1st century AD. Inscriptions record membership of the phratries by both the local and Roman elite, including the emperor Claudius.[35] Membership of Neapolitan phratries is included in lists of honours and offices found on epitaphs, emphasizing their high status. The actual function of the phratries is far from clear, but inscriptions refer to phratry meeting-houses and cults and to officials known as phratrarchs. Their euergetic rôle is underlined by the fact that many inscriptions mentioning phratries are records of dedications to the phratry or its cult, often in the form of statuary or gold and silver plate, or of honours conferred by a phratry. Clearly there had been a change of emphasis comparable to that which took place with the demarchy, in which the original function was modified in favour of an honorific function, extending membership to include patrons and benefactors of the city from Rome and elsewhere.[36]

Although Velia does not have such a quantity and diversity of Greek epigraphy in comparison with Naples, it shows a remarkably similar pattern. *Cursus* inscriptions show that the Greek office of gymnasiarch survived alongside the Roman administrative machinery of quattuorvirs and aediles.[37] As with the *laukelarchos* at Naples, one of the more distinctive and peculiar Greek priesthoods, the office of *pholarchos*, enjoyed a renewed lease of life in the 1st century AD.[38] It was connected with the healing cult of Apollo Oulios, which enjoyed prominence during Velia's brief period as a fashionable cold-water spa.[39] The exact function is uncertain, but the appearance of the title on epitaphs listing official and administrative careers confirms its importance in public life.[40] A further similarity with the Neapolitan evidence is the occurrence of decrees of the Boule, published bilingually or in Greek, which are effectively Hellenistic proxeny decrees, identical in form to those found in Sicily, Athens, and many other cities in the eastern empire.[41]

At Rhegium, there is rather less evidence for the civic constitution, but much the same pattern is repeated, namely the continuing use of Greek language and forms in certain ceremonial contexts. A *proxenos* inscription in honour of the Roman general Gn. Aufidius may pre-date the Social war, but another example in honour of G. Norbanus is rather later, suggesting that this Greek form of honour persisted into the late 1st century BC, or the 1st century AD.[42] A further series of inscriptions connected with the cults of Apollo and/or Artemis, also of the 1st century AD, record state sacrifices made in honour of these gods. The participants listed include holders of the offices of *prytanis*, *archon* and *synprytaneis*, in contrast to cursus inscriptions of similar date which refer to *quattuorviri*.[43] Thus the problem is analogous to that of the Neapolitan decrees. There is no obvious indication as to whether the Greek titles mask Roman magistracies or whether Greek offices survived with a more restricted and largely ceremonial scope of action. However, the same corollary holds true no matter which interpretation is given, that religious and euergetic documents were deliberately couched in terms drawn from the city's Greek past.

The final city which I wish to discuss, Tarentum, is something of an anomaly. Elsewhere, there has been at least some evidence to bear out Strabo's assessment of the survival of Greek culture. At Tarentum, there is very little Greek epigraphy.[44] However, this may be explicable in terms of the type of inscriptions which survive. Most of the Greek texts discussed so far have been from an urban context and are connected with high-status activities conducted by the municipal elite. At Tarentum, a significant proportion of the epigraphy comes from the territory of the city, the most frequently represented social groups being slaves and freedmen or discharged veterans.[45] There are no inscriptions analogous to the decrees of the *Boule* at Naples and Velia or the religious inscriptions at Rhegium which could give clues as to how the elite operated and how they wished to present themselves.

The evidence, then, presents a fairly cohesive picture. Where inscriptions relating to honorific activity by the city have been preserved, these are almost exclusively Greek, both in their language and the terms in which the honours are presented. Honours offered to prominent citizens or outsiders are carefully couched in terms drawn from the Greek history of the region, terms which are in many cases familiar from the Hellenistic conventions of the eastern empire. In all cases, this contrasts with other types of epigraphic evidence from Magna Graecia which is primarily Latin, generated by people with Latin names, in cities operating within a Roman municipal structure. This paradox makes it clear that this is more than simply a residual element of local culture which persisted in an otherwise Romanized society, and gradually died out during the 2nd century. Greek culture was being consciously privileged over Oscan or Roman culture in a very specifically defined context. Far from dying out, there is a possibility that it was deliberately revived under the Julio-Claudians and again under the Antonines.[46] The evidence, therefore, poses some important questions as to the mechanisms which were at work. Why did the municipal elites of Magna Graecia preserve this part of their Greek heritage?

One possible explanation for the persistence of Greek culture can be immediately dismissed. Evidence for the ethnic composition of these cities indicates that by this date, they were very mixed. The ethnicity of elites is a problematic question, but the balance of evidence suggests that they were substantially Romanized or Italicized, whatever their actual origin. One of the most noticeable features of the inscriptions discussed so far is that almost all the high-status individuals named have names of Latin or Campanian origin.[47] Costabile has suggested, specifically in the context of Rhegium although the same argument could be applied equally to other cities, that the apparent disappearance of the Greek aristocracy is simply the result of large-scale and thorough Romanization, including a change of name, on the part of this aristocracy.[48] While this is a very plausible theory on a general level, it does not seem sufficient to account for the disappearance of all traces at all of the survival of the native Greek aristocracy. In any case, there are signs that in many parts of Magna Graecia, the elite was already absorbing Oscan families as early as the 4th century BC. Strabo[49] comments on the admission of Oscans to the ruling elite at Naples, and magistrates with Messapian names occur on the Table of Heraklea.[50] In addition, there must have been an element of natural wastage as families died out or became impoverished, to be replaced by new ones.[51] Therefore, a degree of change is to be expected. By the 1st century AD, the municipal elites of Magna Graecia must have been a mixture of Romanized Graeco-Oscan aristocrats and Roman or Italian newcomers, a factor which further underlines the separation between the predominantly Roman nature of civic life and the Greek flavour which was imparted to it by the elite.

The reason why there was such an emphasis on Hellenism in civic life in cities which were not predominantly Greek in population and were certainly Romanized in their municipal structures lies in the prevailing philhellenism of the Roman elite as a whole and certain emperors in particular. This was a phenomenon which transcended the purely cultural sphere and came to acquire a political status which enabled Greek cities throughout the empire to exploit their history and traditions for political benefits and enhancement of their civic status.

Naples and its environs are perhaps the clearest examples of this process. Many factors, including proximity to Rome and a history of good relations, undoubtedly helped in establishing the Bay of Naples as the centre of what might be termed "villa culture".[52] Cicero's letters demonstrate that this involved many members of the Roman elite by the 1st century BC, who owned at least one, and often several, properties and who cultivated connections with the local Campanian elites.[53] The extensive imperial properties at Baiae served merely to confirm the strength of the connection between the Roman elite and the Bay of Naples. The elements of Hellenism in this area were vital to this development. Greek culture, particularly literature and philosophy, was an essential ingredient of *otium*, the leisured and cultivated lifestyle which was supposedly the ideal pursued by Cicero and his correspondents, and later by emperors and senators of the 1st and 2nd centuries AD.[54] To some extent, this provided the phenomenon of Hellenism with its own momentum. The possibility of gaining imperial or aristocratic patronage attracted large numbers of Greek teachers, philosophers and *litterati* from all over the eastern Mediterranean, of whom the best known examples are perhaps Licinius Archias, citizen of Heraklea and Naples, but originally from Antioch,[55] and the poet Statius, the son of a *grammaticus* from Velia who moved to the more fashionable Naples to pursue his career, a factor which was instrumental in allowing Statius himself to gain the patronage of Domitian.[56] The Greek games founded at Naples in AD 2 and at Puteoli in AD 138 both made their imperial connections explicit in their names (Sebasta and Eusebeia) and provided a further point of focus for Greeks from the eastern empire, as well as being an expression of civic Hellenism for the host cities.[57] The rewards which could be generated by a display of Hellenism were clearly high, and usually expressed as gains in status or patronage for cities or individuals, although this could be accompanied by more tangible benefits, in the form of buildings, *sportulae* and other benefactions.

In this context, the resurgence of Hellenism in the activities of the elite becomes entirely comprehensible, particularly in the voting of honours to prominent Romans or the expression of thanks to civic benefactors. The proxeny decree in honour of Julius Naso at Velia, the honorary demarchate for Hadrian at Naples and the inclusion of at least one emperor – Claudius – and numerous Roman senators and officials in phratries at Naples are all examples of the manipulation of Greek heritage by the local elite to give these honours an extra cachet. The question of whether this represents continuity of Hellenism or a resurgence of elements of civic life which had lapsed and been artificially revived is problematic and ultimately unanswerable, in view of the limited evidence. However, parallels with the history of the eastern empire in the 2nd century suggest that a deliberate revival is very probable.

The high status accorded to cities with a demonstrable Greek past and Greek culture was not a phenomenon which was peculiar to Italy. In reviving Hellenism in civic life, the Italiote cities were participating in a process which is well documented in the eastern empire during the 1st and 2nd centuries AD. There was a renewal of interest in local history and culture during the 2nd century AD in many Greek or Hellenized cities, with a consequent revival of magistracies, priesthoods or festivals which may have lapsed entirely or faded into obscurity.[58] Ancient kinship ties between cities were formally renewed. Sparta revived the ancient cult of the Dioscuri and also the famous *Agoge*. At Cyrene, the sanctuary of Apollo was rebuilt in a predominantly archaic style.

One of the principal reasons for this was the foundation of the Panhellenion by Hadrian in AD 131/2, since proof of Greek foundation and continuing Hellenism was the main criterion for membership of this league.[59] As a result of this, great emphasis was placed on traditional Greek festivals and forms of government, and many cities developed elaborate foundation myths as a means of proving their Greek origins.[60] The Panhellenion itself had few formal powers, but the status which accrued to a city that obtained membership was considerable, further underlining the connection between civic Hellenism, high status and imperial patronage.[61] None of the Italian cities are known to have been members, although there is some slight evidence that Tarentum may have been involved.[62] A Spartan ambassador, Callicrates, was sent to Tarentum in AD 145–50, probably in an attempt to renew the ancient ties between the two cities, and received an effusive welcome. Envoys were also sent by Sparta to Naples and Puteoli, probably in connection with the Greek games there. As at Naples and Rhegium, Greek terminology was revived. Writers adopted Greek titles such as harmost and satrap for Roman officials and used archaic Greek place-names such as Dicaearchia (replacing Puteoli) and Hipponion (instead of Vibo) in preference to their Romanized forms. The principle was even extended to personal names, with the appearance of characters such as Jason of Argos and Theseus of Corinth in the sources for the 2nd century.[63] It seems certain that in a world where the rewards of Hellenism were so great, the elites of the Greek cities of Italy would have had a massive incentive to emphasize their Greek culture and history, particularly in their dealings with the Roman elite and the predominantly philhellene emperors of the 1st and 2nd centuries AD.

To conclude, I shall return briefly to my starting point – the question of cultural interaction and Romanization, and in particular to Strabo's analysis of these. In broad terms, Strabo is clearly right in observing that Greek culture was flourishing in parts of southern Italy, but his rigid bipolar division between becoming Roman and remaining Greek is a gross oversimplification. In the most basic sense, all Italians were Roman by virtue of citizenship. Even where Hellenism continued to flourish, there was a Roman administrative structure and a large Roman and Italian admixture to the population. Nevertheless, the privileged status of Greek culture ensured that it not only survived but enjoyed a revival of importance and was integral to the activities of the elite. Imperial patronage ensured that Hellenism continued to flourish in southern Italy, as elsewhere in the empire. It was an important factor in mediating relations between the Roman and local elites, and as such, was exploited to the full. In terms of elite activities and interaction, therefore, Hellenism and Romanization are not opposed and exclusive processes but are mutually compatible and continued to exist in equilibrium in southern Italy until the end of the 2nd century AD.

Notes

1. I would like to thank the Leverhulme Trust and the British School at Rome for their financial support for the research on which this paper is based.
2. Most notably P. Veyne, *Bread and circuses: historical sociology and political pluralism* (Paris, 1976), tr. O. Murray, 1990; but also E. L. Bowie, The Greeks and their past in the second sophistic, in *Studies in Ancient Society*, ed. M. I. Finley (London, 1974); P. Cartledge, & A. J. S. Spawforth, *Hellenistic and Roman Sparta: a tale of two cities* (London, 1989); G. W. Bowersock, *Hellenism in late antiquity* (Cambridge, 1990), D. Engels, *Roman Corinth* (Chicago, 1990); and G. M. Rodgers, *The sacred identity of Ephesos* (London, 1991)
3. P. A. Brunt, The Romanization of local ruling classes in the Roman empire, in *Travaux du VI Congrès International d'Études Classiques*, ed. D. M. Pippidi (1976); A. Mócsy, *Pannonia and Upper Moesia: a history of the middle Danube provinces of the Roman empire* (London, 1974); H. G. Pflaum, *L'Afrique romaine: études épigraphiques* (Paris, 1979); M. Millett, *The Romanization of Britain: an essay in archaeological interpretation* (Cambridge, 1990).
4. M. H. Crawford, Greek intellectuals and the Roman aristocracy, in *Imperialism in the ancient world*, eds P. D. Garnsey & C. R. Whittaker (Cambridge, 1978), pp. 193–208; E. D. Rawson, *Intellectual life in the late Roman republic* (London, 1985).
5. Strabo, 6.1.2
6. On the subject of Strabo's reliability as evidence for Italy in the 1st century AD and the question of his use of earlier sources, see D. Musti, *Strabone e Magna Grecia* (Padua, 1988), pp. 11–60.
7. Bowersock, *Hellenism in late antiquity*, pp. 1–13.
8. R. D. Whitehouse & J. Wilkins, Greeks and natives in south-east Italy: approaches to the archaeological evidence, in *Centre and periphery: comparative studies in archaeology*, ed. T. C. Champion (London, 1989), pp. 102–26
9. Bowersock, *Hellenism in late antiquity*, pp. 2–18.
10. On the problems of defining Romanization, see D. G. Orr, The Roman city: a philosophical and cultural summa, in *Aspects of Graeco-Roman urbanism: essays on the classical city* ed. R. Marchese (BAR 188; Oxford 1983), pp. 93–109.
11. M. Mauss, *The gift: the form and reason for exchange in archaic societies* (London, 1950), tr. W. D. Halls, 1990; Whitehouse & Wilkins, Greeks and natives in south-east Italy, pp. 102–26

12. R. Macmullen, The epigraphic habit in the Roman empire, *AJP* **103**, 1982, pp. 233–46; E. A. Mayer, Explaining the epigraphic habit in the Roman empire: the evidence of epitaphs, *JRS* **80**, 1990, pp. 74–96; K. Lomas, Local identity and cultural imperialism: epigraphy and the diffusion of Romanization in Italy, in *The archaeology of power: proceedings of the 4th conference of Italian archaeology*, eds E. Herring, R. Whitehouse, J. Wilkins (London, 1991), pp. 231–9.

13. CIL X.3682–3713; M. Mello & G. Voza, *Le iscrizioni latine di Paestum* (Naples, 1968).

14. CIL IX.234–57; X.1–16, 1478–1543; IG XIV.612–29, 714–828; L. Gasperini, su alcune epigrafia di Taranto Romana, in *Seconda miscellenea greca e romana* (Rome 1968), pp. 379–98; Il municipio Tarentino: ricerche epigrafica, in *Terza miscellenea greca e romana*, (Rome, 1971); Tarentina epigrafica, in *Settima miscellenea greca e romana* (Rome, 1980); F. Costabile, *Municipium Locrensium* (Naples, 1978); P. Ebner, Nuove epigrafi di Velia, *PdP* **21**, 1966; Nuove iscrizioni di Velia, *PdP* **25**, 1970.

15. Macmullen, The epigraphic habit in the Roman empire, pp. 233–46.

16. E. Vetter, *Handbuch der Italischen Dialekte* (Heideberg, 1953), nos 108–14.

17. IG XIV.624, 627, 789, 802, 806, 807, 868, 870.

18. IG XIV.660; P. Poccetti, Un Brettio a Cuma, *PdP* **39**, 1984, pp. 43–7; Vetter, *Handbuch der Italischen Dialekte*, p. 112; A. Levi, Camere sepolcrali scoperte in Napoli durante i lavori della diretissima Roma-Napoli, *MAL* **31**, 1926, pp. 378–402.

19. For the alleged suppression of Greek language and customs at Paestum, see Athen. 16.632a. At Cumae, much of the Greek population fled in 421 BC (Livy, 4.44.12; Diod. 12.76.4, Dion. Hal. 15.6.4). By the time the city officially adopted Latin in 180 BC, the main language was Oscan (Livy, 40.42.13)

20. CIL X.3685

21. Mello & Voza, *Le iscrizioni latine di Paestum*, pp. 98–104

22. CIL X.3704

23. CIL X.10, 473, 482, 3685–89; VI.1.1851; Mello & Voza, *Le iscrizioni latine di Paestum*, pp. 100–104

24. IG XIV.766–824; G. A. Galante, Il sepolcro ritrovato in Napoli sotto il palazzo Di Donato in via Cristallini ai Vergini, *AAAN* **17**, 1893–96, pp. 2–24

25. IG XIV.766 (Antioche Alexandrou Laodikeu), 771 (Astragalos Herakleotes), 781 (Hermokles Euphemou Alexandreus), 785 (Heliodoros Alexandrou Antiocheus), 805 (Poseidonios Berytie).

26. Strabo, 5.4.7

27. F. Sartori, *Problemi di storia costituzionale Italiota* (Rome, 1953), pp. 46–53; IG XIV.716, 717, 729 (= CIL X.1481), 741, 745, 760, *ILS* 6460; L. Correrra, Miscellenea epigrafica, MDAI (R) **19**, 1904, p. 185

28. Sartori, *Problemi di storia costituzionale Italiota*, pp. 46–53.

29. Spartianus Vit. Had. 19.1 (Hadrian), IG XIV.729 (Vespasian), CIL X.1492 (L. Munatius Concessianus), *ILS* 6455; CIL X.1478 (P. Vergilius Restitutus).

30. Sartori 1953, 42–55; H. J. Mason, *Greek terms for roman institutions: a lexicon and analysis* (Toronto, 1974), gives the usual term for *quattuorviri* or *duoviri* as *tessares andres* and *duo andres*. An example of the *tessares andres* occurs in IG XIV.745.

31. *AE* 1954, 186; IG XIV. 737, 758, 760, *ILS* 6460

32. A. Hardie, *Statius and the silvae: poets, patrons and epideixis in the Graeco-Roman world* (Liverpool, 1983), pp. 2–14; MAMA 8.408, 409, 410

33. IG III.1.741, 745, 897, 7.342, 505

34. Strabo, 5.4.7, Varro, *LL* 5.85; M. Guarducci, L'istituzione della fratria nella Grecia antica e nelle colonie Greche d'Italia, *Mem. Linc.* 6.6.1, 1936; M. Napoli, *Napoli Greco-Romana* (Naples, 1959); *Napoli Antica*, 1986.

35. IG XIV.721, 724, 728, 730, 743, 748; CIL X.1491, XII.3232; A. Maiuri, La nuova iscrizione della fratria Napoletana degli Artemisi, *Studi Romani* 1, 1913, pp. 21–36.

36. Strabo (5.4.7) identifies the phratries as an important element in the Greek character of Naples. Their function by the 1st century AD seems to be similar to that of collegia in other cities. Each had its own cults, meeting houses and magistrates. Inscriptions include dedications to the phratry or honours offered by a phratry to its patrons. IG XIV.715, 721, 722, 741–44, 748, *ILS* 5082, 6455, CIL VI.1.1851, X.1491

37. P. Mingazzini, Velia. Scavi 1927. Fornace di mattoni ed antichità varie. Elenco di bolli laterizi statale, *ASMG* 1, 1954, pp. 21–55; CIL X.462; *AE* 1978, 260

38. Ebner, Scuole di medicina a Velia e a Salerno, *Apollo* 2, 1962, pp. 125–36; Nuove epigrafi di Velia, pp. 336–41; Nuove iscrizioni di Velia, pp. 262–7; Pugliese Carratelli, Ancora su φωλαρχος, *PdP* 25, 1970, pp. 385–6.

39. Hor. *Ep.* 1.15

40. Ebner, Nuove epigrafi di Velia, no. 18; Nuove iscrizioni di Velia, pp. 262–7; cf Pugliese Caratelli, Ancora su φωλαρχος, pp. 385–6.

41. G. Forni, Intorno alle costituzioni di città greche in Italia e in Sicilia, *Kokalos* 3, 1957–58, pp. 61–70; For parallels, see IG XIV.12. (Syracuse), 256 (Gela), 258 (Segesta), III.1.741, 745, 897 (Athens). The decrees in honour of Pelops Dexiai of Naples (IG VII.342 and 505) are more elaborate examples of the same genre.

42. IG XIV.612, *SEG* I.418.

43. CIL X.6; Sartori, *Problemi di storia costituzionale Italiota,* pp. 136–141.

44. IG XIV.668–71; Viola, *NSc.* 1881.

45. Gasperini, Su alcune epigrafia di Taranto Romana, pp. 379–98; *Tarentina epigrafica.*

46. Macmullen, The epigraphic habit in the Roman empire, pp. 233–46; On 2nd century archaism in the eastern Mediterranean, see Bowie, The Greeks and their past, pp. 166–209; A. J. S. Spawforth & S. Walker, The world of the Panhellenion I, *JRS* 75, 1985, pp. 78–104, and The world of the Panhellenion II, *JRS* 76, 1986, pp. 88–106.

47. IG XIV.760 (Lucius Frugi, Cornelius Cerialis, Tranquillus Rufus), Correrra, Miscellenea epigrafica (Cominia Plutogenia, Paccius Caledus, Castricius Pollio), IG XIV.617 (Sex. Numonius Sex. F. Maturus, G. Hortorius G. F. Balbillus, M. Pemponius M. F. Pulcher, M. Cornelius M. F. Martialis).

48. Costabile, *Municipium Locrensium.*

49. Strabo, 5.4.7.

50. E.g., Daszumos Pyrrhou. IG XIV.645 .

51. K. Hopkins, *Death and renewal* (Cambridge, 1983), pp. 31–118.

52. J. H. d'Arms, *Romans on the Bay of Naples* (Cambridge, Mass., 1971); E. D. Rawson, *Intellectual life in the late Roman republic* (London, 1985).

53. Cic. *Att.* 14.10, 16.5; d'Arms, *Romans on the Bay of Naples.*

54. Rawson, *Intellectual life in the late Roman republic*

55. Cic. *Arch.* 4–7

56. Hardie, *Statius and the silvae,* pp. 2–14.

57. R. M. Geer, The Greek games at Naples, *TAPA* 66, 1935, pp. 208–21; I. R. Arnold, Agonistic festivals in Italy and Sicily, *AJA* 64, 1960, pp. 241–51.

58. Cartledge & Spawforth, *Hellenistic and Roman Sparta,* pp. 105–19; Bowie, The

Greeks and their past, pp. 188–201.

59. Spawforth & Walker, The world of the Panhellenion I, pp. 78–90.

60. *Ibid.*

61. Spawforth & Walker, The world of the Panhellenion I; The world of the Panhellenion II.

62. *Ibid.*, 88–96; L. Gasperini, Un buleuta Alessandrino a Taranto, in *Studi in onore di A. Adriani* (Rome, 1984).

63. Bowie, The Greeks and their past, pp. 198–201.

7

Warfare and urbanization in Roman Italy

T. J. Cornell

"War is the father of all things", as the wise old Greek said.[1] The process of
urbanization in Roman Italy is a good illustration of the truth of this saying.
The distinctive political, economic and social structures that characterized
Italy under Roman rule were brought about by war. In so far as they were the
product of conscious or deliberate planning, they had an exclusively warlike
function. The facts are elementary and familiar, but we need constantly to
remind ourselves of them because they are all too easily overlooked. For
instance, when considering the sophisticated and cultured life of Pompeii in
AD 79, and the secure and comfortable existence of its leisured class, not everyone remembers that at the same time a Roman army under Julius Agricola was
engaged in a destructive and bloody campaign in northern Britain – making a
desert and calling it peace, in Tacitus' immortal words. It is difficult at first
sight to see any connection between these two worlds; and indeed one of the
most striking things about the Roman principate is the huge gap that separated
the civilian society of Italy and the inner provinces from the military life
which was exclusively confined to remote frontier provinces. The demilitariza-
tion of Italy and the creation of a civilian society separated from warfare and
military matters not only by geographical space but also in people's experience
and outlook, are amongst the most striking consequences of the profound
social transformation that we call the Roman revolution.[2]

It was not always like this. During the republican era, as we know, Italy
was the centre of the Roman war machine, a society that was geared to war to
a degree that has few, if any, historical parallels. For centuries the Romans and
their Italian allies made war every year as a matter of course.

Constant warfare required the commitment of a high proportion of Italian
manpower to regular active service; throughout the period of the middle
republic around 10 per cent of adult males were under arms every year, and at
times of crisis the figure was much higher. To achieve this level, every male
Italian would have had to serve for at least four years, and such service almost

invariably entailed active participation in war.

For much of the period of the middle republic, Italy itself was the battleground: during the Roman conquest in the 4th and 3rd centuries, and in the catastrophic years of the Hannibalic war. For most of the 2nd century, Italy was at peace, but the Roman wars of conquest in other parts of the Mediterranean drew upon Italian manpower to an unprecedented extent. In the 1st century BC Italy was the scene of a devastating series of civil wars.

Under the republic, therefore, warfare was part of the normal experience of all Italians, and was embedded in the fabric of their society. The Roman republic's institutions were military in character and function; its religion, and its cultural and moral values, were suffused with a militaristic ethos. This is the warrior society that has been so well described and analyzed in recent studies.[3]

It was against this background that urbanization took place in Italy. The purpose of this paper is to show that the growth of urban society in Roman Italy can be understood in the context of military institutions and the operation of economic factors arising from war. I intend to study the effects of warfare on the process of urbanization in Italy from two points of view: in the first half of the paper I shall examine the ways in which war affected the formation of urban centres, both literally in the form of physical structures such as fortifications, and metaphorically in the form of political development. The second half of the paper will deal with economic factors, and the ways in which war shaped patterns of production and consumption in republican Italy.

From a broad ethno-historical viewpoint, it can be said that in general the effect of warfare on human society is aggregative. It is arguable that at certain stages of human development, for instance in hunter–gatherer societies and in palaeolithic cultures, warfare tends to be *dispersive* – that is, its effect is to push bands apart and keep them separate; but from neolithic times, and in settled agricultural conditions generally, the main effect of warfare is *aggregative*. This distinction has been drawn by the American anthropologist Robert Carneiro, who regards the transition from dispersive war to aggregative war as marking a decisive step in the history of political development. Warfare, in Carneiro's view, brings about the unification of formerly autonomous groupings – villages, chiefdoms, etc. – and gives rise to more complex forms of organization and hierarchy. Only in this way can human groups survive and prosper in a competition for limited resources. On this theory, war is the most important single factor in the process of political development, and in particular in the formation of states.[4] As Carneiro himself acknowledges, this theory has much in common with the ideas of the 19th-century sociologist Herbert Spencer.[5]

Secondly, it can be argued that war is the most important form of interaction between communities, and it is interaction which has been particularly stressed in recent studies of social and political development. I am referring particularly to the idea that interaction can be a dynamic force leading to simultaneous growth and development in neighbouring communities of the same type. This "peer-polity interaction" (as it is called) has been seen as decisive in the rise of city-states in ancient Greece and Italy,[6] and the main element in the process is identified by A. M. Snodgrass[7] as war. In the 7th and 6th centuries BC new military tactics and new styles of combat – in particular, the use of heavily armed infantry soldiers or "hoplites" – spread rapidly throughout the Greek world and adjacent areas, such as Tyrrhenian central Italy.[8] This development was crucial in the formation of the ancient city (the *polis*), which can be defined as a community of equal citizens who qualified for membership by ownership of land and their capacity to arm themselves for service in the army. The political organization of the Greek cities was based on reforms introduced in the 7th and 6th centuries BC which distributed power and political status according to property ownership and military service.

In Italy similar developments occurred in the Greek colonies, and spread to native communities throughout the Tyrrhenian lowland zone. The rise of city-states in Campania, Latium and Etruria is a feature of the common culture (*koine*) uniting these areas, and was itself a product of peer-polity interaction. The most interesting and best documented case of a *polis*-type community in archaic central Italy is of course Rome itself, which emerged as a city-state in the second half of the 7th century BC. In the 6th century, traditionally under king Servius Tullius, Rome formed an army of citizen hoplites based on the census, which divided the people into a hierarchy of groups according to property and place of residence.[9]

Warfare also has an aggregative effect in that it tends to bring about the physical concentration of settlements for defensive purposes, and to prompt the formation of nucleated centres surrounded by artificial fortifications. This proposition is undoubtedly valid in a general way, but the connection between this process and urbanization is neither simple nor straightforward. The case of ancient Italy illustrates this point well. Early settlements in central Italy going back at least to the beginning of the Iron Age were established on defensive hilltop sites, often reinforced by artificial fortifications. The Villanovan settlements of Etruria seem to have been concentrated on hilltop sites (although so far most excavation has been focused on cemeteries rather than areas of settlement), and in Latium the earliest settlements were on defensive sites protected by artificial earthworks, which in some cases can be dated as early as the 8th century BC (e.g. Decima, Ficana).

But the use of defensive hilltop sites is not the same as urbanization, even when the sites in question provide evidence of concentrated settlement. The evidence for settlement is usually in the form of huts, and the communities, although sometimes quite large, are best described as villages (the use of the term "proto-urban" for some of these settlements is unhelpful, in my opinion). There are two reasons in particular for differentiating between urbanization and the development of artificial defences. First, we should note that hill forts are especially characteristic of areas of central Italy that were not urbanized until the 1st century BC, at the earliest. Central Samnium is the best known example. While archaeological research (such as the British survey of the Biferno valley) has revealed a pattern of relatively dense rural settlement in the Samnite valleys, and has substantially modified the traditional picture of the Samnite economy as exclusively pastoral, it still remains true that in the period before the Social war the region was poor and relatively backward with few urban centres, if any.[10] Its political structure was based on a system of rural cantons (*pagi*), each comprising one or more villages (*vici*). The tribal unit known as a *touto* (Latin *populus*) was a federation of *pagi* united under a single elected leader, the *meddiss tovtiks* (in Latin texts, *meddix tuticus*, to be translated, perhaps, as *magister populi*). This official was a military leader, and one suspects that the federation of the Samnite villages in a *touto* had an exclusively military function – that is, they came together only in time of war, which, historically speaking, is another way of saying whenever they were attacked by the Romans.[11] If so, we have a good example of the Carneiro thesis – that war necessitates and promotes more complex and hierarchical political systems.

The settlement pattern in Samnium seems to have been one of scattered villages linked by a network of rural sanctuaries and fortified hilltops. But these three types of site were kept functionally separate. For instance, the elaborate sanctuary at Pietrabbondante, which was developed in the later 2nd century BC with a complex of sacred buildings in the Greek style, including a theatre, remained a purely religious centre, and was never part of a nucleated settlement. It is noteworthy that with the development of truly urbanized communities in Samnium, dated by Gabba to the 1st century BC,[12] the sanctuary site of Pietrabbondante was abandoned. The most significant physical relics of pre-Roman Samnium, however, are the numerous hill forts, of which standing remains can still be seen. The map which I produced for the *Cambridge ancient history*[13] shows no fewer than 56 hill forts in an area of central Samnium measuring some 4,500 km² (there are undoubtedly more of them to be found; I merely listed all those that had been discovered, to that date, by Stephen Oakley). Some of them, for instance those at Monte Vairano, Castel di Sangro and Alfedena, were the sites of substantial permanent settlements; but these places were hardly cities, and are in any case exceptional. For the most part, the hill forts are small and inaccessible, and cannot have been places of permanent habitation. No doubt they were used as temporary refuges, although some of them may have had a more positive strategic purpose as military strongholds.

A similar pattern seems to have prevailed throughout the central Apennines. For instance, the only archaeological trace of the Aequi, the people who fought against Rome in the 5th and 4th centuries BC, consists of ruins of polygonal fortifications that can be seen at a number of hilltop sites in the Monti Prenestini. The forts should presumably be equated with the defensive positions (*oppida*) to which the Aequi retreated whenever the Romans attacked them.[14] That was until 304 BC, when the Romans attacked with overwhelming force and wiped them out in a few days in a campaign of genocide.[15]

The conclusion, that many of the early fortified sites in central Italy were not cities, is paradoxical; but there is an even greater paradox in the fact that in the archaic period most cities were not fortified. This is a difficult issue, on which I should like to discover more information; but at first glance the evidence seems to me to show that the earliest urban centres in Italy were not surrounded by walls.

The case of Rome itself is especially problematic. As is well known, substantial traces still remain of the republican city wall – the most impressive portion being that which stands in the Piazza dei Cinquecento outside the entrance to the main railway station. The ancients believed that this massive *enceinte*, which is over 11 km long and embraces an area of some 427 hectares, was built by king Servius Tullius in the 6th century BC, but in this they were mistaken. Modern research has established that the so-called Servian wall belongs to the 4th century, and should be identified with the wall constructed in 378 BC, according to the notice of Livy.[16]

It is true that there are traces of earlier defensive works, in particular a massive earthwork across the line of the Quirinal and the Esquiline where there is no natural line of defence. The adding of the *agger* is extremely difficult. The discovery of a sherd of Attic red-figure pottery led some scholars to place it in the 5th century, but no certain conclusion can be drawn from such slender evidence; in fact it remains possible that the *agger* goes back to the time of Servius Tullius. But it does not follow that the city was protected by a complete defensive circuit; rather, one might suppose that in the 6th century BC Rome was partly defended against attack from the northeast by a rampart and ditch running from the Esquiline to the Quirinal, but that elsewhere it relied on the natural defences of the individual hills. There was no complete circuit of artificial fortifications. In support of this conclusion it can be argued that if Rome did have effective all-round defences, the Gauls would never have been able to capture it in 390 BC.[17]

We know that earth ramparts were used to defend the vulnerable parts of hilltop sites elsewhere in Latium, for example at Ardea, Ficana and Decima. Some of these earthworks have been dated as early as the 8th century BC (Ficana, Decima, Laurentina), others to the 7th (Satricum, Lavinium, Ardea). At Ardea, there was a complex system of three separate earth banks, defending the three contiguous plateaux that form the site. The largest of the three *aggeres* was 600 m long, 40 m wide and 15 m high, fronted by a ditch 20 m deep. This was clearly a first line of defence, since the plateau it enclosed, now called Casalazzara, was not part of the inhabited area.[18]

The case of Ardea suggests a possible parallel with Rome, where the *agger* was a long way from the nucleus of the city; the area immediately to the west of it is unlikely to have been inhabited in the archaic period. Whether there was an inner line of defence is, at present, quite uncertain.

We may conclude, then, that the ancient tradition is based on a misunderstanding. Although there are good grounds for associating the *agger* with Servius Tullius, it is unlikely that Rome was completely surrounded by walls in the 6th century. But for writers such as Strabo and Dionysius of Halicarnassus it was simply unthinkable that Rome should ever have been without walls.

A similar prejudice seems to have infected some modern writers (and I am not referring only to the alleged discovery of an 8th century wall at the foot of the Palatine which some enthusiasts have associated with Romulus). Recent excavations at Lavinium have revealed traces of a fortified *enceinte* dating from the 7th century BC; in the 6th-century city walls of squared blocks of cappellaccio were erected, apparently surrounding the entire habitation area. If Lavinium had walls in the 6th century, so it is argued, the same must be true of Rome.[19] But this argument is scarcely compelling, because like is not being compared with like. Lavinium was a tiny place, its inhabited area measuring no more than 30 hectares with a perimeter of around 2 km. 6th century Rome was of a different order of magnitude, and belongs in the same category as the larger city states of Greece and Etruria.

Few if any of the major Etruscan cities had complete walled circuits in the 6th century. The walls at Tarquinii and Caere, for example, belong to the 4th century, and do not in either case surround the whole of the site. These cities relied for the most part on their natural defences, as did Veii, which did not equip itself with walls until the late 5th century, shortly before its epic struggle with Rome. On the Greek mainland cities with complete walled circuits were rare in the 6th century. Athens did not surround itself with walls until after the Persian wars, and Sparta and some others never did so. On the other hand, the Ionian cities were surrounded by walls at a very early date (in some cases before 700 BC), no doubt prompted by the threat of attack from the organized kingdoms of Anatolia. The situation in Sicily and Magna Graecia is more uncertain (at least to me: this is a matter on which I should welcome some further information): some cities (Naxos, Leontini, Poseidonia) had walled circuits in the 6th century, while others, including Cumae, seem to have been unfortified towns surrounding a defensible acropolis.

The general impression I have gained from a rather limited study of the available evidence is that for the most part Italian cities, such as Rome, began to fortify themselves in earnest only in the 4th and 3rd centuries BC – the period, that is, of the Roman military conquest. It is also the age of Roman colonization, the primary purpose of which was strategic. The colonies were carefully constructed urban communities, equipped with all the necessary institutional apparatus and hierarchical social divisions to operate as self-governing city-states: they are a fundamental part of the process of urbanization, but it should not be forgotten that their primary purpose was to act as strategic outposts in newly conquered territory (*propugnacula imperii* as Cicero calls them). Naturally, they were all surrounded with defensive walls.

In the later republic, the possession of a walled circuit, complete with towers and formal gateways, became an indispensable symbol of city status. In Samnium and the central Apennine region the process of urbanization began after the Social war, and was, according to Gabba's convincing demonstration, a function of the extension of the Roman citizenship and the formation of self-governing *municipia*. This development was accompanied by a spate of public building in the communities of central Italy, and in particular by the construction, often for the first time, of city walls. In 1972, Gabba was able to list over 20 cities in central and southern Italy in which inscriptions record the construction or reconstruction of city defences in the course of the 1st century BC:[20] the list could, no doubt, be extended. An example is the inscription at Caudium recording the construction of towers in the walled circuit by two *patroni*, the Scribonii Libones, father and son, whom Degrassi identified as the grandfather and father of L. Scribonius Libo, the consul of 34 BC; if so, the construction should be dated a generation earlier, say in the 70s or 60s BC.

Now this was still a period of violence and unrest in Italy, and no prudent community could be certain that civil war might not break out again at any moment; nevertheless one is bound to agree with Gabba, that there might be another motive for this remarkable explosion of city fortification in the middle of the 1st century BC, namely that the city walls had come to represent "l'elemento indispensabile e caratterizzante perché un insediamento umano si qualificasse con la dignità di vera città".[21]

At this point, I should like to turn to the economic aspects of the question, and to the ways in which warfare transformed the economy of republican Italy and fostered the growth of towns.

I should say at once that I do not intend to discuss at length an aspect which has received a certain amount of attention from historians, namely the direct effects of war on the movement of population from the country to the towns in the battle-zone itself. Of course the presence of a hostile army (or its threatened presence) inevitably causes people to take refuge where they can if they have any sense, and this usually means migration to a fortified town. While the effects of such movements would normally be temporary, in certain special circumstances they can be more lasting.

During the Hannibalic war in particular, many country dwellers in central and southern Italy fled to the towns in order to escape the attentions of Hannibal (or of the Romans, depending on which side they were on), and because the danger lasted for years on end, it may be that some took up permanent residence there. But the extent of such a development, if it occurred, and its long term effects, are extremely difficult to assess; and it is only in the case of Rome, which was obviously exceptional, that we know of it happening to any significant degree. In 206 BC, Livy tells us, the senate instructed the magistrates to expel the migrants from the city and send them back to where they came from. This proved rather difficult in the event, because it turned out that the migrants did not wish to go; their reaction was not unlike that of a group of London office workers on receiving notice that they had been relocated to Middlesbrough.

What I am saying is that their attitude is understandable, but it does not necessarily indicate that a major shift had taken place in the pattern of residence of the Italian population, still less a permanent change from rural to urban occupations. Toynbee's argument, in the course of a chapter entitled "Urbanisation and industry in post-Hannibalic peninsular Italy",[22] that they took up urban occupations in trade and manufacture, is speculative and based on modernising assumptions which I for one do not share.

In conclusion, it can be said that the question of direct economic effects of the Hannibalic war on the towns of Italy is even more uncertain than the notoriously controversial issue of its effects on the countryside.[23] Having said that, I shall pass on to a discussion of the indirect consequences of the war on the economy of Roman Italy.

The most important fact about war in a society such as the Roman republic was that military success was the principal means of capital accumulation and economic growth, and consequently the principal cause of changes in the social structure. The immediate profits of war included indemnities and movable booty, which in the 2nd and 1st centuries BC amounted to enormous sums. I need not elaborate this point, which has been extensively studied in recent scholarship (especially by Harris[24]).

The most important economic gains from the war, however, were produced by the subsequent exploitation of conquered territories. This included swift and efficient extraction of their mineral wealth (the Spanish silver mines near Cartagena, for example, were producing 25,000 drachmae a day for the Roman state in the 2nd century BC), and the imposition of an annual tribute, either in the form of a fixed sum, or assessed as a tenth of the annual yield of the province.

These revenues boosted the Italian economy in several ways. The state expended large sums on public works in the city of Rome and elsewhere, and from the later 2nd century BC onwards popular politicians implemented programmes of public spending for the direct benefit of the poor, most notably by subsidizing imports of staple foodstuffs (in 58 BC this became the famous "corn dole"). Surprising as it might seem at first sight, these imports had a positive effect on local agricultural production because Italian farmers did not in general produce grain for the Roman market in competition with overseas suppliers. The effect, rather, was to strengthen the spending power of the city population and to increase the demand for the specialized products such as wine and olive oil that formed the bulk of the output of large commercial estates in Italy.[25]

But the principal means by which the Italian bourgeoisie benefited from successful war was through the administration of state finances. The practical organization of public income and expenditure in the Roman republic was undertaken by private entrepreneurs who contracted for state business. These *publicani* (as they were called) organized the collection of taxes, the construction of public works, and the exploitation of state-owned resources such as mines.[26] They also dealt with military supplies. It was through the profits from these activities that the Italian elite became rich from war, rather than through direct appropriation of war booty, which, though significant, benefited only a small number of highly placed individuals.[27]

The most important effects of successful war on the Italian economy were brought about by the military expenditure of the state. The payment of wages to soldiers serving in the Roman army was an effective mechanism for redistribution of the profits of empire among the population at large. But the greatest benefit was to the propertied classes, whose fortunes were invested in large slave-worked estates producing cash crops and other commodities such as wool and leather for sale. Before the later 1st century BC the greatest demand for these products came from the state itself, in the form of orders for supplies, clothing and equipment for the army.

The requirements of any large military force are always difficult to meet in pre-industrial conditions, and if they are continuously present for any length of time they are bound to be a stimulus to economic growth and development. Although in a modern economy military spending can have negative effects, in that it tends to divert scarce capital, technological and raw-material resources from productive to unproductive (or indeed destructive) uses, it would not have had this effect in the context of ancient Italy, with its primitive technology, rudimentary credit system, and low-level demand. The effect would rather have been to bring underemployed capacity into productive use and to stimulate increased output with a demand for mass-produced goods.

A few figures can be given. Large Roman armies were enrolled every year throughout the last two centuries of the republic. Their numbers averaged around 45,000 men each year in the 2nd century (not counting Italian allies, who always contributed at least as many again, and would have had an important economic impact), rising to well over 100,000 in the early 1st century (when allies were incorporated into the Roman state), and reaching as many as 250,000 in the age of the civil wars.[28] These soldiers needed to be supplied with food, clothing, shelter, arms, and other equipment. These needs, and the state's capacity to pay for them, created a degree of spending power and a concentration of demand that could not (until the late republic) be matched by the diffuse and erratic requirements of the free domestic market. The effects on textile production, for instance, must have been enormous. This is an area of Roman life about which we have little evidence, but a simple comparison can give an idea of what might have been involved. I quote from a standard work on the emergence of the European great powers in the 17th century:

by the end of the 17th century uniforms had become the rule for the soldiers of all nations. The English redcoats, the Prussian blue and the French green, yellow, white and blue regiments won fame on a dozen battlefields. As Sombart has pointed out, this suggests an expansion of the textile industry. Quantities of cloth of standard quality and colour had to be woven and worked into uniforms. The manufacturers of rough woollen cloth were prosperous in France when most of the textile industry languished under the strain of taxes and low demand, and there was a lively trade in woollen cloth from Saxony, Silesia and England to Hamburg, Frankfurt and Holland, where elaborate equipment for dyeing and finishing adapted the material for military use. An estimate for the demand can be derived from the fact that an army of 100,000 men required 20,000 pieces of cloth every two years. Considering that all Brandenburg consumed in this period only 50,000 pieces a year for civilian use, and that 100,000 troops used about half the textile production of the West Riding, this figure assumes its proper importance.[29]

The figures for troop numbers in the last two centuries of the Roman republic would be roughly comparable, and if they were supplied exclusively from Italy, as seems probable, we are dealing with a factor of major economic importance.

The amounts of money required to finance the Roman army must have been immense. It has been estimated that between 75 and 80 per cent of the Roman state's budget in the 2nd century BC was devoted to military expenditure. It has been further calculated that it would have cost around 100 denarii per year to keep a serving soldier fed, clothed and equipped.[30] Supply contracts would therefore have amounted to 4.5 million denarii per year for legionaries alone (that is, without any allowance for the allied contingents, which were financed by their own communities; but the economic effects would have been comparable). An example of the contracts that must have been common is the order for 6,000 togas, 30,000 tunics and 200 horses, together with their transport to Macedonia, made by a praetor in 169 BC.[31] The sums of money involved were very large. An idea of the order of magnitude that can be assumed is given by Livy's report of an event in 209 BC, when the sum of 1.2 million (or 1.4 million: the figure is disputed) was earmarked for the supply of clothing to the army in Spain.[32]

The raw materials for these supplies were produced by the large agricultural estates in Italy, and it seems likely that the requirements of the army accounted for much of their output. It is probable that in peaceful conditions, there would have been a tendency towards overproduction and underconsumption in the free market, and that a regular demand for army supplies by the state was essential for the agrarian economy of Italy as it developed in the 2nd century BC; and the need for regular and continuous military spending implied regular and continuous war. But the necessary political response was always forthcoming, and in the Roman republic, as Harris has eloquently pointed out, there was little serious danger of peace breaking out. Senators, whose income depended on the exploitation of large landed estates, duly allocated military commands to the consuls and praetors, provided for the enlistment of soldiers, and voted the necessary funds for their maintenance.

The contracts were let out by the annual magistrates, the consuls, and, where appropriate, the praetors, who controlled the money voted to them by the senate. The beneficiaries of the contracts, the *publicani*, belonged to the wealthy class outside the senate, a group which dominated the *comitia centuriata*. I mention this simply in order to complete the circuit, and to show how the pork barrel operated. The *comitia centuriata*, after all, was the assembly which elected the consuls and praetors and had the deciding voice in matters of peace and war.

How did all this affect urban development and the growth of towns? It is important for me to be clear about what I am saying and what I am not saying. We have very little direct information about the supply system of the Roman army. Although we can assume that the *publicani* were crucial to the system, their activities are documented only in unusual circumstances – for instance the discovery of a major fraud. Normally the system worked smoothly, as Badian has argued, and was simply taken for granted by ancient historical writers (as it is still taken for granted by most of their modern successors).

We know even less about the units of production for clothing, weapons, armour, boots, etc. which the army required in such large numbers. It might seem that the heavy demands of state procurement would inevitably affect the organization of production, and bring about rationally organized systems in relatively large units (i.e. factories). If so, do we have grounds for supposing that production came to be concentrated in particular places, and that some Italian towns and cities became centres of production? This is possible, but by no means certain. First, the primitive state of ancient technology and the absence of mechanized forms of production mean that there would not be any automatic increase in productivity from the creation of larger units. The basic units of production would remain raw materials, labour, and technical skills.

As far as arms manufacture is concerned, it might have made more sense for skilled artisans to be assembled and made to accompany the army. As it happens this method is attested in one of the few surviving literary passages dealing with this matter, the account of Sertorius' organization of a direct labour system in a fragment of Livy, Book 91. We are told that Sertorius arranged for all the towns in Spain to produce weapons according to their capacity; then his soldiers threw all their old weapons into a heap and took new ones. Sertorius also summoned smiths (*fabri*) from every part of Spain and grouped them in *officinae publicae* to make instruments of war, giving them a daily output target.

In the imperial period, such *officinae* became permanent establishments attached to the principal army bases and employing direct labour, often that of the soldiers themselves. Of course the standing army of the principate was largely a peacetime force, whose principal problem was to find something to do; much of the time and effort of the soldiers came to be spent on organizing their own supply. The Vindolanda letters, for instance, indicate that soldiers spent a great deal of time seconded to the *officinae*.

Under the republic, however, these things had to be organized *ad hoc*, and armies were engaged in the serious business of fighting wars. It is therefore most probable that much of the supply and repair of military equipment was organized by contractors who served the needs of the armies on the spot.

As for textile production, which would have been based in Italy, the most likely reconstruction is that the industry was widely dispersed in small localized units. The reason why the state relied so heavily on the services of the *publicani* was precisely the fact that production was so widely diffused. We might compare the method by which some modern clothing manufacturers and retailers use home-based workers, to whom they supply raw materials and from whom they demand high rates of output at very low rates of pay. The *publicani* could have organized networks of out-workers and small production units to whom they supplied the raw materials; the absence of any alternative market for the finished goods placed them in a monopoly position, and would have enabled them to depress wage rates and increase their own profits.

Even under the empire, when the army took over the organization of its own supplies, we find there was no significant concentration of textile production: quite the contrary. Jones pointed to the evidence of papyri which record the deals between the army and individual weavers and other cloth producers in numerous small towns and villages. Amazingly, many of the orders, which are for tiny amounts – two or three cloaks here, half a dozen tunics there – are earmarked for army units stationed as far away as Judaea and Cappadocia. As Jones rightly points out,

> the army authorities would surely not have distributed their orders to hundreds of villages, an undertaking which involved a heavy burden of administration and clerical work, if they could have placed them in few large centres. It is even more significant that the Judaean and even the Cappadocian commands placed orders in Egypt for woollen garments, which were not an Egyptian speciality. This implies that the weaving industry of Judaea and Cappadocia had little surplus capacity above local needs, and was incapable of supplying the large forces stationed in these countries. The army supply authorities had therefore to distribute their orders over a wider field; Egypt with its large population and small garrison was a suitable area on which to draw.[33]

Returning to republican Italy, it seems most likely that the chief beneficiaries of the Roman military–industrial complex were not the textile manufacturers and industrial entrepreneurs among the urban bourgeoisie, but rather the suppliers of raw materials – that is, the owners of large slave-run agricultural estates – and the middlemen (i.e. the *publicani*) most of whom were also drawn from the Italian landed elite. What I am saying, therefore, is that the army supply system, though extremely important, did not radically affect the *structure* of the urban economy of Roman Italy.

I am still basically an adherent of the consumer city model, if by that we understand an urban economy based mainly on the provision of goods and services for local consumption, the bulk of the demand being provided by the spending power of a landed elite. Urbanization in Roman Italy reached a very high level by pushing this system to the limit; the products of imperialism, of which I would say that the military supply system forms an important and largely neglected item, served mainly to swell the spending power of the elite. If the income of the elite in the consumer city model is derived largely from the agricultural surplus of the surrounding hinterland, imperialism functioned as a mechanism for artificially enlarging the size of the hinterland.

Notes

1. Heracleitus, Fr. 53
2. T. J. Cornell, The end of Roman imperial expansion, in *War and society in the ancient world*, eds J. Rich & G. Shipley (London, 1993), pp. 139–70.
3. K. Hopkins, *Conquerors and slaves* (Cambridge, 1978), pp. 25 ff.; W. V. Harris, *War and imperialism in republican Rome* (Oxford, 1979), pp. 9 ff.
4. R. Carneiro, A theory of the origin of the state, *Science* 169, 1970, pp. 733; Political expansion as an expression of the principle of competitive exclusion, in *Origins of the state*, eds R. Cohen & E. Service (Philadelphia, 1978) pp. 205–23; The rôle of warfare in political evolution: past results and future projections, in *The effects of war on society*, ed. G. Ausenda (San Marino, 1991), pp. 87–102.
5. H. Spencer, *The principles of sociology*, 2 vols (London, 1896).
6. C. Renfrew & J. Cherry (eds), *Peer-polity interaction and socio-political change* (Cambridge, 1986).
7. A. M. Snodgrass, Interaction by design: the Greek city-state, in *Peer-polity interaction and socio-political change*, eds Renfew & Cherry, (1986) pp. 47–58.
8. M. Torelli, Tre studi di storia etrusca, *DdA* 8, 1975, pp. 3–78; B. d'Agostino, Military organisation and social structure in archaic Etruria, in *The Greek city*, eds O. Murray & S. Price (Oxford, 1990), pp. 59–82.
9. C. Ampolo, La nascita della città and La città riformata e l'organizzazione centuriata, in *Storia di Roma*, eds A. Momigliano & A. Schiavone (Turin, 1988), vol. i., pp. 153–80; 203–40.
10. G. W. Barker, The archaeology of Samnite settlement in Molise, *Antiquity* 51, 1977, 20–4; G. W. Barker, J. A. Lloyd, D. Webley, A classical landscape in Molise, *PBSR* 46, 1978, pp. 35–51.
11. T. J. Cornell, The conquest of Italy, in *CAH²* (Cambridge, 1989), vii.2, pp. 351–9.
12. E. Gabba, Urbanizzazione e rinnovamenti urbanistici nell'Italia centro-meridionale del I sec. a. C., *SCO* 21, 1972, pp. 73–112.
13. Cornell, The conquest of Italy, p. 358.
14. Livy 2.48.4, 10.45; Diod. 20.101; Cornell The conquest of Italy, pp. 285.
15. Livy 9.45.17.
16. Livy 6.32.1.
17. A. Alföldi, *Early Rome and the Latins* (Ann Arbor, Mich., 1965), p. 322.

18. C. Morselli & E. Tortorici, *ARDEA* (Rome, 1982).
19. F. Castagnoli, Roma arcaia e le recenti scavi di Lavinio, *PdP* **32**, 1977, p. 346
20. Gabba, Urbanizzazione e rinnovamenti urbanistici.
21. *Ibid.*, p. 108
22. A. J. Toynbee, *Hannibal's legacy* (London, 1965), vol. ii. pp. 332 ff.
23. *Ibid.*, pp. 10 ff.; P. A. Brunt, *Italian manpower, 225 BC-AD 14* (Oxford, 1971), pp. 269 ff.
24. Harris, *War and imperialism in republican Rome.*
25. Hopkins, *Conquerors and slaves*, pp. 73–4.
26. E. Badian, *Publicans and sinners* (Oxford, 1972).
27. A. N. Sherwin-White, *Roman foreign policy in the east* (London, 1983), pp. 12–14.
28. Brunt, *Italian manpower,* pp. 424–5, 432–3, 449.
29. J. B. Wolf, *The emergence of the great powers, 1685–1715* (New York, 1950), p. 180.
30. Badian, *Publicans and sinners*, p. 22.
31. Livy 44.16.4.
32. Livy 27.10.11–13.
33. A. H. M. Jones, *The Roman economy* (Oxford, 1974), pp. 355–6.

8

Religion and rusticity

J. A. North

Introduction

It is a very normal assumption in discussions of ancient religion that certain types of religious activity are "rural" in their character, that they belong specifically to the religion of countryside as opposed to that of the city. The problem of this paper is to assess whether there was such a "country" religion in republican Italy and, if so, how it should be identified and defined.

The discussion is directed to an issue of religious history, not socio-economic history; but this statement is not as radical in its implications as it would be in the context of later "world"-type religions, where the institutional structure of the religion is autonomous enough to provide its own independent point of analysis. The pagan religions of the pre-Christian period were quite differently related to their own societies: they formed an embedded part of city life, rather than a separable area of religious activity.[1] For this very reason, the attempt to identify a "country" religion could be seen as premature. The fact is that we have few if any certainties about Italian peasants of the late republican/early imperial period – not whether they used money, nor whether they were integrated into the market economy, nor even where they lived.[2] If we have no confident picture of their socio-economic location, there might seem to be little chance of making any sense of their religious relationships either.

On the other hand, these problems about life in the country are not going to disappear in the near future. In the meantime, the case might be argued the other way round: religious evidence might be as helpful a way of looking at some of the problems as any other. If indeed religion is an integral part of all activities, then in principle, its modalities should reflect patterns of life as well as any other source of information. However, as will become very clear, although there is no shortage of evidence about religious aspects of country life (references in texts to the country and countrymen,[3] religious sites in remote or rural locations,[4] deities with agricultural duties to perform,[5] rituals carried out in the villages[6]), making use of this information in any spirit other than the antiquarian raises formidable problems of method. At this stage, defining the problems may be as much as can be expected.

135

Religion in the countryside

Literary sources provide the obvious starting point for this study; and, at first sight, Roman poetry in particular seems reassuringly full of countrymen and of observations about their peculiar religious habits. Indeed the contrast between town and country is one of the most familiar themes of Augustan poetry, while attitudes to religion regularly occur as an essential component of the comparison. The countryman of this stereotype is hard working, lives a simple life, keeps to an old-fashioned morality and worships the gods in an unchanging, traditional way. He has to be contrasted all the time with the town dweller, characterized by his degenerate tastes and habits and – it goes without saying – by his lack of piety and his contempt for the gods.[7]

A different version of the same set of attitudes arises from Pliny's famous visit to the shrine of Clitumnus.[8] He describes the beauties of the place and the religious interest of the shrine; but the note on which he concludes is one of delicate ambiguity, which the recipient of the letter is naturally assumed to appreciate and share:

> There is much you will praise, some things you will laugh at: but no, not you: for you are so kindly that you won't be laughing at all.[9]

So there is a temptation, for all but the most indulgent, to smile at the simplicity of these country people. It is important to notice how specific is Pliny's amusement here; it is not a question of reporting what we should regard as some particularly "primitive" survival from the past. What he was looking at represented a rich collection of written texts and dedications.[10] It was the old-fashioned grammar and piety of the record that provoked his patronizing little outburst. Much of what went on in sophisticated Rome would strike a modern observer as at least as curious and archaic as anything that could have appeared on the walls of the shrine at Clitumnus. And meanwhile the fact of the written tradition provides, for us today, significant evidence of how important the act of writing was in the religious expression of pagans in relation to the gods, even in the backwoods; it provides an index of sophistication, not of simplicity.[11]

This firm association of the backward and ignorant with the "rustic" is particularly evident in a passage of Cicero's *Republic*.[12] The subject is an incident before the battle of Pydna, when it was known in advance that there was about to be a lunar eclipse. The speaker in Cicero's dialogue, Scipio Aemilianus, tells how the learned C. Sulpicius Gallus, who was an officer serving under Aemilius Paullus at the time,[13] tried explaining the theory of eclipses to the troops to prevent the panic that might have followed the event, if it had not been anticipated. The interlocutor in the dialogue, Aelius Tubero, expresses his astonishment:

Did he really, said Tubero, try teaching such doctrines to rustics? Did he dare to speak so to the unlearned?[14]

Tubero is referring evidently to the dangers of letting the unlettered masses know that natural phenomena have natural causes, rather than leaving them to believe that such events are controlled by the gods and averted by the skill of the priests.[15] So, *agrestes* here, as often, means ignorant, not specifically country-dwelling at all. But the country dweller stands as the symbol of ignorance and backwardness.[16]

Some ignorant, backward *agrestes* there must have been, of course; but it is difficult to believe that texts such as this can reveal anything except the prejudice of the elite. Even if taken seriously as descriptions of a cultural situation, of a perceived distance in attitude between city and farm life, they provide only the basic message that the simpler, more moral past was expressed in a rural idiom. The country and the past spoke the same fictional language. But imagine, for the sake of the argument, that Cicero and his speakers, not to say Gallus himself, had known that the soldiers addressed before Pydna all came from city life not farm life; that would have made no difference at all to the argument.

The history of Roman religion

The problem is not just a superficial or a theoretical one for the study of Roman religion, because traditional histories of the development of republican religion have always made a good deal out of sets of distinctions based on such categories as the cults of the farm, cults of pastoralism or cults of the wild lands.[17] The gods and goddesses are allocated to particular spheres, as are the rituals and festivals of the old calendar. Where the allocation is not obvious, it is debated as a major problem of understanding.

More remarkably still, the whole historical development of the religion of the republican period has often been reconstructed precisely on a framework provided by this distinction. So the early period is characterized as one in which there was a perfect fit between the simple beliefs of the rural population of the archaic city; but later on, as the city grew and its life became more sophisticated, the old deities and festivals lost their meaning for the now city based proletariat. Consequently, both at elite and popular level, the power of religion became thin and remote, the subject only of meaningless priestly academic elaboration.[18]

It is a corollary of this view that the rural population did believe, as much as ever, in the old cults and festivals, since they still had to face head-on the practical problems of crop failure, pests, bad weather and all the other disasters of farm life. It hardly needs saying that there is no direct evidence to prove any of these romantic hypotheses.

The most telling argument in favour of this view concerns the working of the calendar. At least potentially, it could demonstrate the separation between town-based religion and country-based agricultural or pastoral religion. The argument is that originally all festivals fitted precisely the right moment in the sequence of an agricultural year; but the calendar was controlled by the priests, who allowed the months to get out of phase with the solar year by omitting to insert the necessary intercalary month.[19] As a result, the sequence of religious festivals would have lost its proper relationship to the seasons, so the ceremonies would have been totally meaningless.[20] The Vestal Virgins (to give one example) had an obligation to go out into the fields on a particular day, specified in terms of the calendar (7, 9, 11 May) and pick the first ears of corn.[21] In the 190s BC, for at least 20 years and probably longer, the calendar was approximately four months ahead of itself;[22] so 7 May would have fallen in early February. It is possible that this distortion arose during the Hannibalic emergency, but it persisted for some years afterwards and no urgent measures were taken to correct the error. In other words, on this view, we should infer that the cults had been reduced to total nonsense and that nobody cared. One difficulty is that this argument claims to prove far too much: not merely that a growing cynicism about the gods was undermining "sincere beliefs", but that the Roman authorities as early as the 190s BC were happy to have their irreligion publicly paraded for all to see. At almost the same moment they were proclaiming in the East that the Romans were triumphant because they were the most religious of men.[23]

The apparent paradox is, however, surely no more than a modern construction, interesting only because so much discussion of ancient religion works on the same bogus set of assumptions. Its crucial – unasserted and unbelievable[24] – premiss is that the ancient pagans used religious language and ritual in an entirely literal, everyday sense, utterly innocent of symbolism, so that if the Vestals found no physical ear of corn in the fields, the whole religious system would be confounded. It is true that pagan religious expression, like any other, has to function at a distance from everyday reality (because its propositions cannot be proved in reality), but must constantly refer back to it to sustain its meanings. But it is the crudest reductionism to think that believers become unbelievers because of the merest brush with an awkward fact; still worse, that country people would not, and town dwellers would, put up with such a disjunction.

The right assumptions?

The whole idea under discussion depends heavily, as was pointed out above, on a particular view of the city, its territory and its relationship to the economy: namely, that there was a separate urban community isolated from the countryside and its culture, to such an extent that in the late republic the rituals of the farm and of agricultural production would have been drained of all meaning, for the town dweller, though not for the country dweller. It is true that the population of Rome expanded rapidly in the 3rd century BC and that at some point local food production will have become inadequate to maintain the necessary supply.[25] But some degree of dependence on imported food is not at all the same as loss of interest in agriculture; whether that happened as well depends on the nature of the new population and its lifestyle. The corollary of this is:

(a) If there was a flow of immigration from the countryside, increasing as time went by, then, given the death rates to be expected in an immigrant population under primitive sanitary conditions, this must mean that a high percentage of the poor urban population at any moment, so far from being thoroughly urban, would have been born and brought up in the country. For them at least there can hardly have been any gap of sophistication between their own ideas and those of the villages in which they had been born and grown up.[26]

(b) While it is still a matter of controversy where the majority of the farm-workers would have lived, it seems certain that at least some of the city population would have farmed land in the vicinity of Rome and simply walked out to work in the fields every morning.[27]

(c) In any case, a good deal of food production would have taken place inside the city or at least in the suburbs, wherever there was open land to be used.

These categories are not necessarily mutually exclusive, but between them they must represent a significant proportion of the urban population. If so, then the model of total isolation must be to that extent inappropriate.

As so often, however, it is far easier to make this negative point than to replace the separation model with a better one. It is not difficult to show that local communities very often had their own history, their own jealously guarded traditions as to religious ceremonies, their own cults, priesthoods and so on. It must therefore be a possibility, at least, that their culture and their religious traditions should be seen as a completely separate rural phenomenon. However, there are also local cults – cults of the *pagus* or of the *vicus* – which certainly do belong to the countryside, but also belong within structures that relate the country to the city.[28] In other words, even where it seems that a local cult is operating independently, it is possible that it in fact forms part of wider patterns of religious activity including, not separate from, city ones.

Another possibility therefore is that we should be thinking of local cults, even if they had once been part of an independent religious life, as forming, at least in the late republic, simply part of a town–country complex. If the Italian city-state united town and country – that is to say the built-up area and its territory – the fact that particular cults took place in rural parts of the city-state should not make them any the less part of a religious unity. To put this in its most extreme form, you could say that so far as the countryside was concerned, one of the central functions of the town was to provide the religious centre at which the main festivals took place and where the priests, or at least the most important of them, were located.

The position is of course very much more complicated, as soon as we consider, not the theoretical unity of city and territory, but the actual situation of Roman Italy: it ceased at some point to be clear what the city of Rome was, who the citizens of Rome were, or what or where the Roman countryside was. At any rate, this must have happened by the 3rd century, when the Roman state had already expanded beyond the notional limits of any normal city-state.

Can we learn anything at all from Roman elite accounts?

There are some Roman texts that seem to provide first-hand accounts of what happened at festivals in the country. These have, not surprisingly, tended to play a very significant rôle in descriptive accounts of Roman cult. So, for instance, Ovid in the *Fasti* introduces his account of the Parilia (21 April) by what sounds like a personal recollection:

> Night has passed, Dawn rises. I am asked to tell of the Parilia; the asking will not be in vain if kindly Pales looks upon me favourably: "Kindly Pales, look favourably upon me as I tell of the rituals of the shepherds, as I pay respect to your very own festival. Surely, I too have carried the calf's ashes and the beanstraw, my hands full of the chaste purifying stuff. Surely, I too have leaped through the threefold flames and had the water sprinkled onto me from the moist laurel-branch." The goddess is moved and favours my work . . . [29]

Ovid goes on[30] to give an account of how the shepherds dress up the sheep-folds, light bonfires and then jump through them. The passage itself refers to the mixture of ashes from the unborn calves sacrificed at the Fordicidia (15 April), which the Vestals had to mix with the congealed blood from the genitals of the October horse (previous 15 October).[31] Or again, also from the *Fasti*, under 25 April :

> On that day, as I was returning to Rome from Nomentum, a white-robed crowd blocked the road. A *flamen* was on his way into the grove of ancient Robigo [Mildew] to throw into the flames the entrails of a dog and of a sheep. I went straight up to him to inform myself about the rite.
>
> Your *flamen* pronounced these words, O Quirinus:

There follows the prayer of the *flamen* addressed to Robigo and then a brief lecture by the *flamen* on the aetiology of the cult.[32]

There are many difficulties in the way of accepting that these are simple autobiographical accounts of village festivals and local ceremonies in the Rome area. First, the fact that the narrative voice in the poems claims to have carried ashes and conversed with *flamines Quirinales* does not prove (or even make it plausible) that the poet himself had ever done so.[33] The narrator has to make the claim because he needs to ingratiate himself with the goddess by claiming experiences that make him the right singer for her festival; and to authenticate his antiquarian–legalistic speculations by having them from the very *flamen*'s mouth. Admittedly, Pales seems to have been impressed by the claim; but that does not imply that we should be too. The tone is surely jocular, pseudo-scholarly, and remote from the literal-mindedness that those who strive to re-construct early Roman rituals from Ovid have to wish on him.

To start from the Parilia: if the claim is to be taken seriously, and the argu-ment to begin from the assumption that Ovid for once in his life means exactly what he says, there are still insoluble problems about establishing what he does mean and where he is claiming to be. If the scene is some village outside Rome, as usually assumed, then we have to believe that the Vestals' mixture of ashes and dried blood was distributed, presumably in tiny pinches, around the Ager Romanus to the different shepherd communities of the district. If that did not happen, and none of our sources says it did, then the scene is surely an imagi-native evocation of a ceremony that really happened as part of the central ritual or perhaps at one of the boundary cults of the city.

Ampolo[34] has observed that it cannot be an accident that the foundation of Rome was celebrated primarily at the Lupercalia and the Parilia, precisely the leading pastoral festivals in the Roman calendar. The connection between herdsmen and city-foundation reflects (he argues) not some historical phase, but the cultural theory that pastoralism belonged to the primitive stage of human development, to be succeeded by cities and agriculture. From the point of view of this discussion, the most interesting point is that once again we find an inextricable mixture of rusticity and the past.

In the case of the Robigalia, the claim to autopsy is just as deeply suspect. Indeed, the fiction of the mini-lecture by the *flamen* cannot be anything except a device of presentation. What is worth noticing in this context is that the Robigalia is one of a number of cults which occur at specified points outside the Roman complex, on the roads out of Rome. The Robigalia took place at the fifth milestone on the Via Claudia.[35] The best known of these milestone cults is the Grove of Dea Dia on the fifth milestone of the Via Campana, if John Scheid's analysis is right, as I believe it must be.[36] From the point of view of this subject, it is important and interesting to find a series of these agricul-tural cults placed at the boundaries of the city. The Grove of the Arval Brethen is of particular interest and importance for a series of reasons:

(a) The boundary cult in this case is linked to the centre by ritual performances which we happen to know about because of the survival of the Arval record.[37]

(b) Like the Parilia this rustic performance is strongly linked to the foundation myth of the city, in this case because the Arvals are strongly connected with Romulus himself. So once again we find a combination of foundation and rusticity.

(c) The cultic performance seems to connect with the definition of the city in space because it is a boundary cult, as well as in time, because it is a foundation cult. We find, in other words, the same relationships arising in this context as well. It is a shame that Ovid never wrote his piece on the ceremonies of the Grove of the Dea Dia, if indeed he came across them or thought them important enough to include in the *Fasti*.

Questions to ask

The general lines of the argument so far can be summarized:

(a) There was a high degree of integration between the religious life of town and country.

(b) Elite accounts that might seem to give us any guidance in fact exploit the idea of country life and of its religiosity in the interests of a moralizing discourse associating the moral, the past and the rustic.

Was there in fact a separate "country" religiosity at all? The situations that offer some hope of a conclusion are those where there is reason to detect powerful religious forces, operating outside the approved pattern of civic life.

Deities independent of any city?

The classic example of a cult that attracted high levels of attention and support in the Roman world, without ever becoming a state cult, was that of Silvanus.[38] Under the republic, Silvanus received no temple or official recognition and relatively few dedications either;[39] but there is enough mention of him to make it clear that he was in fact an important figure and a patron of the herds and the herdsmen, a protector of agriculture, but also a power in the uncultivated wild places.[40] So the list of his functions and powers associates him strongly with the countryside, not the city; and he receives little or no attention from the city authorities.[41]

There is good reason to suspect that what we know about this cult in the republican period is only a small part of the full story; but the argument operates only by retrospective inference from later evidence. The cult became widespread in the middle imperial period both in Rome itself and in Celtic north Italy, Gaul and the Illyrian provinces.[42] It is of course very possible that the

Silvanus of the provinces was a useful *interpretatio Romana* of local deities who happened to correspond to him. The best parallel would be the Saturn of the African provinces, where again a less prominent Italian deity takes on high status among the gods because he is essentially the representative of a local high god.[43]

So the argument is that this explosion of support for Silvanus makes sense only if the Italian cult, about which we know so little, was in fact deeply rooted in the allegiance of ordinary country people. It was they who carried the cult with them into the cities and into the provinces, either worshipping him in his own right or identifying him with the local deities of the areas in which they settled. So the paradoxical conclusion is that Silvanus became such a popular cult in the city, precisely because he evoked the world outside the city.

It may be quite legitimate to argue along these lines and reach the conclusion that a great popular cult of Silvanus should be inferred despite the lack of evidence. However, even if this is a sound argument, there remains a major problem for the project of this particular article. The tendency of the points made so far is indeed, in my view, to suggest that Silvanus had a great following and that he is excluded from conventional accounts of Roman religion. But we still have no means of making the differentiation of town and country. Indeed as we have seen, the bulk of the evidence comes from an urban context, not from a rural one. We can postulate an earlier period in which this was not true and in which there was indeed a separation between town and country. But this is a mere postulate without evidential value. It is of course possible that, in the 5th century BC, the people who lived in the town knew and cared nothing about Silvanus, and that he was purely a country figure. But it is equally possible that in the 5th century, as in the 4th or the 3rd, there was much interchange between town and country, that the city and its territory were essentially a unity and that the cult of Silvanus was never particularly a country cult, but simply a cult of the poor as opposed to the elite. That seems to have been the case in the Roman imperial period; we have no way of proving that it had not always been the case.

Centres independent of any city?

The evidence for the existence of Italian rural sanctuaries in the middle republic consists essentially of discoveries at many sites within a coherent area of central Italy, including Latium, Etruria and Campania, of votives of parts of the body. The votives consist for the most part of cheap terracottas. There is some variation as to the parts of the body represented and it is possible that the different sites "specialized" to some extent in particular bodily areas. The sites all fall within a rough chronological period starting from the 4th century BC and ending by the close of the republican period.

The interpretation of the data has not given rise to much dispute in its general outline. The implication seems to be accepted that the terracottas were dedicated as offerings to the gods or goddesses with prayers or vows for the curing of illnesses, and that the terracottas represent the afflicted parts. In other words, this is a widely disseminated health cult common to quite large areas of Italy.[44] It is an extremely important observation that the terracottas are not purely local products, site by site, but come from centres of production covering a substantial area.[45]

At first sight, we seem to have found exactly the situation that we need. That is, the archaeological evidence has revealed a phenomenon of the countryside, which the elite sources on whom we normally depend either ignore or of which they were perhaps unaware.

In fact, however, the position is not really quite as clear as this. For one thing the context of these discoveries is not always rural, or at least not always rural in the same sense. Examples such as the great find in the Tiber itself in the centre of Rome, and the similar substantial finds at the temple of Diana at Nemi offer two examples – one actually inside a city, the other in a sanctuary closely adjacent to a city – which put into question the rural character of the sanctuaries. It remains, of course, true that a number of the sites where anatomical votives are found are quite isolated and cannot be immediately associated with a particular urban centre, though they may in fact have belonged to one.

Even if this difficulty can be overcome, however, the problem of method is in fact very similar to that set by the different evidential picture over the cult of Silvanus. The question here is: are we dealing with a local cult of local people in rural areas? Or are we dealing with holy places with alleged curative powers to which people came from widespread areas of Italy because of the power of the place and its deities? If the latter is the case, then these are not so much characteristically country sites as places of pilgrimage to which you came to get a cure for yourself or for your loved ones. There seems no way of proving this, but we meet the same difficulty – that there can be no compelling argument in favour of separation. So here, as with Silvanus, the hypothesis of separate country religiosity must stand or fall with the hypothesis of separation between town-folk and country-folk. We are not making significant progress.

It could be argued that the ending of the rural shrines provides the best argument for their rural character. The fact is that just as the phenomenon has a beginning, in the 4th century BC, so it has an ending in 1st century BC. After that date, the terracotta votives no longer turn up. That might imply that they share in the collapse of local cultures, local languages and traditions, all over Italy after the Social war. Now if the sites had been simply holy places to which pilgrims came from all over central Italy in search of a cure, there seems to be no reason why they should not have been sought out by city dwellers just as much as they ever had. On the other hand, if they shared in the collapse of local cultures, that implies that they must have formed part of local cultures.

Movements of rural discontent?

The third and final example is the most dramatic, but perhaps also the most problematic of the three. The first two cases have been alleged expressions of popular religion, independent of, but consistent with, the established life of the city religions of Roman Italy. They may have expressed or derived from needs that the city religion had not met; but they do not themselves imply any defiance, still less hostility, towards the religion of the city. It must have been different with the celebrated affair of the Bacchanalia.[46] But once again, it could be argued that a form of cultic life unwelcome to the Roman ruling elite has been eliminated from the historical record. In this case, the silence was broken as it was not for Silvanus or the rural cults; but only so that the destruction of the cult could be recorded and implicitly defended by the authorities.[47]

If the situation was, at least to a certain extent, the same in all three cases, so the problems are the same as well. In fact, the Bacchanalia accounts provide a certain amount of material to test the model. The victims of Roman persecution included many country people and slaves from rural areas, but also, as Livy makes very clear, city dwellers of high status; while the very revealing Etruscan archaeological evidence indicates a cultic centre in the heart of an Etruscan town.[48] Perhaps too, the very structure of the cult implies a relationship between civic structures and conventions and the wild and unconfined, which means that the opposition of town and country has little to do with the case.

Conclusions

There are two main methodological difficulties in the way of making any substantial progress towards fulfilling the programme set by this contribution: the local nature of paganism and the argument from silence.

The local nature of paganism

It is inherent in the basic structure of traditional Italian cults that they have strong links with specific places. This is most obviously true of the city of Rome, where it is very clear that particular divine tales, deities and places are inextricably mixed together and would make no sense apart.[49] But the same is evidently true of the Roman countryside and, indeed, of Italian religion generally in this period.

It follows from this that where we find local traditions, ceremonies and holy places, however isolated they may be from centres of power or population, we need direct evidence of their being locally, not more widely, significant. Thus, the so-called rural sanctuaries might have seemed to be specially cults of the countryside rather than of the city; but as we have seen, proof is hard to come by.

The argument from silence

All three of the possibilities considered above derive from the same basic argument. They all rest on the contention that the tradition about the religious history of the Romans is heavily biased so as to reveal certain kinds of religious activity and to conceal other kinds. So that where it is a question of the state and its official religious practices, we receive full information; but about any other activity, whether those of unofficial prophets or of secret groups or in locations of power not under state control, the sources have nothing to tell us.

How reliable are such arguments from the weakness of the official Roman tradition? There can be no doubt at all that the tradition we have received is indeed a highly artificial construction.[50] The only doubt can be how it was constructed and what it was constructed to exclude.

It could, as one possibility, be seen simply as a reflection of a specific recording tradition: the early priests were amongst other things recorders of the past, the keepers of books of their own laws, but also, at least in the case of the *pontifices*, of other historical traditions as well.[51] So a tradition was established early that the doings of the priests – unusual religious events, the deaths of the priests themselves, the official acceptance of new cults or of changes of any kind in cultic life – these were the materials of a proper religious record.

Another possibility, more directly related to issues of political power, would be that the ruling elite recognized from an early date, though not necessarily at a very explicit level of awareness, that their power depended on the control of the religious rituals and traditions of Rome; they perceived all religious forces not within their control as threats to their monopoly and ultimately to the whole basis of their authority. So far as possible, they eliminated such outside forces in reality; where they could not succeed, they either appropriated them or excluded them from notice. The main conclusion of this study must be that the search for an alternative religion in the republican period does find some degree of justification in the evidence considered here. It is highly plausible that the main tradition conceals from us a richer variety of religious experience that was not to the taste of those who determined and dominated the nature of the tradition. To this extent, the quest for an alternative is well worth pursuing.

However, the interpretation of these results is not so easy. In particular, it provides no real grounds for making a distinction between town and country in this respect. If a choice has to be made, it seems a more feasible hypothesis about the followers of Silvanus or of the health cults in the republican period or of the Bacchic groups of the 3rd to 2nd centuries BC, that their membership cut across the distinction between town dwellers and country dwellers.

So, the programme from which the argument started has to be turned on its head. It does not turn out at all that we can use the religious evidence to try to improve our grasp on the social situation. Rather, the argument is forced back again on the analysis of the social situation to interpret the religious evidence. In the end, it is precisely because the social distinction we are looking for is implausible that the evidence cannot be forced into the town–country pattern. If there were a serious reason to believe that country people formed a separate sector of the population, then in terms of the expectations of ancient religion, it would be quite likely that we should be able to discover their religion.

It follows that, to make progress at all beyond this point, the requirement will be for a thorough examination of the epigraphic and archaeological local cults of specific regions of Italy. This alone can provide new material to break the circle. The work of C. Letta[52] is now seeking to show for one area that a distinction can be made in terms of pattern of development between the cults associated with a city and those of the *pagi* and *vici* of the area. This will provide a basic tool for further analysis. It is still important to see that it does not in itself evade the methodological problems of this subject. Cults associated with the countryside may retain their archaic forms, but who controls them? And whose expectations are enshrined in their religious patterns? It may be possible to find answers, but we are far from them at the moment.

Notes

1. J. A. North, Religion in republican Rome, in *CAH²* , vol. vii.2 (Cambridge, 1989), pp. 598 ff.
2. P. Garnsey, Where did Italian peasants live? *PCPS NS* **25**, 1979; K. Greene, *The archaeology of the Roman economy* (Berkeley, Calif. & Los Angeles, 1986), pp. 98–141; W. Jongman, *The economy and society of Pompeii* (Amsterdam, 1988), pp. 108–23; J. Patterson, Settlement, city and elite in Samnium and Lycia, in *City and country in the ancient world*, eds J. Rich & A. Wallace Hadrill (London & New York, 1991), pp. 147–65; J. A. Lloyd, Farming the highlands: Samnium and Arcadia in the Hellenistic and early Roman imperial periods, in *Roman landscapes*, eds G. Barker & J. A. Lloyd (Arch. Monograph of the BSR no. 2; London, 1991); C. Howgego, The supply and use of money in the Roman world, 200 BC to AD 30, *JRS* **82**, 1992, pp. 20–22.
3. See e.g., Virgil, *Georgics* 2.490–542.
4. For instance, the rural shrines of Hercules, which may have been connected with transhumance routes: F. Van Wonterghem, Le culte d'Hercule chez les Peligni, *L'Ant. Class.* **42**, 1973, pp. 36–48; A. Di Niro, *Il culto di Ercole tra i Sanniti Pentri e*

Frentani: nuove testimonianze (Doc. Ant. Ital. e Rom. 9; Rome, 1977); M. Pasquinucci, La transhumanza nell'Italia romana, in *Strutture agrarie e allevamento transumante nell'Italia Romana (III-I sec. A.C.)*, eds E. Gabba & M. Pasquinucci (Pisa, 1979), pp. 79–182; or the remote cult of Jupiter Atratus: K. Kajava, J. Aronen, H. Solin, Atratus, a new epithet of Jupiter: CIL × 5779 reconsidered, *Chiron* 19, 1989, pp. 103–15.

5. Survey in K. Latte, *Römische Religionsgeschichte* (Handbuch der Altertumswissenschaft V.I; Munich, 1960), pp. 64–94; for Ceres in particular, H. Le Bonniec, *Le culte de Cérès à Rome* (Paris, 1958); for reservations about the specifically agricultural identity of deities, North, Religion in republican Rome, pp. 603–4.

6. For the rustic celebrations of the Liberalia, see Varro, *ap.* Augustine, *De civ. Dei* 7.21; Latte, *Römische Religionsgeschichte*, p. 70; A. Bruhl, *Liber pater* (Paris, 1953), pp. 13–29. For the Parilia, see below p. 140.

7. Though the theme is of course often exploited by the elegists for its ironic potential, as by Propertius, 2.19, fantasizing his Cynthia into a rural environment, free from the gaze of rival lovers and busy with humble tasks: "atque ibi rara feres inculto tura sacello/ haedus ubi agrestis corruet ante focos."

8. Pliny, *Letters* 8.8.

9. "Plura laudabis, non nulla ridebis: quamquam tu vero, quae tua humanitas, nulla ridebis."

10. M. Beard, Ancient literacy and the function of the written word in Roman religion, in *Literacy in the Roman world*, ed. J. Humphrey (*JRA* Supp. no. 3; Ann Arbor, Mich., 1991).

11. *Ibid.*, n. 10.

12. 1.23

13. T. R. S. Broughton, *The magistrates of the Roman republic*, I (New York, 1951), p. 429.

14. "Ain tandem?" inquit Tubero, "docere hoc poterat homines paene agrestes, et apud imperitos audebat haec dicere."

15. The distinction is commonly made, most frequently by Cicero, between what can be discussed in private and what stated in public: see Cic. *De nat. deorum* 1.61, 118; *De div.* 2.28, 70 (with Pease *ad loc.*, for more texts).

16. *TLL* 1.1418–19.

17. So, e.g. G. Wissowa, *Religion und Kultus der Römer*² (Handbuch der Altertumswissenschaft, V.I; Munich 1912), pp. 141–53; W. Warde Fowler, *The religious experience of the Roman people* (London, 1911), pp. 131–4; G. Dumézil, *Archaic Roman religion* (Eng. tr.) (London & Chicago, 1970), pp. 205–45.

18. The thesis of Latte, *Römische Religionsgeschichte*, pp. 195–212.

19. Pontifices and intercalation: A. K. Michels, *The calendar of the Roman republic* (Princeton, NJ, 1967) 1967, pp. 101–103, 145–72.

20. Cf. North, Religion in republican Rome, pp. 601–603.

21. A. Degrassi, *Inscriptiones Italiae* XIII, ii (*Fasti Anni Numani*) (1963), p. 454, quoting Servius auct. *ad Virgil. Ecl.* VIII.82.

22. J. Briscoe, *A commentary on Livy XXXIV–XXXVII* (Oxford, 1981), pp. 17–26; for detailed discussion: P.Marchetti, Le marche du calendrier Romain de 205 à 190 (Années Varr. 551–564), *L'Ant. Class.* 42, 1973, pp. 473–96; La marche du calendrier Romain et la chronologie à l'époque de la bataille de Pydna, *BCH* 150, 1976, pp. 401–26; P. Derow, The Roman calendar 190–68 BC, *Phoenix* 27, 1973; The Roman

calendar 218–191 BC, *Phoenix* **30**, 1976, 265–81.

23. Inscription from Teos (= R. K. Sherk, *Roman documents from the Greek East* (Baltimore, 1969), no. 34, pp. 214–16); see R. M. Errington, Röm, Antiochus der Grosse und die Asylie von Teos, ZPE **39**, 1980, pp. 279–84; J. A. North, Roman reactions to empire, *Studia Classica Israelica* (1993).

24. Though see the comments of D. Potter, Pagans and Christians (review of R. Lane Fox, *Pagans and Christians*, (London, 1987)), *JRA* **1**, 1988, pp. 208–10.

25. P. Garnsey, *Famine and food-supply in the Graeco-Roman world* (Cambridge, 1988), pp. 188–95; T. J. Cornell, Rome in the age of the Italian wars, in *CAH*² vii.2. (Cambridge, 1989), pp. 408–9.

26. For discussion of the development of the city, P. A. Brunt, *Italian manpower 225 BC to 14 AD* (Oxford, 1971), pp. 376–88.

27. Garnsey, Where did Italian peasants live?

28. M. Frederiksen, Changes in the pattern of settlement, in *Hellenismus in Mittelitalien*, ed. P. Zanker (Göttingen, 1976), vol. ii, pp. 341–55; M. Cristofani, Città e pagus nell'Italia peninsulare, in *Popoli e civiltà nell'Italia antica 7*, (1978) pp. 88–102.

29. Ovid, *Fasti* 4.721–29.

30. Ovid, *Fasti* 4.731–82.

31. Ovid, *Fasti* 4.731–4. H. H. Scullard, *Festivals and ceremonies of the Roman republic* (London, 1981), p. 105.

32. Ovid, *Fasti* 905–42.

33. M. Wyke In pursuit of love (review of P. Veyne, *Roman erotic elegy* (Chicago & London, 1988)), *JRS* **79**, 1989, pp. 165–73.

34. C. Ampolo, Rome archaique: une société pastorale, in *Pastoral economies in classical antiquity*, ed. C. R. Whittaker (Camb. Phil. Soc. Supp. vol. 14) (Cambridge, 1988).

35. Robigalia: Degrassi, *Inscriptiones Italiae*, p. 448; Scullard, *Festivals and ceremonies of the Roman republic*, pp. 108–9.

36. J. Scheid, *Romulus et ses frères: le collège des frères arvales, modèle du culte public dans la Rome des empereurs* (Rome, 1990), pp. 96–8.

37. J. Scheid, Les sanctuaires des confins dans la Rome antique, *L'urbs: espace urbain et histoire* (CEFR no. 98) (Rome, 1987), pp. 583–95.

38. A. von Domaszewski, Silvanus auf Lateinischen Inschriften, *Philologus* **61**, 1902, pp. 1–25 (also *Abhandlungen zur Römische Religion* (Leipzig, 1909), pp. 58–85); P. F. Dorcey, *The cult of Silvanus: a study in Roman folk religion* (Leiden, New York, Cologne, 1992).

39. He is mentioned in the middle republic (Plautus, *Aulularia* 674 f.; Cato, *De agricultura* 83), though not even then in terms that necessarily prove him an independent god.

40. Dorcey, *The cult of Silvanus*, pp. 14–32.

41. *Ibid.*, pp. 3 ff. – arguing that Silvanus should be seen as a folk deity.

42. C. Pascal, *The cults of Cisalpine Gaul.* (Collection Latomus, 75; Brussels, 1964), pp. 170–76; Dorcey, *The cult of Silvanus*, pp. 49–83 (list of inscriptions at Appendix II).

43. P. Leglay, *Saturne Africain* (Paris, 1966), pp. 409–78.

44. M. Fenelli, Contributi per lo studio del votivo anatomico: i votivi anatomici di Lavinio, *AC* **27**, 1975, pp. 206–52; Pensabene *et al.*, *Terracotte votive dal Tevere* (Studi Miscellanei, 25; Rome, 1980); A. Comella, Complessi votivi in Italia in epoca medio- e tardo-repubblicana, *MEFRA* **93**, 1981, pp. 717–803; T. W. Potter, A republican healing sanctuary at Ponte di Nona, *JBAA* **138**, 1985; T. F. C. Blagg, The cult

and sanctuary of Diana Nemorensis in *Pagan gods and shrines of the Roman empire*, eds M. Henig & A. King (Oxford University Committee for Archaeology, Monograph no. 8) (Oxford, 1986), pp. 211–20.

45. See A. Commella, Complessi votivi in Italia, for detailed analysis of the distribution of types over central Italy.

46. C. Gallini, *Protesta e integrazione nella Roma antica* (Bari, 1970); J. A. North, Religious toleration in republican Rome, *PCPS* **25**, 1979; J-M. Paillier, *Bacchanalia: la répression de 186 av. J.-C. à Rome et en Italie: vestiges, images, tradition* (BEFAR 270; Rome, 1988) (with exhaustive bibliography); E. S. Gruen, *Studies in Greek culture and Roman policy* (Cincinnati Classical Studies, NS 7) (Leiden, 1990), pp. 34–78.

47. North, Religious toleration in republican Rome, pp. 87–92.

48. J-M. Paillier, *Raptos a diis homines dici* (Tite-Live XXXIX) Les Bacchanales et la possession par les nymphes, *Mélanges Heurgon* II, 1977, pp. 731–42.

49. For the Roman view, or at least that in the Augustan period, see especially Livy, 5.51–55, the speech of Camillus arguing against the proposal to move the city to the site of Veii after the Gallic sack. Cicero makes the same point, in a concise, telling phrase, when faced with Pompey's abandonment of the city in 49 BC: "non est in parietibus res publica, at in aris et focis." (Pompey says the republic does not consist of house-walls. No, but it does consist of altars and hearths).

50. J. A. North, Diviners and divination at Rome, in *Pagan priests: religion and power in the ancient world*, eds M. Beard & J. A. North (1990), pp. 65–71.

51. North Religion in republican Rome, pp. 585–87.

52. C. Letta, I santuari rurali nell'Italia centro-appenninica: valori religiosi e funzione aggregiativa, *MEFRA* 104, 1992.

9

The Roman *villa* and the landscape of production[1]

Nicholas Purcell

The Roman view

Beyond the city, everything – behaviour, culture, decisions, religion, perception – was in antiquity about producing livelihood from the environment.

Greed, refinement and Varro's villa *satire*

We begin, however, with a text which has endlessly been used against that proposition. The passage is the scene-setting of the strange third book of Varro's *Res rusticae*: the date is 50 BC and the occasion is the assembly for the election of aediles outside the gates of Rome at a place called the People's Farm, Villa Publica (3.2.1–18).[2] In it we meet Appius Claudius Pulcher, head of one of the oldest and noblest families in Rome, brother of the infamous demagogue P. Clodius and the no less notorious Clodia, Lesbia to Catullus, and are not surprised to be told (3.17.1) of his *villa*, which stood nearby on the level ground to the northwest of Rome between the city and the Tiber, that it was plastered with fine paintings and statues, including works by Greek old masters, and that it was expensively equipped for the life of luxury, *deliciis sumptuosa*.[3] Much has been made of the contrast that Varro's speaker draws between this and the ancient Villa Publica, and between this and the productive farms of the Italian countryside: Pulcher has no farmland, no mares, no oxen; his *villa* is useless, *inutilis*.

Before we take the discussion of the relative merits of usefulness and elegance as a symptom of terminal disease in Roman agriculture, it is worth looking a little more carefully at the quite complex construction of this passage as a whole. Pulcher's estate, which should be called *horti* (cf. Cicero, *Dom.* 112), rather than *villa*, which is a less specific word, only came into the argument as a riposte from a wealthy, but not noble, landowner, Q. Axius, who has been himself accused of luxury by Pulcher (3.17.1). Pulcher himself has advanced the Villa Publica as a model of frugal restraint, usefulness to the citizen body, and public ownership to be contrasted with the display of Axius' *villa*, which is "elegantly finished with stucco" (3.2.9: "polita eleganter opere tectorio"), and has exotic wood, precious metals and luxury paintwork, and the finest of mosaic floors (3.2.4). This is no unseemly display of charge and countercharge by equally compromised tycoons: there is a real difference between the estates, which Axius makes clear. His *villa*, opulent though it is, is more admirable than Pulcher's because it has productive functions which are part of its visible character, integral to the kind of statement that it is making. There are pigs (3.2.12), and fine breeding horses and donkeys (3.2.4); the peak of luxury represented in the *horti* of the Claudii Pulchri by the paintings of Antiphilus and the statues of Lysippus has its counterpart in the visible traces, *chez* Axius, of the husbandman and the shepherd (3.2.5: "vestigium ubi sit nullum Lysippi aut Antiphili, at crebra sartoris et pastoris").

So where Appius Pulcher shows off Greek works of art, Axius shows off his farmhands. The contrast is not just a rhetorical antithesis. It is repeated when Varro makes Pulcher go on to describe the estate in which he is thinking of investing on the coast near Ostia. This provides a new problem case for the agronomical philosophers of Varro's dialogue: this estate lacks both forms of definition that we have so far encountered, both the works of art and elegance, and the machinery and equipment of production (Cornelius Merula on M. Seius' estate, 3.2.8–9). The two sides are paired as a comparison: *membra rustica* vs. *urbana ornamenta*. Each is equally capable of advertizing the intentions of the proprietor. The same visibility of the productive side features in a third comparison, which Axius draws between Pulcher's new *horti* and the farms of his Claudian forebears: "this estate has never seen a crop of hay in its loft, a vintage in its cellar or in the granary a harvest" (3.2.6 "nec enim . . . faenisicia vidit arida in tabulato nec vindemiam in cella neque in granario messim"). In other words, the choice of the *villa* owner is not between on the one hand quietly getting on with the agricultural job and on the other making a splash through elegant decoration; agriculture and elegance are alternative forms of display. Pure elegance on its own, moreover, is revealed as a very unusual choice; the elaboration of the multiple contrasts reveals the freakishness of such display: it is of the inner circle of wealth, birth and power.

The discussion also shows us the choices of the wealthy landowner at work. The uselessness of Pulcher's *horti* must be seen against the background of his other plans. We see that he is not so innocent of the profit motive, and are made to feel, by the way in which he wryly responds to the accusations of Axius, that it is actually through a deep involvement in productivity that he can afford the luxury of the sterile ornament of his *horti*.[4] For the *villa* that he is buying from M. Seius at Ostia, the one which had neither *urbana ornamenta* nor *membra rustica*, is one of the most advanced examples of the new fashion for investment in the rearing of luxury foodstuffs for the prestige delicatessen market, the *macellum*, and for prestige eating on the part of the elite and its favoured dependants. Here Pulcher will own huge flocks of geese, hens, pigeons, cranes, peacocks, dormice, fish, bees, wild boar and other game; but, as another patrician involved in the discussion explains, this is also a fine *display*. He has been entertained there by Seius' secretary; and we hear later in the book (3.13.2–3) of the *fête champêtre* in the neighbouring game reserve of the orator Hortensius at which a tableau of Orpheus charming the wild animals was put on to entertain the dinner-guests. This new enterprise is called *villa* pasturing, *pastio villatica*.[5] The phrase is an oxymoron: *villa* agriculture and pastoralism occupy quite distinct zones of Roman imaginative landscape.[6] The place itself assists the effect: the *litus Laurentinum*, the wilderness in which the Trojans had landed, was proverbial for its sterility,[7] and to turn the coastal desert to profitable productivity was a splendid *coup*.

Anecdotes about the profitability of this enterprise abound; the anecdotal tradition itself, importantly, is part of the publicity which is characteristic of Roman production. A comparison related to Varro's is found in Martial (3.58), when he attacks modish sterility in a suburban estate by comparison with a productive farm – but although he uses the language and commonplaces of the comparison we have heard made between Pulcher's *horti* and the old farms of the Claudii, the comic effect is that the reader quickly comes to see that the object-lesson in this case is devoted to the profitable raising of table delicacies, and is situated at Baiae, the pleasure resort, of all places![8] It is obviously significant that this subject with its extravagant hopes, easy delusions, risk, ostentation and excitement is the raw material for satire, from Catullus (*Carm.* 104–5) on "Mentula's" farm onwards,[9] and there is no difficulty about endorsing the view that Varro's *Res Rusticae* was written to some extent in the jocular but ethically concerned tone that derives from the Lucilian tradition. Even at a superficial level, the animal or bird names of the participants, the realism of the scene-setting, the moral characterization of the principal debaters, the badinage between them, the allusions to the somewhat *demi-mondaine* society of agricultural profits and the type of people, often from the middle strata of Roman society, who are involved in it – all this sets us in the same sort of world as the satires of Horace and Persius and, more tellingly, has direct reflections in Varro's own *Menippea*, where we know that he examined the implications of great granaries, the pressing-room which complements the vineyard, the feeding of great flocks of peacocks.[10]

In the first book of the *Res rusticae*, where the names again give a satiric tone (1.2.1–2; 1.2.9; 1.2.11) – it is Fundilius' party, and Fundanius, Agrius and Agrasius are later joined by Stolo "the shoot", and Scrofa "the sow" – we find another instance of what is most strikingly to be contrasted with productivity. Scrofa's estates are much visited and admired for their spectacular productivity; a contrast can be drawn with the lavish estates of the proverbial Lucullus, where the spectacle consists, as it does in the *horti* of Appius Claudius Pulcher, in the Greek paintings. In Scrofa's *villa* it is a *galérie de beaux fruits*, an *oporotheca*, rather than a picture gallery, *pinacotheca*, which impresses (1.59.2); the productive again lends itself to display and even to showy Hellenization just as much as the useless but beautiful paintings.[11] Even more importantly, however, nobody is ashamed of the fact that the fruit, just like the pictures, succeeds in being a spectacle because of how much it is worth. "The top end of the Sacred Way, where apples fetch their own weight in gold, is the very likeness of this man's orchard" (1.2.10). The glory of Scrofa's estate is the glory of the urban market-place, and in both the pictorial language is highly appropriate. "There was nobody who did not rush to see the piles of grapes in the vineyards of Palaemon", says a later anecdote, famous enough to feature in more than one text, about a new highly profitable form of viticulture.[12] The sudden and amazing profit is the objective of the sorts of agriculture which lend themselves to the satirical raconteur, and there is a colloquial term for it in the language of the seamy side of life in the Roman city – *bolum*, a lucky throw of the dice.[13] This kind of agriculture can be a huge gamble, and the risks are great. For serious profits, according to Varro, the good fortune of a moment of artificially high prices for luxury foodstuffs is necessary, like the celebratory public banquets which went with a triumph: though he notes that the escalation in public banqueting is making the prices of the provision market inflate "to the point of incandescence". "Incan – I must say – descent is what your talk of making 60,000 on the sale of little aviary birds makes me" says Q. Axius, picking up the word and breaking it into colloquial Latin fragments in his slobbering greed.[14]

And with that piece of satirical caricature we must pass from Varro out into the wider world. What we have begun to perceive is that the sterility of certain *villae* in the literary tradition is no general phenomenon to set against the omnipresence of agricultural production with which I opened; rather it is a highly specialized and problematic refinement which actually throws into higher relief the generally overwhelming centrality of the pursuit of yield. We have also been able to locate the debate about sterility and different sorts of productivity in the world of spectacular, theatrical self-presentation. That helps us in turn to put in its proper setting the concept of the estate which is so luxurious that it does not even produce snails, peacocks or turbot; and to begin to perceive the associations of the world of theatrical display with the aleatory life of the *demi-monde*, the subjects of satire, the parasite or *scurra*, the rich man's agent, the excitement of risk and the prospect of enormous enrichment.

Suburban agriculture and the dependent cultivator

This set of associations is of course very closely linked with the life of the city, and is to be illustrated, as we have indeed been seeing, above all from the estates of the urban periphery. It is in this zone immediately around the city, especially in the smaller properties, that the problems of the market and the social relations of agency, clientage and dependence – a second theme that needs to be stressed – are seen at their most intense. The unproductive small-holding is a commonplace, either because of the risks of disease or disaster – Martial has a poem (1.85) on an estate near Rome which is unsaleable because it has become labelled as *noxius* – or because the profit simply proved an illusion. Other poems on this theme present a *pragmaticus* who lives in a crumbling cottage with a hectare or two of land wedged in among the tombs and finds himself buying the same cheap foodstuffs which he had been involved in selling when he was in business in the city (12.72); and another suburban land-owner who is pictured gaily travelling along the road laden with country produce, a wonderful scene except that he is not off to sell his wares in the market but is going the other way, to consume them at home (3.47, cf. 3.58 and n. 7). The disappointments are no doubt real enough, and are the natural subject of epigrammatic verse in the satirical tradition: but the scenes presuppose the atmosphere of fervid activity producing for the urban market which we have already met in Varro and which is amply attested in the literary sources and by the evidence of the inscriptions, especially those which define the productive plot around a tomb in the immediate environs of the city.

This is not the place for even a superficial account of this material, which is copious enough for us to get a detailed picture of the horticultural landscape of the environs of cities and the degree of intensification of effort involved in catering for the urban market.[15] What concerns us more here is the connection between this phenomenon and the estates of the elite. To what extent did this activity, often on small enough a scale to be the preserve of Romans of very modest means, exist in isolation from the programmes of self-presentation involved in the laying out of larger lots by the wealthiest members of Roman society? It might be thought that this frenzied activity was an extension of the life of the Roman back-streets on which the senator would be pleased to turn his back. That that is not in fact the case is apparent from the debate in Varro. *Pastio villatica* represents the acceptable face of suburban productivity. Everything is done here and elsewhere to make a distinction between the serious investments of the great noble and the greedy profiteering of the *plebs*. Dye plants are known only to the *sordidum vulgus* because of their extreme profitability (Pliny, *NH* 19.47). Freshwater fishtanks are common among plebeian proprietors; salt-water pisciculture is the preserve of the *locuples* (Varro, *RR* 3.17.2–3). Anyone can rear swine in wild woodland on the margins of an estate; real *pastio villatica* involves buying in the best acorns and feeding the pigs on that (3.2.12). And so on, with watering sterile plane trees with wine,[16] feeding fish with expensive fish-pickle (*RR* 3.17.7). The negation of self-sufficiency which Martial mocked in the smallholder can become a gesture of pride in the great.

Non-productivity, useless sterility, of the Appius Claudius kind, is only one of the games with farming the Romans played: gleeful overinvestment for its own sake or as part of a cultured and playful parody of "ordinary" agriculture, like Lucullus' transhumant fish (Varro, *RR* 3.7.9), was just as widespread. I must insist, however, that the really expansive gestures should be used by the historian only as indicators of tendencies: the archaeological evidence, which attests *pastio villatica* through the remains of numerous fishponds and even the occasional dormouse hutch – peacocks and snails are more difficult to identify on site – shows that this form of investment agriculture was anything but confined to a whimsical coterie.[17]

Agency of various kinds was a solution to the problem of unseemly profit and also represents a specific instance of the brokerage between town and country practised by the *locuples*. The urban periphery was a landscape of patronage, in which grants of small or large plots were frequently made in tight accord with the prevailing philosophy of service, dependence and reward in the patron–client relationship. The productivity of the plot is part of the theory of such relationships, again something that is clearly seen in the poetical self-portraiture of Horace. The complex ways in which freedmen and other clients fed the fruit of their labours – or their own dependants' labours – into a chain which benefited the wealthy at the top applied as closely to rural production as to the domain of the urban *officina* or the roving *negotiator*.[18]

Neither the classification of agricultural techniques as smart or sordid, nor the hiding behind the activity of the agent, actually succeeded in distancing the high elite from the world of production. The anecdotal evidence, combined with common sense, persuades us that making a huge amount of money was in practice as attractive to a *consularis* as to a *colonus*. Cicero betrays his concern for the behaviour of his Tusculan dependants whose market-gardening enterprise is not functioning as smoothly and untroublesomely as he would like (*Ad fam.* 16.18). The point is rather that the efforts that were made to create these deceptive façades are actually signs of the extent to which the compulsion to make money from the productive environment was all-pervasive in the Roman elite. The pursuit of sterility and the expensive investment are gestures which only work against this background. We cannot understand why the Romans chose to call their suburban palaces vegetable gardens, *horti*, unless we give proper weight to the real horticultural world first. When we have done so, moreover, we are probably going to be less tempted to say that the phenomenon of *horti* such as Pulcher's or those of so many others is a symptom of agricultural decadence. Coming to grips with the real and pastoral associations of dairying enables us to make a stab at understanding Marie Antoinette's dairy; when we have done so, we are not going to be tempted to attribute a decline in milk and cheese production in *ancien régime* France to the frivolous behaviour of princesses. What we have heard of horticulture may help us to perceive the nuance of Diocletian's growing of vegetables in retirement,[19] but that taste on the part of the emperor is not an economic datum in the story of the Decline and Fall.

I must plead guilty to misunderstanding the evidence myself. The article

"Wine and wealth in ancient Italy",[20] took too seriously the noteworthy Roman tradition of caution, reserve and hostility about the risks and profits of viticulture and rashly suggests that this might mean a real reluctance to be involved on the part of the high elite. That view has been criticized.[21] We cannot of course quantify any of these preferences, but it now seems to me unlikely that Roman senators and *equites* were seriously swayed by the opinions that they voiced so emphatically. The phenomenon of anxiety remains an important one, though it should be seen not in a literal sense, but in the context of attitudes to production. The negative tradition about vines and wine is a facet of the response to the imperative to produce and to intensify production. Alongside it, and to be compared with the celebration of horticulture and *pastio villatica*, stands the positive impact that this form of production made on the layout and décor of Roman *villae*.

The celebration of production

The literary *locus classicus* is the scene in Fronto in which Marcus and Fronto participate in the vintage at the imperial estate of Lorium, working up a good sweat as they help to press the grapes, and enjoying the spectacle of the rustics hurling abuse at each other.[22] On a less than imperial scale, a press-room and vat-space which seems to have been designed with such antics in mind was discovered in a *villa* on the Via Cassia at Muracciola;[23] the apsidal plan seems to be dictated much more by *elegantia* than by *utilitas*: comparable is the elaborate apsidal *calcatorium* of a *villa* excavated at Cinecittà.[24] Another example is the 3rd–4th century decorated courtyard in the *villa* at Casal Morena on the Via Latina, in which scenes of the making and storage of wine are given a Dionysiac quality.[25] This is the heart of the wine belt of the Roman *suburbium*, and the religious celebration of the importance of production may perhaps be seen in the remarkable Dionysiac cult-association in a senatorial estate of the mid 2nd century not far from Casal Morena attested by the inscription in the Metropolitan Museum of Art usually called the *thiasos* of Pompeia Agrippinilla.[26] Turning back into the inner *suburbium*, the funerary vineyards, which are well attested epigraphically,[27] deserve mention in this context: there is little need to elaborate the way in which these combine *utilitas* and *elegantia*, whether in the humblest *cepotaphion* garden-tomb or in the pretentious funerary estate of Herodes Atticus' Triopion on the Appian Way. In the latter, long flowing poems inscribed on *stelae* burlesque the usual warning-inscriptions on suburban tombs.[28] They describe the vines and other lavish plantings, but however learned and opulent the display, the whole ensemble is set by the form of the description in the productive world of the inner *suburbium*.

Viticulture was characteristic of agriculture near cities, but is conspicuous in another environmental zone of the Roman countryside too – the wetland. The coastal marshes in which grew the grapes from which Caecuban wine was made are a case in point, but other instances are not hard to find in a tradition that goes back to the Homeric vine-ground of *Odyssey* 1.193.[29] This is just one instance of the importance of the coastal landscape as a setting of production. *Saxa et solitudo maris*, crags and the deserted seashore, in Tacitus' phrase,[30] are only a limited part of the story. The coastal strip, especially where a sandy beach separates the sea from a coastal wetland, is a prime location for the exploitation of the environment. The association of the wetland with the special interests of the wealthy who could afford to exploit it, and, in particular,[31] to improve it, intensifying the management of the environment, is, once again, a very ancient tradition, going back to the holdings of the Homeric heroes. The *villae* of the coast of west central Italy are not town houses transposed into the wilds for the sake of solitude, but estates such as that of M. Seius south of Ostia, centres for the management of the unique resources of the uncultivated environment. The fowler, the hunter and the fisherman (cf. Varro, *RR* 3.3.4: "tria genera artificum paranda, aucupes, venatores, piscatores") reinforce the shepherd and the husbandman in doing the productive work in this milieu, but it is clear from the literary texts and to some extent from the inscriptions that this is what the *villa* in these places is intended to achieve. The younger Pliny's remarks about the quality of the figs and mulberries at his Laurentine *villa* where little will grow (though note that it has an *apotheca* and a *horreum*), and his eagerness to point out that, even in the absence of really exciting fish, the soles and prawns are of the very highest quality, reminds us of the normal expectations of the coastal proprietor (*Ep.* 2.17.28: "mare non sane pretiosis piscibus abundat, soleas tamen et squillas optimas egerit").

Fish are particularly significant: the *piscinarii* of the late republic are not to be taken as simply whimsical, choosing pisciculture as a random pastime for reasons of fashion (cf. the sober account of Columella, 8.16–17). The elaboration of coastal fishponds fitted well into the ideology of *Pastio villatica*, as we have seen, and the product is prominent in the anecdotal tradition about vast profit and extravagant investment (e.g. Pliny, *NH* 9.7, Asinius Celer's 8,000 HS mullet; cf. *NH* 170 4,000,000 HS yield of Lucullus' ponds). Long before the great *villae* of the late republic the fisherman had become a picturesque character who belonged in the supporting cast of the parasitical urbanites of Greek comedy, and the Romans were keen to have grotesque statues of weather-beaten emaciated *piscatores* in their *villae*, whether or not they also had fishponds.[32] If they did, that was an excuse to employ droves of real slave fishermen (Varro, *RR* 2.17.6), and a passage in the *Digest* (33.7.27, Scaevola), of republican origin, reveals a troupe of these workers accompanying the owner when he migrated from the *praedia maritima* to the city or elsewhere. The point, whether in marble or real life, was to harp on the theme of the productivity of the estate. If possible, this message should be broadcast in terms appropriate to the urban world of the parasite or *scurra*: there is an unlikeable but revealing description in Varro of what Hortensius did when storms made it impossible for him to get the live small-fry on which he usually fed his fine fish. In these conditions it was necessary to send to the luxury food-market for pickled fish; the everyday diet of the fishponds on the other hand, missing in bad weather, is identified as "the dinner of the poor" (Varro, *RR* 3.17.7). The story, told thus, puts the *piscina* of the orator in the context of the ordinary life of the seashore and its wretched inhabitants, of less account than the great man's investment. The opportunity to make a point like this was coveted. Cicero has an account (*Off.* 3.58–60) of a man who is tricked into buying a coastal *villa* in Sicily by a carefully orchestrated display of fishing offshore when he visits the property. He is convinced that this will be part of his regular landscape, and when he turns up on completing the purchase is so completely duped as to think that the absence of fishermen in his view must be due to some local fisherfolk's festival which has taken them all from their normal occupation.

Fish in the ancient world were not an everyday commodity – they have been seen as a "cash crop" rather than as a means of survival for their producers,[33] and the spectacle of production in this case should be seen as deriving from the exotic, like the English landowners who planted vineyards on their estates in the 18th century.[34] But more ordinary enjoyment of the spectacle of production is well attested, most unashamedly by Cassiodorus in the 5th century (*Var.* 12.15), praising a *villa* whose main rooms give the chance of seeing people "charmingly labouring". This is in the context of the arable harvest, vintage and olive crop, and many *villae* are arranged so as to command views not of distant hills but of the fertile terrain which belongs to the estate. The *locus classicus* is Pliny's description of his estate at Tifernum, carefully outlining all the different terrains which are represented in the single property, but also the easy communications which themselves form part of the desirable view from the well placed house – the *spectaciuncula* of people going about their ordinary activities, as Cicero calls them in the context of a *villa* near Pompeii (*Fam.* 7.1.1). We are reminded of the view over the Tiber of Martial's Janiculum *villa* (4.64), and of the view of highways which orients the layouts of several *villae* in the Roman *suburbium*.[35]

Descriptions which depict the estate in terms of its productive landscape, even if they are not as detailed as Pliny's, are common in the language of benefactors in East and West alike – the legal description abuts the literary *ecphrasis topou* in the rhetoric of administration – "I give and alienate to my sweetest home-country my estate in the locality Paunalloi", reads one document from Lycia in southern Asia Minor (IG III.422, Ariassus) "in the hill-country, in vineyard and in arable, plain and mountain, all as it is, with nothing taken therefrom". A bequest to a civic association at Petelia in southern Italy takes a similar form, describing the vineyards which are to support the Augustales not just with revenue but with wine for public banquets (*ILS* 6468–9, benefaction of M' Megonius Leo). Nearby a freedman of Domitian consecrates a game preserve, described in some detail, to the appropriate god

Silvanus, for the benefit of another local association (*ILS* 3546 "fundi cum suis villis" and "locus sive pars agri silvaeque": cf. *ILS* 8375–6, a late example from Praeneste). The productive estate, with its production – we recall Agrippinilla's *thiasos* once again – emphasized in the language of cult, is for deployment in the service of the ideology of benefaction as well as for the private enjoyment of the *dominus*. So some estates were known simply by the name of their principal crop: *seges*, a corn harvest, defines estates on the route of an aqueduct near Amiternum, alongside *vineae*, vineyards (*ILS* 5792). The *horti* are of course another example. We are reminded of the way in which some of the grandest estates of 18th century England bore names such as Woodburn Farm or Hall Barn.

It is not only in the agronomists that the productive element in the *villa* is normative. For Vitruvius likewise (6.6.5), it is assumed that although parts of the *villa* will be built *delicatius*, in a lavish and stylish way, that should not impede *utilitas*: both are expected to coexist. Columella sees no harm in *elegantia* in a farm, provided that the owner does not get carried away and become an *aedificator* (1.4.1). If elegance gets out of hand, it is likely to affect the storage facilities as much as the dining-room: Vitruvius again – "those who are interested particularly in the produce of the countryside will need stalls and booths in the outer court and in the main part of the building *cryptae*, storerooms, depositories and all the other things for preserving crops, and these are to be built in a utilitarian rather than an elegant style" (6.5.2). But the archaeological remains show us that the storage areas of *villae* were by no means always so utilitarian in their design: *cryptae*, which we call "crypto-porticus", are a fine feature of many a *villa*, and the lavish provision of the *pars fructuaria* at Settefinestre reminds us of the care that could be taken.[36]

There is no difficulty in seeing why. The schematic separation between *utilitas* and *elegantia* notwithstanding, there was in practice no incompatibility between the care with which the dwelling house and the agricultural facilities of a country estate were designed. Columella (1.6) famously divides the *villa* into three – *partes urbana, rustica, fructuaria*; the typical *villa*, then, has all these. At Settefinestre again, although the excavators are right to emphasize the practical division between the slave areas and the *percorso padronale*,[37] from the architectural point of view the striking thing is the organic union into which they are both planned.[38] That *villa* looks two ways – a main façade to the farmyard, another looking over gardens to a vista. The two directions do have different architectural/landscape nuances, but it is not a question of rustic production versus urbane sterility. The *hortus* is productive, or at the least relates closely to the idea of productivity; and beyond it lie the fields which give the *villa* its *raison d'être*. Both sides of the *villa* thus relate to the centrality of production. And that is true of the whole productive landscape; as in Strabo's description (5.4.8) of the Bay of Naples in the Augustan period, the whole scene is one continuous intermingling of buildings and plantations.[39] Even in the *crater delicatus* there is no serious dichotomy between production and the elite lifestyle of luxury. *Aedificatio* itself was a productive activity. English gardeners in the 18th century made their own bricks on the estate,[40] and it is not clear that the brick and tile kilns of Roman villas[41] were shunned as a banausic part of the estate. We know of one rather fine pilastered tiledrying works in a coastal *villa* near Nettuno.[42] I have been stressing that the Roman *locuples* was used to living surrounded by the activities which supported his lifestyle, and that this is not the least urban aspect of the landscape of production.

That is also revealed in a little known but interesting text of nearly two centuries earlier. This is one of the oldest testimonies to the *villa* landscape as a whole, but has perhaps been rather overshadowed by Cato's slightly earlier treatise on agriculture. It dates from 140 BC and is a fragment of Scipio Aemilianus' Fifth Oration against Claudius Asellus (Gellius, *Noct. Att.* 2.20.6; Malcovati, *ORF²*, p. 129).

> Where he saw the fields most intensively cultivated and the *villae* most elegantly finished, there, on the highest eminence, he would regularly say that the measuring-pole should be set up: and from it he laid out the track, in some places smack through the vineyards, in others through the game reserve or the fishpond, in others through the *villa* itself.[43]

This damage to the landscape cannot be the result of a centuriation scheme. Asellus, not yet even tribune, was too junior to take decisions about the orientation of a whole network of land division, and in any case infringement of the rights of previous owners would hardly have been a surprise in such a case. The "track" must be a through route, but I do not think it likely that it was the line of a great Roman highway; it is not just that we know of no suitable candidate at this time, but again, wilful diversion of the path of a great long-distance road seems beyond the competence of an Asellus. A much more attractive context would be the renewal of the Anio Vetus and Tepula aqueducts and the construction *ex novo* of the Aqua Marcia (voted 144).[44] The complex settlement pattern of the *suburbium* and the ramifications of an aqueduct network make the abuse much easier to understand. The uneasy relationship between the landscape of property and the phenomena of water supply is a subject to which we will return; here what is important is the right that this passage gives us to retroject to the age of Aemilianus (and Lucilius) so much of what was characteristic of that of Varro; and most of all, the conjunction yet again of Varronian *pastio villatica*, Catonian cash-crop agriculture and luxury *villa* architecture in a complete, harmonious and unified landscape description. The rhetoric makes us see, as the malicious Asellus is alleged to have seen, a whole landscape of wealth which he proceeded to disrupt with an iconoclastic and populist fervour.

The problem

Moses Finley taught us that we must not commit the fallacy of thinking that there was in antiquity no middle ground between subsistence production and capitalist economics on a developed scale.[45] In his detailed examination of the economic ideologies of the age of Cicero, which he held to be an essential test-case period, he emphasized the greed of the ancient elite.[46] But into the gap he had made between the toiling peasant and the modern rationalist he put, explicitly, the "gentleman farmer", and the result was stagnation. "There is nothing mysterious about this 'stagnation', no serious reason for disbelief: large incomes, absenteeism and its accompanying psychology of the life of leisure, of land ownership as a non-occupation ... all combined to block any search for radical improvements."[47] This seems to me to be a missed opportunity. Failing to find modernity in the new aperture, Finley seems to have been less concerned to scrutinize more carefully what actually was there. The presence or absence in antiquity of harbingers of the modern world such as double-entry book-keeping is not of great interest; the progressivist philosophy represented by that investigation is now increasingly seen as unhelpful and unsympathetic. Finley's triad – peasant, gentleman farmer, capitalist – is not going to be much advance on the old pair. The stagnation theory deters research into what should be a fascinating and important topic: the actual responses of greedy aristocrats – if even this social classification is a helpful one for the Roman period – to productive opportunities. All wealth came from agriculture; all aristocrats were greedy; the consequence should be a proposition about aristocrats and agriculture which is more interesting and arresting than the caricature that they were stagnant gentleman farmers. The colourful, even hectic, examples of the previous pages may serve to draw our attention to some of the obsessive cultural responses of the Romans to the world of production. The economic and social circumstances behind those responses are considered in more detail below, but first we should explore briefly the centrality of the *villa* to the stagnation theory.

It seems very likely that it is principally the archaeology of Roman *villae* which has created the supposition that the rural interests of anyone who could afford them were dominated by the "psychology of the life of leisure". The emphases of Cicero and Pliny, which lay behind the creation of early modern reconstructions of Roman country homes in accordance with the princely taste of the day, before archaeology had revealed anything much more than Hadrian's Villa at Tivoli (though that was quite enough!), do corroborate this picture at first sight.[48] There is a moral indignation in the reaction, shared by Finley, which is still present in the influential definitions earlier in the 20th century of Rostovtzeff (*The social and economic history of the Roman empire*, p. 564) and Heitland (*Agricola*). Later authors, even if they feel bound to play down the unproductive element in Roman landscape architecture, and the importance of the *villa urbana* (so-called), tend to do so in a tentative and apologetic way.[49] Here are a couple of quotations from Heitland. Firstly (p. 246), on Seneca, *Ep.* 123: "here we seem to have an instance of what was now probably an ordinary arrangement: the *villa*, homestead with some land around it, kept as a country 'box' for the master by his steward who would see to the garden and other appurtenances, while the rest of the land is let to a humble tenant farmer." Or again (p. 366): "a man who could afford to own vast unremunerative estates was a great personage". This unwarranted extension of the *topos* of spectacular sterility also illustrates a more general fallacy, that any reference to an unproductive estate is legitimate evidence for the rapid and disastrous spread of underproduction. One of the texts quoted by Heitland neatly shows the process of misunderstanding.

This is a complicated case in the law of usufruct (*Dig.* 7.1.13.4) which raises a special difficulty (unusual therefore) concerning a *praedium voluptuarium*, a pleasure estate, "with gardens or terraces or walks whose ornamental trees give shade or amenity". Whereas the law of usufruct normally permits the *fructuarius* to improve the property, in this case any changes such as the removal of the amenities to create vegetable gardens are considered illegal – the general principle is that the usufruct of such a property is abused if anything is done to it which will yield a return.[50] As it happens, this passage of a 3rd century lawyer tells us nothing whatsoever about the spread of the unproductive *villa* – if anything, it reinforces the impression which we have already gained that the totally unproductive estate is seen as something of an extreme case – but it does illustrate the nature of the rejection of production in such cases. Such a property is so overwrought a gesture of luxury that *any* productive enterprise, even if it does not involve the destruction of the ornament, spoils the perfect uselessness of its programme. As for planting real *horti* in Horti, that would be an obvious breach of the responsibilities which derive from the law. The old maxim about exceptions proving the rule has often been used by sophistic scholars to write themselves a blank cheque, but there does actually seem to be a case for suggesting that these attitudes imply that the rejection of productivity, far from being a general sign of a creeping stagnation, is a highly specialized gesture whose existence and elaboration depend on and prove a general passionate interest in the maximization of returns from the environment.[51]

The reason why texts such as this have been misinterpreted probably lies in the interpretation, from the Renaissance on, of the remains of the Roman *villa*. Ackerman's recent brilliant monograph on the history of the Renaissance *villa* takes "the pleasure factor", the contrast with the city, the architectural elaboration of the buildings, the element of fantasy, to be defining characteristics.[52] His book traces admirably how these principles have worked from the end of the Middle Ages on, and how they were based on a reading of the ancient literary tradition about country estates. He tends to assume, however, that that reading was correct, and makes the Roman *villa* Chapter One of a saga in which an outstanding continuity is discerned. This continuity is the result of a circular argument: of course Roman *villae* seem like post-medieval ones if we approach them with the preconceptions of the authors of the latter age.

In fact the preoccupations of the ancient elite and their social and economic and political behaviour are now understood in a very different way from the ideas of the Renaissance. We are today in a position to reinterpret the *villa* and the texts that refer to it. It should be observed, *en passant*, that even Castell, despite magnifying Pliny's *villae* to a ludicrous degree of splendour, never lost sight of their agricultural function:

> If the Romans (which with justice cannot be believ'd) ever divided Architecture into two branches and had separate Professors for City and Country Buildings; I believe . . . it does not appear that the studies of those that profess'd the latter requir'd less Care and Judgement than the former; for it may be observed that in the Choice of the Situation for a *villa* there is as much Knowledge of Nature requir'd as in that for a City: And if those Buildings that were in Cities rais'd for publick Conveniences, Religion & Diversions, were necessarily more magnificent and requir'd the Knowledge of some particular things not necessary to the Country Architect; yet the latter, in the Care he was oblig'd to take in providing for all Things that were dependent on Agriculture had certainly as many different Things to look to not needful to be known to the Architect that was wholly employ'd in the Buildings of the City.[53]

In the study of the physical remains of the *villa*, the elaborate life of luxury creeps to the fore, perhaps because the palatial elements are often the best preserved.[54] Until the excavations of the late 18th century in the Vesuvian cities, reconstructions of ancient *villae*, such as Castell's own, significantly, erred wildly in the direction of symmetry, magnificence, scale and display. Pliny's *villae* were imagined to be on the scale of Badminton or Chiswick, grander than Hadrian's Villa. It remains a simple and apparent fact that the overwhelming majority of *villae* were mixed in type in some way, and the more limited truth would have perhaps encouraged interpreters to play down the productive element less.

Villae rusticae, equally, have too often been studied in isolation; those who know that they are not interested in more evidence for the life of the rich focus high-mindedly on the economic side and exclude the *ornatus*. There is too little investigation of the interrelationship between the different *partes* of *villae*. In fact, as we shall see, what can be seen tends not to support a firm separation. When there are *rustica membra* of elegant *villae* they are not discussed or are assumed to be part of a quite different phase of occupation. There has been little discussion of the tendency which seems to be apparent in relatively many Italian *villae* of the increasing utility of their appointments during the 1st century AD: the Villa of the Mysteries at Pompeii is a case in point.[55]

Why should we assume, after all that we have heard about the attitudes to choice of the Roman landowner, that this represents a radical change of function or ownership for the building? Nobody is too surprised to see a "sacral-idyllic" scene with a plough propped against a wall; why should the real plough in the House of the Menander[56] make us worry about the fortunes of the owning family?

These difficulties surface above all in the agony scholars go through over the definition of a *villa*. In the sensitive account which John Percival published in 1976 he was inclined to a culturally deterministic view, in which he is not alone, that the *villa*, properly so-called, is specifically Roman.[57] If true, that should bother us. So closely intertwined were the cultural and ideological characteristics of the elites of the ancient Mediterranean by the Augustan period, that a distinctive form of the principal vehicle for the principal economic concern of those elites would be very striking, especially if the discussion is focusing on the "psychology of leisure and landownership as a non-occupation". It is worrying that so much of the distinctiveness of the "Roman" *villa* of the West seems to be based on silence from the East, especially when literary sources tell us, for example, of the typical estates of the territory of Pergamum, such as that of the father of the physician Galen, with the central hearth and ovens, *exhedra* and retiring rooms along the wall behind, symmetrical arrangement with farm buildings to left and right, and the *cella vinaria* centrally located over the exhedral reception area.[58] Just as the Lycian benefactor and the euergete of Petelia seemed to be speaking the same language, so here we are dealing with an estate centre on very much the Vitruvian model, as represented by various of the Vesuvian *villae rusticae*. The prototype in the literary tradition for the aristocrat's interest in productive arboriculture in an idyllic setting removed from the worries of politics is, moreover, not Italian but Greek – Odysseus' aged father Laertes, pottering among the fruit trees that he loves.[59] The *villa* and its surroundings owe a good deal equally to the oriental *paradeisos*, with its productive trees and control of precious water; the four-square terraces of the Roman estates are in a tradition which goes back to Persepolis and Pasargadae.

The same problem – the tyranny of architectural typology – is to be seen at work within the study of *villae* in the west as a whole and even region by region. The excavator of a *villa* beside the Via Tiberina north of Rome some years ago spoke[60] of a visible difference between *villae* with an atrium, the complete *domus-villa* closely related to the town house, and the Campanian style *villa rustica*. She was able to claim a quite different typological development for the *villae* of the region of Rome from those of Campania, and concluded confidently that at this particular *villa* "non tratta della *villa* suburbana di un ricco ... la costruzione nacque come dimora di un proprietario di campagna non privo di agiatezza, *che vi abitava e vi laborava insieme ai suoi servi*, ricavando le rendite dai prodotti del suolo, fra cui certamente vino e olio" (my italics). This hopeful image of co-operative and comfortable independence, with its preoccupation with the issue of the owner's presence, is of course arbitrary.

Sensible typologies of *villae* still elude us, as they did our predecessors, because there were so many ingredients which could be mixed in so many different ways for all sorts of reasons. Take an allusive passage like this, about a *villa* in 54 BC: "As for the place in the *porticus* where they say you wrote to have a little atrium built, I like it better as it is. There doesn't seem enough room for a little atrium and it isn't usual to have one except in buildings where there is a big atrium which could not be fitted with *en suite* bedrooms and fittings of that sort. As it is this site will get a nice vault or a really good summerhouse. But if you disagree, let me know by return" (Cicero, *Ad Q. fr.* 3.1.2). The difficulty we have in discerning the nuances of this sort of statement makes one reluctant to put too much weight on Vitruvius' technical but not necessarily standard terminology (Vitr. 6.8). Apart from anything, it is crucial to be sure that we know the whole *villa* – the excavators of Settefinestre might easily, had they been less complete or careful, have missed the granary or the pigsties, for instance.[61]

Most importantly, however, we should recognize that even if the site is completely and expertly excavated, and compared with far more similar instances than we have currently at our disposal, the flexibility of Roman *villa* design is going to make it impossible to deduce anything about the owner. The procedural difficulties which Andrew Wallace-Hadrill has drawn to our attention in the context of the Pompeian house apply equally here.[62] It is noteworthy that we experience the utmost difficulty in relating epigraphic evidence for proprietors, even when it is found almost *in situ*, and slanted towards the high elite as it tends to be, to particular archaeological sites. Consider the *villa* of M. Seius where a freedman scribe could entertain a patrician, and where there were no *rustica membra* or *urbana ornamenta*: what would its remains be taken for today? How do you tell a functional-looking *villa rustica* in a rescue excavation from Q. Axius' *villa* at the bend of Velinus (Varro, *RR* 3.2.9) "which no painter or stuccoist ever set eyes on"? No Roman *villa* was isolated; part of a portfolio or part of a landscape, it played its part in a productive *ensemble* and should always be interpreted, whether we know it from archaeological or literary evidence, in that way. The Roman *villa* is not just the accidental address of a rich family who happen to find themselves out of town. Country and town, production and consumption, are more than simple members of the set of polarities against which the elite oriented itself. Productive management of the environment is the necessary condition for all of life and society. It is thus the logical background to the landscape control which is central to the idea of the *villa* – great or small, "sterile" or ultra-productive.

When faced with evidence for differences in amenity between Roman rural establishments, our response should not be to hive off the world of values in which these differences mattered as something to be isolated hermetically from the economic realities. The two domains are irrevocably interlinked.[63]

Alternative suggestions

Some steps forward have of course been made in the interpretation of the *villa*. Practically, the publication of *villae* has proceeded so rapidly that we have a much better dossier of information, and the best known *villa* today, Settefinestre, has of course made available a spectacular instance of the coexistence in the same estate of production on the most varied and innovative model and of up-to-date *otium*.[64] Theoretically, we have moved through from the first doubts about applying what we thought we knew about the *villa* in the literary tradition to the remains, which surfaced in articles by Skydsgaard and Harmand in 1969–70, to the more sensitive accounts of White's *Roman farming* (1970), Rossiter's *Farm buildings* (1978; see esp. 2–3 and 35–7) and Percival's *Roman villa*. Percival (1976, 15) hesitantly accepted in 1976 the insistence of Rivet that a defining element in the *villa* should be integration into the economic and social organization of the Roman world – a vital principle, but one which he did not develop far. More recently, Leveau has put the principle more firmly: "la *villa* est un mode chronologiquement définissable et historiquement évolutif de l'occupation et de la mise en valeur de la campagne."[65]

The question is, what kinds of phenomena are covered by those definitions? They seem to need more detailed and complex answers than Finley's gentleman farmers can provide. We may wholeheartedly agree with Ackerman, who concludes his study of the *villa* thus: "what distinguishes a villa ... is the intense programmatic investment of ideological goals".[66] But unlike Ackerman, we must see, in the Roman *villa* at least, that those ideological goals are inseparable from the business of production. In conclusion, therefore, it may be useful to examine briefly three ideological aspects of the Roman *villa* which I think deserve more attention: the *villa* and the public landscape; the *villa* and the romance of storage; the *villa* as the locus of intensification.

My account so far has been critical of much of the traditional approach to the archaeology of the *villa*. My principal charge is that we have been obsessed with the country estate's function as residence: who lived there, for how long, what their relationship was to the owner, and so on. This view is a rustic survival of the idea that the elite family lived if they could in dignified detachment, forming a polite nucleus carefully sealed off, such as Jefferson at Monticello, from the scurrying domestics. Roman town houses are now being understood in new ways:[67] as different sorts of spaces for different kinds of living from our modern familial burrows; the same is true of the country residence. Patterns of occupancy – which I have not space to examine – make a *villa* more like a hotel than a modern house, and open the way to greatly varied use, much of it connected with production. Personal mobility and its relationship to abode have different modalities in all cultures, and our preoccupations with absenteeism are not easily mapped onto Roman realities. If we are prone to approaching ancient artworks in the spirit of auctioneers, we approach Roman *villae* in the guise of real-estate agents. Instead we should ask what the country estate of an ancient *locuples* was actually for. If they *were* residences, then what does that mean? Were they farms? Production in the environment is only very misleadingly called "farming" in English: farm and to farm are very culturally determined concepts, nearly as much as gentleman! Let us attempt to strip away automatic assumptions and look for things which ancient estate centres actually *did*.

The villa and the public landscape

Unlike the place in the early modern landscape of northwest Europe of the domains of the post-feudal aristocracy,[68] the Roman landscape of property depended on the spectacular visibility of a series of focal points in the view which announced the power of that series of proprietors.[69] The effect is intended to function in a landscape that has already been ordered. The Roman *villa* of antiquity was not conceived as a pioneer establishment taming new soil; it was epiphenomenal to the centuriated landscape which had already been divided and allotted. It is a later development of that landscape, often no doubt replacing the lots and dwellings of the original *coloni*, but still logically dependent on the fact that the land had previously been assigned in that way. In ancient societies, with their residue of citizen ideology, private wealth accumulated by the *primores* was seen against the background of the common weal, whether positively or negatively: positively if it is the source of euergetism, negatively if it is abusively gained or abused in the disposal. The consolidation of landholdings is analogous; there is an ideology of citizen estates, closely linked at Rome with the ideology of colonial centuriation; the *villa* landscape is a specialized by-product of that world, and the generosity of the rich with their land and its products, as we have seen it several times in this paper, is part of the natural consequence. Just as the *domus* is in form an allotment in the town, the *horti* in the suburb and *villa* in the country, even though they may be vastly elaborated, do not become wholly free of the memory of an egalitarianism which they have transcended. The great *villae* of Sabinum or the change in the settlement pattern which Andrea Carandini has traced[70] in the Ager Cosanus are deliberate creations out of the world of the allotment. That can be seen more readily now that recent scholarship has taught us to see no difference of kind in the agricultural objectives of the *colonus* and the *villa* owner; both are concerned with cash-crop production by way of intensification. Recent archaeological work has shown that considerable coexistence between properties of all sizes is normal, as we would expect. The contrast with which we began, between Pulcher's *horti* and the old Villa Publica, is emblematic. Tradition claimed that the public domain of the Campus Martius had once been the *temenos* of the Tarquins.[71] The Villa Publica – "communis universi populi" – itself had been built in grander form at the same time as the Atrium

Libertatis by the censors of 194 BC,[72] just at the time that the estates of the rich were being made ever more splendid and extensive. We note that there was on the southern outskirts of Rome also a *vinea publica*.[73] Aristocratic estates, at least until the 2nd century AD, are in dialogue with publicly owned land and with allotted land, and the *villa* landscape reflects that fact. To some extent imperial estates may take over this function of foil to the wealthy *villa*. But a consequence of the earlier relationship is the firm location of the *villa* in an urban continuum: among the holdings in the hinterland which support in theory the livelihood of every citizen.

The villa and the romance of storage

Not least among the ways in which the *villa* was seen to function as the visible place where wealth was produced was its obvious and visible rôle as a store. We should see *villae* as so many great warehouses dotting the landscape – the very apparent centres to which so much of what the landscape produces is gathered, the places where, in times of shortage, everyone knows that abundance is immured. Villas are the barns which define the power of control over the surplus in ancient agriculture, as in Matthew 6: 26: "the birds of the air sow not, nor do they reap and they gather not into store". Roman proprietors certainly did; and their *villa* architecture, with vast ramified *cryptae* and *apothecae* under the platform of the residence, or enormous decorated granaries such as that at Settefinestre, emphasized this function.[74] Lin Foxhall has shown recently how huge were the quantities of grain and olive oil envisaged by the storage specifications of Cato's estate: at least three crops-worth of oil and grain for the whole *familia* for three years.[75]

The circumstances of Mediterranean production make storage a central strategy for survival. The circumvention of risk in conditions of great interannual variation of weather determines much of the strategy of environmental management. Storing against the greatest imagined need is a prime response. It links – once again – the ancient single-family household on its arable lot with the swollen *oikos* that is the great Roman *villa*. Indeed, control of storage has been advanced as one of the principal ingredients in the very formation and maintenance of elites in Mediterranean history.[76] The place of the *pars fructuaria* in the design emphasized these functions. Storerooms, in the Roman tradition, were intended to impress, especially through the ordered ranks of vats or *dolia* which formed remarkable interiors, central to the plans of *villae* such as Boscoreale Pisanella or Scafati.[77] These eloquently geometrical displays are equally the theme of the decoration of the monument of the master baker Eurysaces at the Porta Maggiore in Rome. There was a rhetoric of *quaestus* made visible which placed the *villa* clearly in the network – of distribution, of human contacts, of ideas – that joined the *villa* to the places in the city where its product was transformed, put on sale, or shipped elsewhere – to the bakery, the *macellum*, or the harbour. Some *villae* were indeed equipped with their own harbours in order to stress the part their economy played in storage and redistribution.[78] There is a continuity of atmosphere between the urban *horrea, officina* and *taberna* and the rural *ergastulum, cryptoporticus* and press-room. The standard repertoire of forms in the *villa*, the *macellum* and the Roman port are coeval. The *tholos* depicts the suburban estate on wall-painting at the same time as being characteristic of the *macellum*.[79] The first great public granaries at Rome – those of C. Gracchus – answered to the contemporary flourishing of the great *villae* (something similar could be argued for the Villa Publica a half century before). The imperial estates and the great holdings of late antiquity developed the display of storage still further: the great granaries of the Castel Giubileo *villa* on the Fidenae estate, or the Horrea Nervae at Annunziatella on the Via Ardeatina are examples of the former, and the granaries at Torre Angela (Via Gabina 12) of the latter; but this is not a complete innovation.[80]

The school of Aristotle[81] already noted that participation in a developed market-economy was an alternative to long-term storage; as a buffer against risk, the market complements the store. Roman *villa* owners needed to be conscious of their relationship to this possibility, and to display it. Decorative tables of market-day cycles at neighbouring towns were cut on fine marble. Market centres and fairs were encouraged by proprietors.[82] A *villa* was intended to be seen as a great reserve of accumulated production, and the centre from which it is sent on its way into the world of the consumer. The Romans themselves[83] fancied that the word *villa* was derived from *vehere*, to haul "because the crops are hauled in to it". The tall *villae* on their platforms filled with produce, as we see them, for instance on the Avezzano landscape relief, spoke to the dependent producer of the realities of agriculture as clearly as do, in the modern world, the great grain-elevators of the prairies.

The villa as the locus of intensification

But storage of what has been collected is only part of the productive display: the *villa* aims to be seen as the centre of the effort to manage the environment and produce from it, the intensification of agricultural effort which is basic to the production of a surplus in the Mediterranean lands. Two of the ways in which the intensificatory effort is most visible are technological improvement and changes in labour management. Both are on display in the Roman *villa*. Whether in the forecourt at Settefinestre, or in the functional parts of Lucus Feroniae, or at many other *villae*, or in the serried ranks of cottages which line the approaches to great Gallo-Roman *villae*, the workforce is on show to the visitor. Agricultural slaves are intended to be seen, and the tenant as a client is likewise visible, even if he is not often so specifically publicized as he is in the letters of the younger Pliny.[84] We may go so far as to say that the evidence discussed above for the structures of dependency in the *villa* landscape and the *horti* landscape actually reflects the intentions of the proprietors with power in those settings. Certainly this was apparent to the *agrimensor* Frontinus, who wrote (53 Lachmann) of the *vicos circa villam in modum munitionum*. The dependent smallholder is as much part of the Roman landowner's portfolio of prestige as his peacocks, paintings and plantations.

Alongside the living tools, the other hardware is also intended to be noticed. In 70 or 55 BC one landowner in the Campagna thought it worth putting an inscription of the consular date on his olive-oil settling-vat![85] From Cato's detailed instructions on where to go to buy the best machinery (*Agr.* 135) to the long catalogue of improvements in know-how in the elder Pliny,[86] there is abundant evidence for the stress on the plant necessary for intensification – again, something which bridges the gap between the *pars fructuaria* of the *villa* and the world of the urban *officina*.[87]

It is against this technological display that we should put the most important aid to intensification of all, the control of water. When we look at a Roman *villa* we should see it in a hydraulic landscape – in close association with springs and wells or lakes and rivers managed by dykes, culverts, sluices, bridges, dams; or defined by its place on an aqueduct network such as those in the Amiternum or Aquae Passeris inscriptions, and above all perched on vast cisterns which are often the storage area of the *villa* best preserved today.[88] The *villa* represented a focus of water-management, of a specialized kind when it was for the control of watermeadow or fishpond on the coast, sometimes as a gesture towards debonair uselessness for the maintenance of sterile ornamental plants or the proprietor's bath, but always in the context of the environmental control which the owner of the building and the land exercised over this most precious of resources, the resource on which all the subsequent production and intensification depended.[89] It is for this reason that the wetland edge is perhaps the most characteristic setting for Roman *villae* as it is for the Homeric *temenos*.[90]

In an earlier article,[91] I have attempted to explore the ways in which the Romans differentiated between different landscapes, and in particular between town and country. Those ways were found to be closely related to the productive management of the environment, and to be reflected in the design of country houses. It was possible to outline a rather schematic progression between the heart of the city and the outer wilderness. In practice the Roman landscape was far more complex. The various stages of urbanity were all juxtaposed, and where the natural landscape permitted, elements of forest, seashore, suburb, pasture, vineyard, garden, ploughland could be set up side by side in a kind of modular way that was assisted by the mentality of the allotment. The result is a continuum between town and country which makes it futile to identify as alien to the rustic setting certain architectural elaborations which are more familiar from the town.

That continuum equally should deter us from arguing that the relationship works the other way round and from seeing the life of the *villa* as the guiding principle in the formation of the tastes of the town.[92] Communities such as Stabiae or Antium, which were all *villae*,[93] or places such as Pompeii where the topography and institutions are those of a town but the social and cultural fabric is that of a cluster of *villae* and their dependencies, are therefore not anomalous – but neither are they typical. All *villae* are *villae urbanae*:[94] they reflect a world of production which stretches from the *tabernae* around the *domus* on the Carinae to the tenants around the estate in the Apennine valley.[95] Production is designed for the *macellum* or for benefaction; it is part of the way in which the aristocrat fits in to a citizen community, and the *villa* is the location of that sort of production. The urbanity, in this sense, of the *villa*, is an important factor in promoting the ambiguity between *villa* and town which is so prominent in the literary sources.[96]

What *is* typical about these Roman resorts is that they function as intermediaries in the process of enhancing the status and amenities of the centres on which they depend. They are subordinate to the centres from which the wealthy come for their *villeggiatura* and they act as centres for the accumulation of the produce, luxury and everyday, which makes the high life possible. The *villa* and the town resemble each other in both being centres for storage and intensification along the lines which we have explored: note Cicero on Capua, "cellam atque horreum Campani agri" (*Leg. Agr.* 2.89). There is a settlement hierarchy here, movement within which takes the form both of economic dependence and of social promotion.

It was important to keep in touch with your peers; *villae* in the Sallentine peninsula or the remoter parts of Bruttium are considered extraordinary by Cicero in that messages arrive from them only three times a year.[97] Even Trimalchio received formal statements of account from his huge estates,[98] which points up the density of contact that was expected of more accessible properties. Even a junior senator might well depend on his productive *villae* in his home city, in the *regio Romana*, on the coast at Cumae. The economic dependence of a Roman consumer on grain from the one, wine from the second and fish from the third has its counterpart in the social relations which result from the political success of the senator and his family in gaining office at Rome and in exerting their new influence in the richest, most populous and most famous parts of Italy. In this sense, the Roman *villa* phenomenon in the age of Cicero and Augustus could be called the physical expression of Peter Wiseman's thesis in *New men in the roman senate* (1971). This landscape of production is not static: its dynamism derives from the use to which the owners put their resources, and their degree of success.

It is at this type of issue, rather than the typology of plans or the details of residence, that we should look in order to see more clearly what a *villa*, great or small, really stood for and how it was perceived. From the coast of Campania to the heart of Rome, property was for production, and what gave the landscape of the *villa*, the landscape of production, a coherence from Britain to Syria, was patterns in the attitudes of producers and consumers to what was to be produced and how and by whom it was to be consumed. For my "landscape of production" is indissolubly embedded in that landscape of consumption which is formed by stratification, patronage and euergetism in the Roman city. If there is a coherence in the estates of the ancient countryside, it derives only secondarily from architecture and much more from the effect that ancient city society had on producing coherence in the patterns of exploitation.

It should be stressed that exploitation is indeed the *mot juste*. The Roman landowner was not an economic *fainéant*, but that does not mean that his economic activities produced overall economic growth. His interest in production may have been underestimated precisely because it overtly took the form of squeezing more out of labour or out of the environment, or of taking advantage of the political power given to the accumulator of food: it was not wrapped up in the jargon of alleged economic rationalism, and for whatever reason, did not conduce to many of the processes which we associate with economic modernity. If we want to know why, as Jongman[99] has recently stressed, we must look for the answers in the structures of society. The town, as we have seen again and again, is inseparable from the territory. Another reason for missing the essential productiveness of all Roman *villae* has been to imagine that the city was totally unproductive, and that the *villa* can somehow be regarded as a little island of urban uselessness marooned in the real countryside. But both productivity and consumption permeate the whole society. We are unlikely to find in the temple or the amphitheatre the answer to why the Roman world never achieved economic critical mass, and we shall certainly not find it in the Euripus or the *glirarium*.

Notes

1. An earlier version of this paper was presented at a symposium on the Roman Villa at Philadelphia in the spring of 1990: I am grateful to the organizers for their kind invitation to participate. Some of the material used in this paper is the product of research pursued as Fellow in Landscape Architecture at Dumbarton Oaks in 1988–9.
2. 54 and 50 BC are the possible dates: for the latter, E. Badian, Additional notes on Roman magistrates, *Athenaeum* **38**, 1970, pp. 4–6; for the former, I. Shatzman, Four notes on Roman magistrates, *Athenaeum* **36**, 1968, pp. 350–3; J. S. Richardson, The triumph of Metellus Scipio and the dramatic date of Varro *Res Rusticae* III, CQ **33**, 1983, pp. 456–63.
3. For Pulcher and his family, see T. P. Wiseman, *Catullus and his world* (Cambridge, 1985) pp. 22–4; Pauly-Wissowa, *RE*, vol. iii, s.v. Claudius, p. 247; and, recently, W. J. Tatum, The poverty of the Claudii Pulchri: Varro, *De re rustica* 3.16.1–2, CQ **42**, 1992, pp. 190–200.

4. 3.2.7. Pulcher pretends not to know what a *villa* is: "Appius subridens, Quoniam ego ignoro, inquit, quid sit villa..."; but his remarks at 3.12–15 and his view on the problems of stock mortality (3.2.18) suggest that Varro does not mean us to take him for an amateur.

5. W. Rinkewitz, *Pastio villatica: untersuchungen zur intensiven Hoftierhaltung in der römischen Landwirtschaft* (Frankfurt, 1981).

6. N. Purcell, *The gardens of Rome* (London, forthcoming).

7. See e.g. Martial 10.37, and N. Purcell, The *Litus Laurentinum* and the creation of a Roman resort-coast; Castelporziano III (Rome, forthcoming).

8. W. E. Heitland, *Agricola: a study of agriculture and rustic life in the Greco-Roman world from the point of view of labour* (Cambridge, 1921), pp. 309–10, misunderstands this epigram: he sees it both as a contrast between sterile *suburbanum* and "a genuine unsophisticated country farm" and as a portrait of a place which can "only by courtesy be styled a farm since the intrusion of . . . refined and luxurious urban elements . . . destroyed its character". Despite the evidence for expected high prices in the *macellum* he concludes "that it really paid its way . . . is utterly incredible".

9. P. Harvey, Mentula bonus agricola, *Historia* **28**, 1979, p. 329.

10. For the satiric tradition and farming, J. E. Skydsgaard, *Varro the scholar: studies in the first book of Varro's De re rustica* (Copenhagen, 1968), pp. 117–21); J. Linderski, Garden parlors: nobles and birds, in *Studia Pompeiana et classica in honor of Wilhelmina F. Jashemski*, ed. R. I. Curtis (New Rochelle, NY, 1988), vol. ii, pp. 113–20. Varro's own Menippea touched on this in the *Gerontodidaskalos* (frs. 10–13 Riese); cf. E. Rawson, The Ciceronian aristocracy and its properties, in *Studies in Roman property*, ed. M. I. Finley (Cambridge, 1967), pp. 85–102, n. 43.

11. The *oporotheca* is another joky *hapax*, also occurring at 1.2.10 and 2 *pr.* 2, but nowhere else. Note that the use of fruit-store as diningroom is acceptable unless you bring in fruit from the market at Rome to decorate it: "ut Romae coempta poma rus intulerint in oporothecen instruendam convivi causa", 1.59.2.

12. Pliny, NH 14.48–52; Suet., *Gramm.* 25; cf. N. Purcell, Wine and wealth in ancient Italy *JRS* **75**, 1985, pp. 4–5, 18–19.

13. Varro, *RR* 3.2.16; 3.4.15, snails; 3.4.1, Axius' greed.

14. *RR* 3.3.10: "sexaginta enim milia Fircelina excande me fecerunt cupiditate"; cf. 3.2.16 "collegiorum cenae quae nunc innumerabiles excandefaciunt annonam macelli". The same passage discusses the demand for 5,000 small birds for the triumphal banquet of Metellus Scipio (for the date, see n. 2).

15. A. Carandini, Orti e frutteti, in *Misurare la terra: centuriazone e coloni nel mondo romano. Città, agricoltura, commercio: materiali da Roma e dal suburbio* (Modena, 1985), pp. 66–74; N. Purcell, Tomb and suburb, in *Römische Gräberstrassen – Selbstdarstellung –Status – Standard (Abhand. Bay. Akad. Wiss., Ph.-Hist. Kl. 96)*, eds H. Von Hesberg & P. Zanker (Munich, 1987) pp. 25–41; *The gardens of Rome*.

16. Pliny, NH 12.8, cf. Macr., *Sat.* 3.13.3: Hortensius at Tusculum.

17. *Piscinae* near Rome, *NSc.* 1924, pp. 55–60 (vigna S. Carlo dei Barnabiti, Via Portuensis, 42 × 19 m. and fed by the Aqua Alsietina); *NSc.* 1947, p. 136, probably supplied from the Tiber, in the Via Giulia (southern Campus Martius). Cf. Varro, *RR* 3.17.2–3. For real *gliraria* (dormouse hutches) *NSc.* 1968, pp. 12–15; *Misurare la terra*, p. 151.

18. Urban periphery as a landscape of patronage: M. W. Frederiksen, I cambiamenti delle strutture agrarie nella tarda repubblica: la Campania, in *L'Italia: insediamenti e*

forme economiche (= *Società romana e produzione schiavistica)*, eds A. Giardina & A. Schiavone, vol. i. (Rome & Bari, 1981), p. 282. For *villae* in this area, L. Quilici, La villa nel suburbio romano, problemi di studio e del inquadramento storico-topografico, *AC* **31**, 1979, pp. 309–17.

19. Aurelius Victor, *Epit. de Caes.* 39.5–6.
20. Purcell, Wine and wealth in ancient Italy.
21. A. Carandini, L'economia italica fra tarda repubblica e medio imperio considerata dal punto di vista di una merce: il vino, *Amphores romaines et histoire économique* (École Française de Rome; Rome, 1989), p. 517; P. A. Brunt, *Italian manpower*, 2nd edn (Oxford 1987).
22. Fronto, *ad M. Caes.* 4.4, cf. 4.6, dinner in the pressing-room.
23. *Misurare la terra,* p. 127.
24. *Ibid.,* pp. 117–18, 120–21.
25. For the Casal Morena *villa*, F. Coarelli, *Dintorni di Roma* (Bari, 1981), p. 155; G. M. de Rossi, *Bovillae (Forma Italiae,* I, 15, 1979), no. 103.
26. A. Vogliano, La grande iscrizione bacchica del Metropolitan Museum, *AJA* **37**, 1933, pp. 215–31. Domestic cults in *villae* frequently reflect the landscape as it is conceived by the owner: Silvanus is relatively frequent, but there are parallels for Liber Pater; note *NSc.* 1925, p. 387 (Acquatraversa).
27. Purcell, Tomb and suburb.
28. G. Pisani Sartorio, & R. Calza, *La villa di Massenzio sulla Via Appia* (Rome, 1976); IGR I.194.
29. A. Tchernia, *Le vin de L'Italie romaine* (BEFAR 262; Paris, 1988), s.v. Cécube; G. Traina, *Paludi e bonifiche del mondo antico: saggio di archeologia geografica (Cent. Ric. e Doc. sull'Ant. Class.* 11) (Rome, 1988), pp. 83–4, 104
30. Tac. *Ann.* 4.1, cf. 4.67.
31. W. Donlan, Homeric *temenos* and the land economy of the Dark Age, *Museum Helveticum* **46**, 1989, pp. 139–43.
32. E. Bayer, *Fischerbilder in der hellenistischen Plastik* (Bonn, 1983); H. P. Laubscher, *Fischer und Landleute* (Mainz, 1982).
33. T. W. Gallant, *A fisherman's tale: an analysis of the potential productivity of fishing in the ancient world (Miscellanea Graeca* 7; Ghent, 1985).
34. N. & B. Kitz, *Pains Hill Park* (London, 1984), p. 35.
35. The *villa* has been largely destroyed but was recorded in considerable detail in the 19th century: L. Fortunati, *Relazione generale degli scavi e scoperte fatte lungo la via Latina* (Rome, 1859), cf. Coarelli, *Dintorni di Roma,* pp. 138–40.
36. A. Carandini & A. Ricci (eds), *Settefinestre, una villa schiavistica nell'Etruria romana* (Modena, 1985), vol. ii, for the *pars fructuaria* of Settefinestre; cf. N. Purcell, review of Carandini & Ricci, *JRS* **88**, 1988, pp. 194–8. For excessive investment in a country estate, see above all the elder Pliny on Tarius Rufus: NH 18.37.
37. For a parallel, see the Massaciuccoli *villa, NSc.* 1935, p. 212.
38. Carandini & Ricci, *Settefinestre.*
39. Cf. P. Miniero, Ricerche sull'Ager Stabianus, in *Studia Pompeiana et classica in honor of Wilhelmina F. Jashemski,* ed. R. I. Curtis (New Rochelle, NY, 1988) vol. i, pp. 262–5.
40. Kitz, *Pains Hill Park,* p. 87.
41. See *Misurare la terra,* pp. 131–7.
42. *Ibid.,* p. 110.

43. "Ubi agros optime cultos vidisset, in his regionibus excelsissimo loco gromam statuere aiebat; inde corrigere viam, aliis per vineas medias, aliis per roborarium atque piscinam, aliis per villam." A. E. Astin, *Scipio Aemilianus* (Oxford, 1967), pp. 175–7, takes this simply as Scipio's counter-attack, focusing on Asellus' "irresponsibility".

44. The last great road building project before this date seems to have been the Via Postumia in Cisalpina (148 BC, *ILLRP* 452). For the aqueducts, S. B. Platner & T. Ashby, *A topographical dictionary of ancient Rome* (Oxford, 1929), s.vv. On compulsory distraint for aqueduct building, cf. Tacitus, *Ann.* 1.75.3; but note Livy, 40.51.7, M. Licinius Crassus obstructs the building of an aqueduct by the censors of 179 BC by refusing to allow it to pass through his farm (*fundus*).

45. M. I. Finley, *The ancient economy*, 2nd edn (London, 1985), pp. 188–9.

46. *Ibid.*, p. 58.

47. *Ibid.*, p. 109, cf. 58 and, on Cato's ignorance, famously, 110; cf. M. I. Finley, *Ancient slavery and modern ideology* (London, 1980), p. 137.

48. The *locus classicus* for the reception of the Roman *villa* in England is R. Castell, *The villas of the ancients illustrated* (London, 1728); see J. D. Hunt, *Garden and grove: the Italian Renaissance garden in the English imagination: 1600–1750* (London, 1986), pp. 30–41.

49. E.g. Shatzman, Senatorial wealth and Roman politics, p. 26; *Misurare la terra*, pp. 107–9, noting with surprise that only a few *villae* in the territory of Tibur appear to be solely for *otium*.

50. "Et si forte voluptarium fuit praedium, viridaria vel gestationes vel deambulationes arboribus infructuosis opacas atque amoenas habens, non debebit deicere ut forte hortos olitorios faciat vel aliud quid, quod ad reditum spectat."

51. Heitland also makes much of *Dig.* 7.4.8 and 10, on the question of whether the *fundus* belongs to the *villa* or vice versa. But logically, the fact that the question is difficult would not have arisen if everyone knew simply that the principal meaning of *villa* was a largely or totally unproductive luxury home. This evidence reinforces the case for taking the sterile *villa* as untypical. Note, on the terminology, R. J. Buck, *Agriculture and agricultural practice in Roman law* (Wiesbaden, 1983), pp. 9–14; the normal term is simply *praedium*, which does not even discriminate between town and country. The word *praetorium* for *villa* is an interesting development, but it does not reflect on the question of production.

52. J. S. Ackerman, *The villa: form and ideology of country houses* (Washington DC, 1990), pp. 9–34.

53. Castell, *The villas of the ancients illustrated*, p. 77.

54. A. G. McKay, *Houses, villas and palaces in the Roman world* (London, 1987), ch.5; K. M. Swoboda, *Römische und Romanische Paläste: eine architekturgeschichtliche Untersuchung*, 3rd edn (Böhlau, 1969). Note also Rostovtzeff's Type One, in M. I. Rostovtseff, *The social and economic history of the Roman empire,* 2nd edn (Oxford, 1957), pp. 59–66. J. Percival, *The Roman villa: an historical introduction* (London, 1976), pp. 57–8, develops the idea of "urban influence", which he sees as functioning in inverse proportion to the extent to which sites were "primarily working establishments". On the actual preponderance of mixed sites in the area of Rome itself, *Misurare la terra*, p. 83.

55. K. D. White, *Roman farming* (London, 1970), pp. 438–9; W. Johannowsky (ed.), *Le ville romane dell'età imperiale (Itinerari turistico-culturali in Campania 3)* (Naples,

1986), pp. 13–20.

56. J. Kolendo, Le attività agricole degli abitanti di Pompei e gli attrezzi agricoli ritrovati all'interno della città, *Opus* 4, 1985, pp. 111–24.

57. Percival, *The Roman villa*, pp. 14–15.

58. Galen, *Antid.* I.3 = Kühn XIV 17–18. Cf. Boscoreale "Stazione", J. J. Rossiter, *Roman farm buildings in Italy* (BAR Int. Ser. 52; Oxford, 1978), pp. 12–14; Vitruvius 6.6.1–2. For Greek precursors of the Italian *villa*, note the luxury prison of Demetrius Poliorcetes in the lush plain below Apamaea, with its walks and *paradeisos*, Plutarch, *Dem.* 50.

59. Homer, *Od.* 1.190, 11.187, 24.205, 336.

60. B. M. Felletti Maj, Roma (Via Tiberina) – *villa rustica*, *NSc.*, 1955, p. 207, cf. *Misurare la terra*, pp. 124–6.

61. Compare the luxury *villa maritima* at Barbariga in Istria whose grand section was explored in 1901; the large-scale and monumental oilpressery was only discovered in 1953–4. See R. Matijasic, Roman rural architecture in the territory of Colonia Iulia Pola, *AJA* 86, 1982, pp. 57–9.

62. A. Wallace-Hadrill, The social structure of the Roman house *PBSR* 56, 1988, pp. 44–50.

63. Finley, *Ancient slavery and modern ideology*, pp. 132–7, returned to the question of units of exploitation in Roman agriculture and here distinguished it from the patterns of owner-residence. He might have regarded the ideological investigations of the present essay as equally clearly distinct from the economic questions. For the move towards more holistic interpretations of *villae*, J. J. Rossiter, Some recent books on Roman *villae*, *JRA* 6, 1993, p. 449.

64. Carandini & Ricci, *Settefinestre*, vol. i, cf. Purcell, review of Carandini & Ricci.

65. Ph. Leveau, Villa ville village: la ville antique et l'organisation de l'espace rurale *Annales (ESC)* 38, 1983, p. 923. See also now H. Mielsch, *Die römische Villa – Architektur und Lebenform* (Munich, 1987), with the review by P. Gros, *Latomus* 48, 1989, pp. 708–9; and M. Oehme, *Die römische Villenwirtschaft. Untersuchungen zu den Agrarschriften Catos und Columellas und ihrer Darstellungen bei Niebuhr und Mommsen* (Bonn, 1988).

66. Ackerman, *The villa*, p. 286.

67. Wallace-Hadrill, The social structure of the Roman house.

68. Cf. E. Bellamy & T. Williamson, *Property and landscape: a social history of landownership and the English countryside* (London, 1987).

69. Thus N. Brockmeyer, Die villa rustica als Wirtschaftsform und die Ideologisierung der Landwirtschaft, *Ancient society* 6, 1975, pp. 227–8: "bekam die villa rustica im Rahmen der kaiserzeitlichen Socialordnung eine über ihre ökonomische Bedeutung hinausgehende systemstabilisierende Funktion".

70. Carandini & Ricci, *Settefinestre*.

71. Livy, 2.5.

72. Livy, 34.44.

73. CIL VI 933 = 31208.

74. For the granary at Settefinestre, Carandini & Ricci, *Settefinestre*, vol. ii, pp. 189–208; for some spectacular instances of enormously ramified storerooms in substructions, Coarelli, *Dintorni di Roma*, pp. 126, 45, 156. There is a vivid illustration of the complexity and importance of the storage function of *villae* throughout the discussion *De instructo vel instrumento legato*, *Digest*, 33.7.

75. L. Foxhall, *Olive cultivation within Greek and Roman agriculture: the ancient economy revisited* (Diss., Liverpool, 1990), pp. 348–51; cf. Columella 2.20.6
76. T. W. Gallant, Crisis and response: risk-buffering behaviour in Hellenistic Greek communities, *Journal of Interdisciplinary History* **19**, 1989, pp. 393–413, on the connection between risk-buffering and accumulation by elites or states.
77. Rossiter, Roman farm buildings in Italy, pp. 18–21, 31.
78. The best case is Pliny, *Ep.* 6.31 (Centum Cellae): "cingitur viridissimis agris: imminet litora cuius in sinu fit cum maxime portus".
79. I owe this point to Ann Kuttner.
80. Granaries on imperial estates: the Horrea Nervae, CIL VI 8681; Castel Giubileo *NSc.* 1976, p. 224; Via Gabina, W. M. Widrig, Land use at the Via Gabina Villas, in *Ancient Roman villa gardens,* ed. E. B. MacDougall (Washington DC, 1987). In general see Rossiter, *Roman farm buildings in Italy,* Ch. 6.
81. Aristotle, *Oec.* 1.1394b 31–3.
82. J. Nollé, *Nundinas instituere et habere* (Hildesheim, 1982); J. M. Frayn, *Markets and fairs in Roman Italy* (Oxford, 1993), pp. 121–3.
83. Varro, *RR* 1.2.14.
84. Pliny, *Ep.* 3.19; 5.14; 7.30; 9.15, 36–7; 10.8; cf. J. R. Patterson, Crisis: what crisis? Rural change and urban development in imperial Appennine Italy, *PBSR* **55**, 1987.
85. *Misurare la terra*, pp. 150–1 "CN. POM. M. LIC. COS." Given the troubles of the 50s, the first sensational consulship of the two dynasts might be thought the more likely moment for commemoration; the threats of Sertorius and Spartacus were now satisfactorily laid to rest.
86. Cf. Purcell, Wine and wealth in ancient Italy, pp. 18–19.
87. N. Purcell, The city of Rome and its people in the late republic, in *CAH*[2], vol. ix (Cambridge, 1994).
88. E.g. *Misurare la terra*, p. 91.
89. The dichotomy between "recreational" and "utilitarian" in Roman engineering is in some ways parallel to that between "sterile" and "practical" in Roman agriculture. In fact the advanced technology of Roman hydraulics – and the same can be said of agricultural processing techniques – straddles the divide: it is expensive and learned and spectacular as well as being useful and functional, but it also bridges the gap between town and country. Vats and tanks are the common paraphernalia of the uban *officina* and the *villa*; hydraulic wizardry is the sign of the privileged city and the prestigious country estate. For a splendid example of show hydraulics in a setting of *pastio villatica*, we may note A. M. McCann, *The Roman port and fishery of Cosa* (Princeton, NJ, 1987), pp. 98–128 (the Spring House at the Portus Cosanus); this is also the context of the famous epigram (Anth. Pal. 9.418) on the waterwheel, not the paradoxical connecting of industrial banality and high poetry that it can seem to us: cf. also Strabo, 12.3.30 (King Mithridates). For a parallel in English landscape management of the 18th century, Kitz, *Pains Hill Park*, pp. 51–2, 111–17.
90. Donlan, Homeric *temenos*, pp. 129–45; cf. also C. Parain, *La Méditerranée: les hommes et leurs travaux* (Paris, 1936), pp. 56–9.
91. Purcell, Tomb and suburb.
92. P. Zanker, Die Villa als Vorbild des späten pompejanischen Wohngeschmacks, *JdI* **94**, 1979, pp. 460–523.
93. Strabo, 5.3.5; Pliny, NH 3.70.
94. Cf. Cato, *Agr.* 4.

95. Ackerman, *The villa*, pp. 9, 12, makes the link with the town define the *villa*.
96. N. Purcell, Town in country and country in town, in *Ancient Roman villa gardens*, ed. E. B. MacDougall (Washington DC, 1987b), pp. 185–203.
97. Cic. *Sext. Rosc.* 132.
98. Petr. *Sat.* 53.
99. W. Jongman, *The Economy and Society of Pompeii* (Amsterdam, 1988).

10

The idea of the city and the excavations at Pompeii

Martin Goalen

O what a great adventure of our times that we discover not just another ancient monument but a city.[1]   Scippione Maffei, 1748

Introduction

"The ancients", Moses Finley tells us, "were firm in their view that civilized life was thinkable only in and because of cities." To the ancients a city "must be more than a mere conglomeration of people; there are necessary conditions of architecture and amenity".[2] The discovery and excavation of the two buried ancient cities of Herculaneum and Pompeii in the 18th century offered, for the first time since antiquity, a glimpse into just those "conditions of architecture and amenity" referred to by Finley – that is to say, into the physical structure of the ancient city,[3] with its walls, streets, tombs, public and private buildings. It is all the more surprising therefore that it took half a century after the identification of Pompeii in 1763 (digging had been in progress since 1748),[4] for Pompeii to be published *as a city* in François Mazois's (1783–1826)[5] magnificent *Les ruines de Pompéi*, published from 1812 onwards.[6]

At Pompeii, wrote the authors of a work claiming[7] to be the first *in English* to describe the ruins (Sir William Gell and John Gandy's *Pompeiana*, of 1817–19), "in the mind of the liberal antiquary the loneliness of the ruins may be animated by learned recollection". It is a sense of that "civilized life . . . thinkable only in and because of cities", noted by Finley, that Mazois, Gell and Gandy seek to recreate. "Animation" of the ruins by "learned recollection" is suggested, for instance, by the frontispiece to *Pompeiana* (Fig. 10.1), "wholly compiled from paintings and bronzes found at Pompeii".[8] An image is created through the combination of the artefacts of everyday life, the chairs, the tables, the lamps, the paintings, the marbles, with "pavements and distant

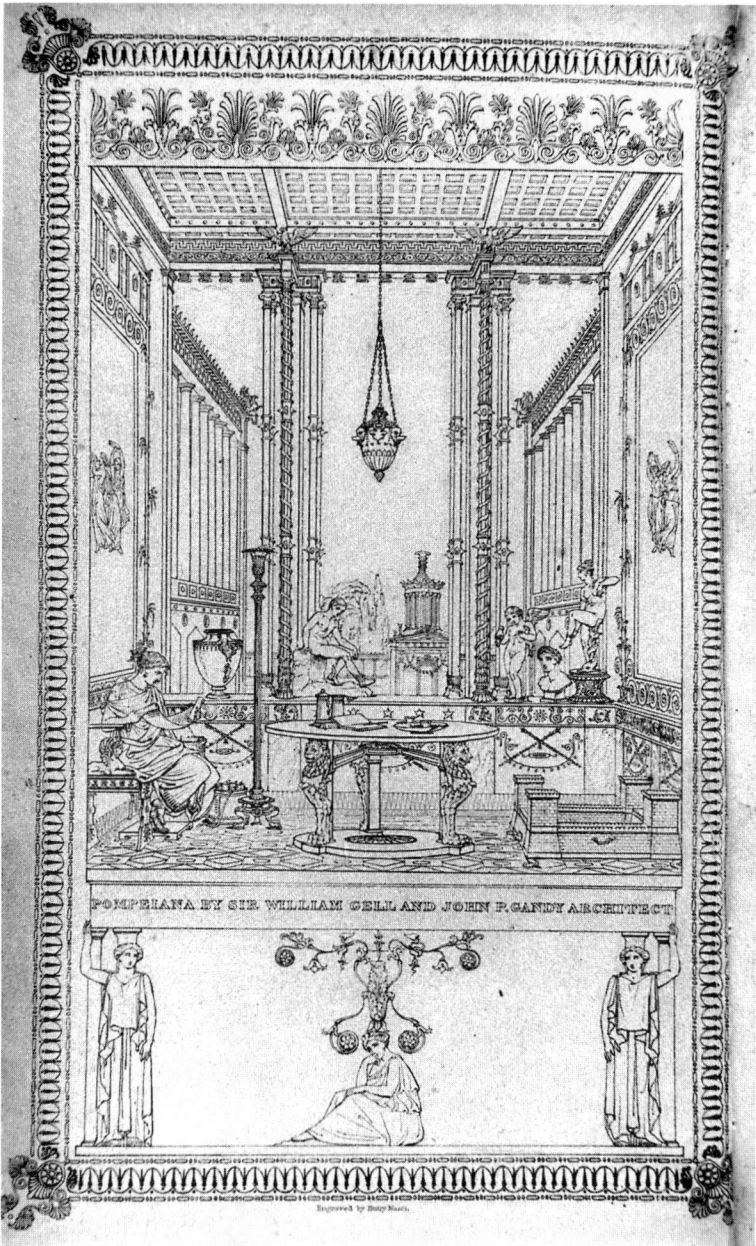

Figure 10.1   Gell & Gandy, Pompeiana *(1817–19), frontispiece.*

buildings".[9] Images from different sources are composed, rather in the manner of 20th century *collage*, to create a new composite image. The second volume of Mazois's work, *Habitations* (published in 1824), has a similarly *composed* frontispiece (Fig. 10.2):

Figure 10.2   Mazois, Ruines de Pompéi, *frontispiece.*

The disposition of the door, the inscription, the mosaic threshold can be seen in several dwellings. The Pilasters and the capitals belong to house no. 27,[10] the entablature and the stucco which decorate it, the paintings which ornament the interior frieze, the portico at the end and several other details are taken from various buildings. The fountain can be seen in house no. 46, called *L'Actéon*;[11] the motif of the garden which completes the *tableau* was given to me by a painting existing in the same place; the two herms are kept at the *Musée des Études* at Naples; in short all the elements of this composition are antique, and the arrangement in which I offer them gives an exact view of the entry into one of the principal houses of Pompeii.[12]

The tradition of compositions and vignettes drawn from the elements of Pompeii continued. In 1851, for instance, Jules Bouchet (1799–1860) published a book of such *Compositions antiques* freely modelled on Pompeii. It is the making, the transmission, and the absorption of such images of ancient city life into the modern world that is the subject of this essay. These images combine, on the one hand, "the figure reading a volume, the chair upon which she sits, the footstool ... manuscripts at her feet.... marble table",[13] with, on the other hand, Pausanius' "government offices, ... gymnasium, ... market-place, ... water descending to a fountain"[14] – linking the world of the individual with that of the community, the microcosm represented by the house with the macrocosm represented by the city.[15]

Vitruvius

"To the ancients", writes Moses Finley, "the urban underpinning of civilization"[16] was self-evident. When one turns to the only ancient exposition of the discipline of architecture that has survived, Vitruvius' *De architectura*, it is indeed the idea of the building of a *city* that underpins the structure of the book. For Vitruvius the art of building is the art of building the city – his exposition proceeds from the choice of site (1.4), to the building of the city walls (1.5), to the laying out of the broad streets and the alleys (1.6.1), and continues with the division into building plots:

> After apportioning the alleys and settling the main streets the choice of sites for the convenience and common use of the citizens has to be explained; for sacred buildings, the forum and the other public places.(1.7.1)[17]

After the public buildings, he moves to the *private* ones and then to a discussion (an opinionated one, it will be recalled: 7.5.3–4) of wall-paintings, showing for instance, "the battles of Troy and the wanderings of Ulysses over the countryside" (7.5.2). In other words, the work of Vitruvius' architect ranged over every aspect of the city – from the choice (and defence) of the site to landscape painting in the *cubiculum* of a private house.

Alberti and Palladio

Of the ancient works on architecture that we know[18] to have been written, the sole survival of Vitruvius' *De architectura* into the Renaissance gave that work an extraordinary, perhaps undeserved, influence. The idea, though, that architecture is structured as a discipline by a hierarchy of tasks involved in the building of a city is one that remained pivotal. The two key architectural treatises of the *quattrocento* and the *cinquecento*, those of Leon Battista Alberti (1404–72) and Andrea Palladio (1508–80), both depend upon it. Alberti's *De re aedificatoria*[19] reveals a critical study of Vitruvius:

> For I grieved that so many works of such brilliant writers had been destroyed by the hostility of time and of man, and that almost the sole survivor from this vast shipwreck is Vitruvius, an author of unquestioned experience, though one whose writings have been so corrupted by time that there are many omissions and many shortcomings. (6.1)

Alberti's treatise sets out to provide what Vitruvius lacks. The result, abstract and analytical compared to Vitruvius, has as its starting point patterns of association in the family and in society:

> In the beginning, men sought a place of rest in some region safe from danger; having found a place both suitable and agreeable, they settled down and took possession of the site. Not wishing to have all their household and private affairs conducted in the same place, they set aside one space for sleeping, another for the hearth, and allocated other spaces for different uses. *After this* [my emphasis] men began to consider . . . shelter from the sun and rain. (1.2)

For Alberti the art of building consists of six things: "(1) locality, (2) *area* [the site], (3) compartition, (4) wall, (5) roof, and (6) openings" (1.2). In this sequence "compartition", the division into public and private, is the more fundamental operation than the provision of shelter. It is the primacy of the social operation of architecture that defines it, for Alberti, as the building of the city – and analogously the house:

> If (as the philosophers maintain) the city is like some large house, and the house some large city, cannot the various parts of the house . . . be considered miniature buildings? (1.9)[20]

Both Alberti and Palladio acknowledge dual sources for their work: Vitruvius and the ancient ruins.[21] Palladio in turn is deeply indebted to Alberti,[22] but what distinguishes Palladio's *Quattro libri* is its dependence on the visual image. The aim of the *Quattro libri* is, Palladio tells us:

> to publish the designs of those [ancient] edifices, (in collecting which,
> I have employed so much time , and exposed myself to so many dan-
> gers) . . . and . . . those rules which I have observed . . . that they who
> shall read these my books, may be able to make use of whatever may
> be good therein. . . .[23]

When, as he must in a complete presentation of architecture through the
context of the city, Palladio turns (in book II) to the description and illustration of building for individuals, the town houses and country villas, he tells us:

> as we have but very few examples from the ancients, of which we can
> make use, I shall insert the plans and elevations of many fabrics I have
> erected . . . [as well as] the designs of ancient houses, in the manner
> that Vitruvius shews us they were made.[24]

At this critical point in his book, then, Palladio has no ancient houses to
illustrate. Instead he must fall back, first, on his attempts to reconstruct, from
Vitruvius' *written* description, what an ancient house might have looked like,
then presenting images of houses that he himself had built. It is perhaps not
surprising that there is a resemblance between Palladio's version of the ancient
house and contemporary work. Vitruvius' ancient house is reconstructed in
the classicizing language of Palladio's own practice; past and present are elided
in a passion to represent the ancient city. François Mazois clearly understood
this aspect of Palladio:

> The descriptions which Vitruvius and Varro . . . have given of the
> atrium become extremely clear once one has seen ancient houses, but
> before any had been discovered it was difficult to understand these
> authors. However, Palladio had guessed the form of the atrium, and
> applied it to modern buildings so ingeniously, that it must be
> regarded in some ways as a new invention.[25]

Mazois

After 1748 – or more importantly perhaps, when the excavations at Pompeii
had been adequately published – such misprision was no longer possible. Excavations reached their first peak during the French occupation of Naples in the
period between 1806 and 1815,[26] and it was as a result of this work that
Mazois's book, presenting the city as a whole, became possible.

The earlier publication of Herculaneum, the *Antichità d'Ercolano* (8 vols,

1757–92), had, like the early excavations themselves, focused on the movable objects, the paintings, sculptures, bronzes, candelabra (all this, of course, having its influence: Ferdinando Bologna has described the volumes as "models for the very modern production of ornaments and tools.").[27] In contrast to the impact of the 18th century discovery and measurement of ancient Greek buildings which led, at first, only to the construction of delicately scaled garden temples, in the manner of the Hephaisteion, the Tower of the Winds or the Arch of Hadrian,[28] the discovery of Herculaneum and Pompeii created a fascination for their objects and interior decoration; motifs were simply grafted onto existing types.[29] (The study of Greek architecture was of course to develop through the 19th century; by 1830 and Schinkel's *Altes Museum* we see Greek architecture so thoroughly absorbed and interpreted that it is becomes, as Palladio's ancient house, almost re-invented.)[30]

Mazois's aim in publishing *Les ruines...* is clear. It is to replace partial with complete publication:

> Les monuments de Pompéi ne sont encore connus que par l'ouvrage de l'Académie de Naples sur les mosaïques et les peintures . . . aussi les savants, les artistes, les amateurs, attendent-ils avec impatience, depuis près de cinquante ans, un ouvrage exact et complet sur les antiquités de cette ville. . . .[31]
>
> Les plans sont tout réduits sur une même échelle, ainsi que les élévations et les coupes . . . en un mot j'ai cherché à ne rien omettre de ce qui peut aider à expliquer clairment chacun des édifices, et servir à les comparer entre eux.[32]

And as we have seen (above, p. 186) Mazois is aware, too, of the importance of Pompeii in transforming knowledge of the ancient house (and hence of the fabric of the city). He placed his study of the ruins of Pompeii in the context of thoughts about the relation of the discipline of architecture to the city and to the house, a context that links Vitruvius, Alberti, and Palladio. The manner of Mazois's presentation makes these connections clear; the first volume describes the walls, the gates, the roads that lead to them (and the tombs that line them); the second volume, the houses; the third volume, secular public buildings; the fourth, temples (and theatres). The city is presented to us in a Vitruvian sequence; Mazois's division into volumes closely parallels that of Palladio's *Quattro Libri* (book II, houses; book III, fora and basilicas; book IV, temples). Mazois, like Vitruvius, describes the ancient city through the whole range of its elements, from the walls and streets (Fig. 10.3) to the buildings, both public and private, and then, like Vitruvius, to detail of painted decoration (Fig. 10.4):

> Les ruines de Pompéi permettent de remplacer désormais les conjectures par des certitudes, et les restaurations hasardées des artistes

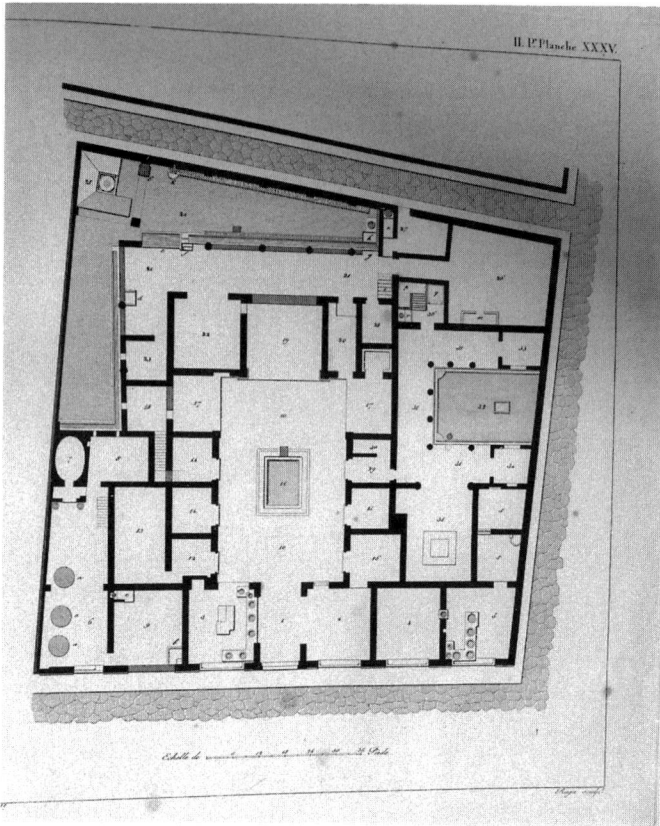

Figure 10.3   Mazois, Ruines de Pompéi, *detail of plan.*

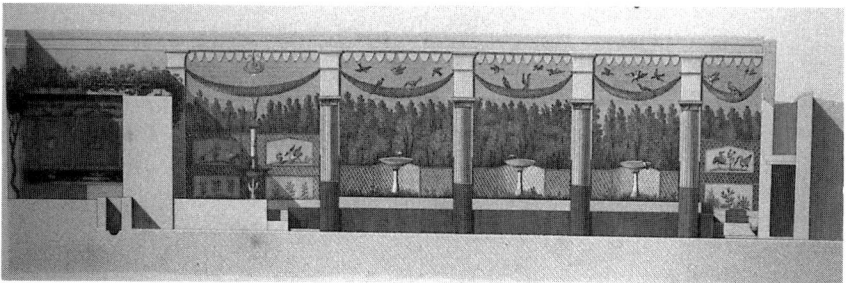

Figure 10.4   Mazois, Ruines de Pompéi, *House of Sallust, plan.*

modernes par le portrait fidèle des monuments demeurés presque
intacts jusque dans les parties les plus fugitives de leurs décorations
brillantes.[33]

188

Figure 10.5   Mazois, Ruines de Pompéi, *House of Sallust, section.*

And so in discussing, for example, the House of Sallust, Mazois' shows the way that, in the pergola garden, the painted walls with their painted plants, painted birds, and painted fountain contribute to the charm of the whole (Fig 10.4 & 5):

> Les parois du mur, qui entoure de deux côtés ce délicieux réduit, sont peintes avec une goût exquis . . . la décoration . . . rapelle cette pièce de la maison de Pline en Toscane: "ou l'on voyait des oiseaux perchés sur des ramaux verdoyants et au-dessous une petite fontaine dont l'eau tombait dans un bassin avec un agréable 'murmur'."[34]

The same attention to the indissoluble effect of architecture and decoration is evident when Mazois describes the peristyle of the house with the rooms that surround it. The group must, he says, be, "un appartement secret, consacré au plaisir et à l'amour"[35] with its:

> Cabinets: dans l'un d'eux existe encore une peinture qui indique assez

la destination de ces boudoirs; on y voit Mars enchaîné dans les bras de Vénus, tandis que l'amour joue en riant avec les armes terribles du dieu de combats.[36] . . . Cette decoration est d'un goût délicieux; les ornements ôtent au fond noir, ce qu'a de trop lugubre cette colour dont on fit choix, sans doute, a fin de donner plus d'éclat au tient et aux vêtements des femmes admises dans ce volupteux séjour. . . . Le tableau au fond de la cour représente . . . Actéon découvrant Diane au bain, et . . . le même personage dévoré par ses chiens. Ce sujet semble avoir été choisi, et placé dans l'endroit le plus apparent pour avertir tout indiscret qui eût tenté de pénétrer les mystères de ce lieu des châtiments inévitables qui l'attendraient.[37]

Mazois returned finally to Paris in 1820 (where he built little, this little however including the Passages Choiseul and Saucède); he died in 1826. The remainder of the century saw a continuous stream of studies and reconstructions from the students of the Villa Medici[38] – but none of this work, though, goes beyond Mazois in conception. Perhaps inevitably, due to the particular requirements of the *Envois*,[39] the concentration was on the details of the orders, painted decoration, or monumental groups of buildings, such as the forum[40] or the theatre district,[41] but not with the city as a whole. Not until the turn of the century did *pensionnaires* concern themselves with the study of a complete[42] town with, most notably, Tony Garnier's study of Tusculum of 1903 and Jean Hulot's reconstruction of Selinus of 1904–1906.[43] Of prime importance for the 20th century is the work of Tony Garnier.

Tony Garnier

Tony Garnier (1869–1948) seems to us now to stand between two worlds – the world of the great French academic system of architectural teaching and practice, represented by the École des Beaux-Arts in Paris and the Villa Medici in Rome – and the world of the beginning of what we now call Modern architecture. Garnier's time as *pensionnaire* at the Villa Medici, between 1900 and 1904, precisely marks this transition.[44] In the first year of his tenure, in addition to the required (but according to the academy, inadequate)[45] study of an ancient monument (in his case the *Tabularium*) Garnier submitted drawings of an Industrial City invented for a site near Lyons ("a daub of pencil marks", reported the academy).[46] Garnier's final *envoi*, too, was an urban study – a restoration of the town of Tusculum (which for Garnier had the advantage of very few remains to constrain him).[47] That restoration (Fig. 10.6) clearly borrowed from Pompeii, where Garnier's fellow *pensionnaire*, Chifflot, had made restoration drawings of the House of the Centenary in the previous year.[48]

Study of ancient cities by the *pensionnaires* of the Villa Medici was, as we

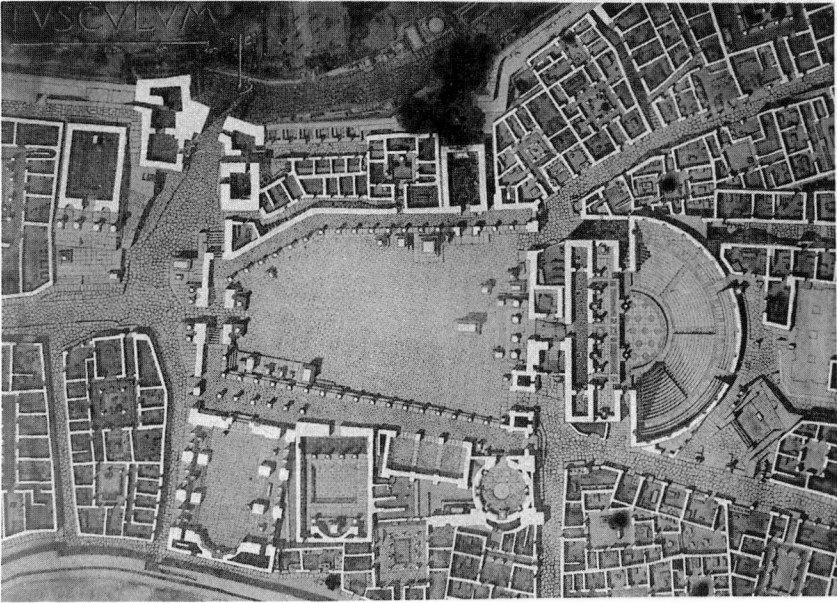

Figure 10.6   Tony Garnier, *Tusculum.*

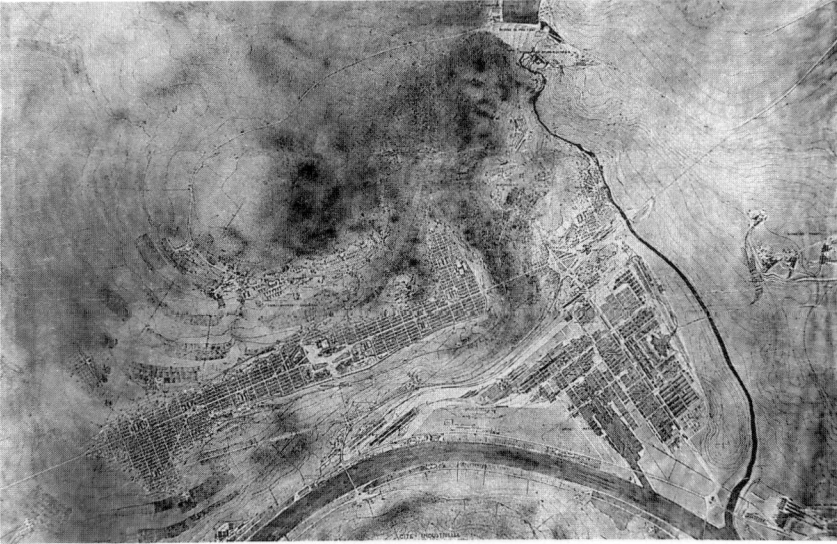

Figure 10.7   Tony Garnier, Cité industrielle.

have seen, part of a continuing trend by the turn of the century (and was to continue with studies of Delos, 1910, and Priene, 1911)[49] but Garnier, in his final *envoi*, went beyond the study and restoration of the ancient city and presented again, in a revised and enlarged and form, his *Cité industrielle* (Fig. 10.7).

Following his return to his home town of Lyons in 1904, a further enlarged and revised version of the *Cité industrielle* reached publication in 1917,[50] this publication now being augmented by built work carried out in Lyons, presented uniformly as if part of the development of the earlier proposals. The house and studio, of 1909–10, that Garnier had built for himself at Saint-Rambert, is included in the plates (Fig. 10.8),[51] a house that, without columns or classical detail, is an abstraction of a Pompeian house. Garnier's *atelier* is as symmetrically related to its atrium as, say, the *tablinum* of the House of the Faun to its atrium and peristyle, and the house is photographed (plates 121 and 122 of *Une cité industrielle*) with all the attention to ways in which a sense of light and greenery suffuses from atrium and garden that so delighted Mazois at the House of Sallust. A half-size nude statue of Madame Garnier facing the atrium seems to play the same rôle in suggesting the intimacy of domestic life

Figure 10.8   Tony Garnier, house in the Cité industrielle.

as does the painting of Mars and Venus in Mazois's description of the peristyle at the House of Sallust (p. 189 above).

In the 1917 publication, the industrial and public elements, too, are supplemented by examples from Garnier's practice in Lyon; but the real point here is not the separate elements, but that *all* elements are presented together as part of a total organization – the visual equivalent of a social organization – and there is indeed a social as well as a cultural programme in the work. Garnier proposes the inscription of passages from Zola's *Travail* on the walls of his "Chamber of Assemblies" (*Travail* was first published Garnier was searching for a topic for his work at the Villa Medici).[52]

Anthony Vidler has discussed this social programme in the catalogue of the 1990 exhibition of Garnier's work at the Centre Pompidou[53] but my concern here is to note that Garnier presents the city as an organic whole, a collective work of art – proceeding, in a way reminiscent of Vitruvius, from the establishment of the settlement on its site, to the various types of public buildings: the assembly halls, the sports buildings, the schools, the factories, each finding a place within a structure articulated by streets and alleys, with individual houses, like Garnier's own, offering at once a retreat from, and by analogy, a connection with, the organism as a whole.

Garnier's period at the Villa Medici had been a turbulent one. The inscription on his 1901 drawing of the *Tabularium*, "Ainsi que toutes les architectures reposant sur des principes faux l'architecture antique fut une erreur. La vérité seule est belle",[54] is indicative (and duly enraged the academy). Garnier's pugnaciously critical attitude to antiquity released him from its sway. What he did take from antiquity became his own.

Le Corbusier

Garnier's work was widely transmitted to the architectural world through the most influential architectural text of the 20th century, Le Corbusier's *Vers une architecture* of 1923, which presented, with approving comments, plans and perspectives of the housing areas of the *Cité*.[55] Le Corbusier had met Tony Garnier in Lyons in 1907 and tells us:

> He had won the "Grand Prix d'Architecture" and it was from Rome that he sent his project the "ville industrielle". This man discerned the approach of a new architecture based on social phenomena. His plans show great sophistication. They stand at the end of a hundred years of architectural evolution in France.[56]

Four years after that meeting, Le Corbusier was himself in Pompeii,[57] and responding in a way that is close to the abstracted interpretation of the atrium

193

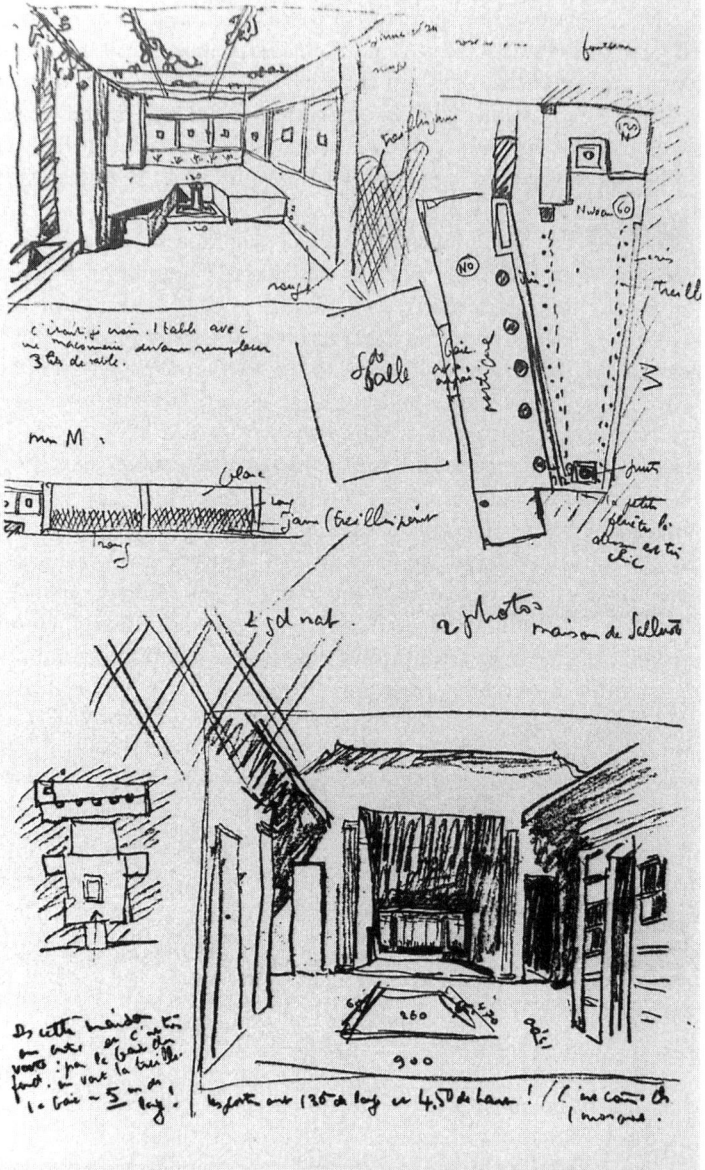

Figure 10.9   Le Corbusier, House of Sallust. Dessin extrait de l'oeuvre complete, © DACS
1995. Taken from Tony Garnier: l'oeuvre complète *(Paris, 1989, p.19).*

house that Garnier created at Saint-Rambert. Le Corbusier describes his experience of the House of the Silver Wedding thus:

> And then you are in the atrium; four columns (four *cylinders*) shoot upwards towards the shade of the roof . . . but at the far end is the brilliance of the garden seen through the peristyle which spreads out this light with a large gesture, distributes it and accentuates it, stretching widely from left to right. . . . Our elements are walls. . . . The walls are in full brilliant light or in half shade or in full shadow . . . your symphony is made. . . . Have respect for walls. The Pompeian did not cut up his wallspaces. He was devoted to wall spaces and loved light. . . . The impression of light is extended outside by cylinders (I hardly like to say columns, a worn out word)[58]

Pavillon de l'Esprit Nouveau

Le Corbusier conducted much of his research, in architecture, in painting, and in what he called the aesthetics of modern life, through the pages of the review

Figure 10.10   Le Corbusier, Pavilion de l'esprit nouveau L2(8)1–3, © DACS 1995.

195

Figure 10.11   Le Corbusier, immeubles-villas, *Pavilion de l'esprit nouveau,   L2(8)1–19, © DACS 1995.*

Figure 10.12   Le Corbusier, Pavilion de l'esprit nouveau (interior) L2(8)1–15, © DACS 1995.

L'Esprit Nouveau, produced in Paris between 1920 and 1925. The *parti pris* of the review (from June 1922, Le Corbusier[59] and the painter Amédée Ozenfant were directors) was summarized in a tiny exhibition pavilion, the Pavillon de l'Esprit Nouveau in the Paris Exposition des Arts Décoratifs of 1925 (Fig. 10.10). Designed by Le Corbusier, and incorporating his own version of a *Cité industrielle*, the pavilion itself was in the form of a prototypical apartment dwelling, arranged round a hanging garden. Within the pavilion is presented a diorama of the city, of which the apartment blocks – Le Corbusier called them *immeubles-villas* (Fig. 10.11) – were the elements, the *insulae*, of the city. As well as this presentation at the city scale were shown the paintings, rugs, furniture and equipment conforming to that new spirit, *l'esprit nouveau*, which Le Corbusier and his collaborators were exploring and promoting through their magazine – the final issue of which served as a catalogue for the pavillion.[60] "We were not concerned with frivolities," wrote Le Corbusier; "we went from the everyday object to the urbanisation of great cities – an enormous undertaking."[61] Within the pavilion, arranged around the atrium-like *jardin suspendu*, as in a Pompeian house, or Garnier's studio at Saint-Rambert, the visitor's mind was focused on the one hand, by means of the diorama, to the scale of the city of which the pavilion was a microcosm, and on the other to the scale of the objects of everyday life – most particularly to works of painting and sculpture (Fig. 10.12):

> Painting: We have placed on the wall-paintings of Picasso, Braque, Léger, Gris, Ozenfant, Jeanneret, and arranged sculptures by Lipchitz; easel paintings in frames and free standing sculpture, independent of the wall. We are not, at the moment, partisans of fresco painting . . . It is better that painting or sculpture is not made to order but is a direct product of the imagination. We want to create an architectural terrain made from matter, from light, and from proportion, in which works with high emotional potential are at ease. We detach painting and sculpture from the wall so that they are free to act with the charge that they contain.[62]

These "purist" paintings (as their authors christened them) presented an imaginative reflection of images of everyday and industrial life, surely the equivalent in the Pompeian house of paintings of "poultry, eggs, vegetables, fruit",[63] "the battles of Troy and the wanderings of Ulysses over the countryside", or "Mars locked in the arms of Venus". This equivalence is not, of course, to be taken as an exact one; in what is for Le Corbusier a characteristic strategy of disengagement, or articulation, of elements, the wall and its modulation of light[64] are separated from the figuration of representational painting. The continuum between the macrocosm of the city and the microcosm of the dwelling (and the imaginative world re-created through its decoration), so powerfully presented by Mazois, has been taken apart and reassembled. The desire for that continuum, though, remains. In the introduction to his *Aspects of antiquity* Moses Finley cites John Jones, in turn citing Fustel de Coulanges: "Rien dans les temps moderne ne leur [Gréce et Rome] ressemble. Riens dans l'avenir ne pourra leur ressembler".[65] The responses, in the modern world, to the ruins of Pompeii that I have discussed may show resemblances to the ancient city but, to echo Mazois's comment on Palladio's atria, each "must be regarded in some way as a new invention". One might say that it is when most thoroughly and critically transformed, in the work of a Le Corbusier or a Garnier, that responses to the ancient city have had most resonance. The *Nachleben* of the ancient world does not flow simply as a stream.

Acknowledgements

Figures 10.6, 10.7 and 10.8 were taken from *Tony Garnier. L'oeuvre complète*, Paris: Centre Georges Pompidou, 1989. Figures 10.9, 10.10, 10.11and 10.12 were taken from *Le Corbusier and Pierre Jeanneret. The complete architectural works. Volume 1, 1910–1929*, London: Thames and Hudson, 1964, but are the original property of the Foundation Le Corbusier in Paris.

Notes

1. S. Maffei, *Tre lettere del Signor Marchese Scipione Maffei* (Verona, 1748), cited in F. Bologna, The rediscovery of Herculaneum and Pompeii in the artistic culture of Europe in the eighteenth century, in *Rediscovering Pompeii* (Rome, 1990), p. 85. The passage continues: "by excavating and leaving everything in place the city would become an unequalled museum".
2. M. I. Finley, The ancient city: from Fustel de Coulanges to Max Weber and beyond, in *Economy and society in ancient Greece*, eds B. D. Shaw & R. P. Saller (London, 1983), p. 3.
3. *Ibid.*, p. 4, draws the distinction between "'town' in the narrow sense and 'city-state' in a political sense." The ambiguity of the word city seems appropriate here and I shall use it throughout even though, mostly, it is indeed the physical structure, the "town", that I shall be discussing.
4. A summary of the history of excavation at Pompeii is given in E. C. C. Corti, *The destruction and resurrection of Pompeii and Herculaneum* (London, 1951). The basic source is G. Fiorelli (ed.), *Pompeianarum antiquitatum historia*, 3 vols. (Naples, 1860–64). F. Furchheim, *Bibliografia di Pompei, Ercolano e Stabia*, 2nd edn (Naples, 1972), has a chronological list of publications, xiii–xxx. C. Grell, *Herculanum et Pompéi dans les récits des voyageurs Français du XVIIIᵉ siècle* (Naples, 1982), pp. 212–19, has a useful table showing excavation and publication in the 18th century.
5. There is a necrology *Notice sur M. Mazois* by Artaud in the posthumous vol. iv of *Les ruines des Pompéi* (1837), and biographical notes in *Pompéi: travaux et envois des*

architectes Français au XIXe siècle (Paris, 1980), pp. 291–2. F & J. B. Piranesi, *Antiquités de Pompeia*, 2 vols, (Paris, 1804), might be said to herald Mazois's work but, compared to Mazois, is neither complete nor systematic; there is no text.

6. Vol. i, *Voie, tombeaux, murailles et porte de la ville* (1812); vol. ii, *Habitations* (1824). The work was completed posthumously, vol. iii, (1829); and vol. iv (1838).

7. W. Gell & J. P. Gandy, *Pompeiana* (London, 1817–1819), pp. ix–x: "Pompeii was begun upon in 1748; and it may at first excite our surprise that from this date to the present day, no work has appeared in the English language upon the subject of its domestic antiquities, except a few pages by Sir William Hamilton.".

8. *Ibid.*, p. xviii. The passage continues: "The figure reading a volume, the chair upon which she sits, the footstool and scrinium, or capsa, for manuscripts at her feet. The marble table, and implements for writing; the pavement and distant building, are all from the same source."

9. *Ibid.*, p. xviii.

10. The reader is referred to a plan at the end of the work for the numbering of the houses. In fact the numbering in the general plan at the end of vol. iv, by H.Roux *ainé*, 1837, does not correspond to the numbers in this passage; no. 46, for instance, is *not* the House of Sallust!.

11. I.e. The House of Sallust (VI.2.4).

12. F. Mazois, *Les ruines de Pompéi*, 4 vols, (Paris, 1812–38), vol. ii, p. 35: "Cette planche, qui sert de frontispiece à la seconde partie, représente l'entrée d'une maison antique. La disposition de la porte, et l'inscription en mosaïque placée sur le seuil, se remarquent dans plusieurs habitations. Les pilastres et leurs chapiteaux appartiennent à la maison n°.27; l'entablement et les stucs qui lui le décorent, les peintures qui ornent la frise intérieure, le portique du fond, et plusieurs autres détails, ont été pris de divers édifices. La fontaine se voit dans la maison n°.46, dite d'Actéon; le motif du jardin qui fait le fond du tableau m'a été fourni par une peinture existante dans le même lieu; les deux termes sont conservés dans le Musée des Études à Naples; enfin tous les éléments de cette composition sont antiques; et l'arrangement dans lequel je les offre donne une idée exacte de l'entrée d'une des maisons principales de Pompéi." There is a similar composition at the heading to the Chapter, Essai sur les habitations des anciens Romains, vol. ii, p. 3, described by Mazois as a "Muséum composé de fragments et d'objets antiques du cabinet de la Reine, existant au palais Royale de Naples avant 1815". vol. ii, p. 102.

13. Gell & Gandy, *Pompeiana*, p. xviii.

14. Pausanius, 10.4.1. It was, of course, the absence of these elements that prevented Panopeus from being considered a city; cf. Finley, The ancient city, pp. 3–4.

15. Palladio, *Quattro Libri* 2.12: "the city is as it were but a great house, and, on the contrary, a . . . house a little city."

16. Finley, The ancient city, p. 3.

17. English translations are taken from Frank Granger's translation in the Loeb edition (1931).

18. E.g. from Vitruvius himself: 7.11–14, preface.

19. Written in the mid 15th century, first printed 1486; quotations are taken from the most recent English translation by J. Rykwert, N. Leach & R. Tavernor: L. B. Alberti, *Leon Battista Alberti: on the art of building in ten books* (Cambridge, Mass. & London 1988).

20. Echoed in 5.2: "The atrium, salon, and so on should relate in the same way to the

house as do the forum and public square to the city" Cf. Palladio, no. 15 above.

21. E.g. Alberti: "Examples of ancient temples and theatres have survived that may teach us as much as any professor, but I see – not without sorrow – these very buildings being despoiled every day. . . . No building of the ancients that had attracted praise . . . but I immediately examined it carefully, to see what I could learn from it. Therefore I never stopped exploring, considering and measuring everything, and comparing the information through line drawings, until I had grasped and understood fully what each had to contribute in terms of ingenuity or skill . . ." (6.1). Cf. Palladio: "I . . . set myself to search into the relics of the ancient edifices that, in spite of time, and the cruelty of the Barbarians, yet remain . . . and . . . began very minutely and with the utmost diligence to measure every one of their parts" Bk I, preface.

22. R. Wittkower, *Architectural principles in the age of humanism* (London, 1962), pp. 21, 65, 110.

23. A. Palladio, *The four books of architecture* (New York, 1965), preface.

24. *Ibid.*

25. Mazois, *Les ruines de Pompéi*, vol. ii, *Essai sur les habitations*, 20: "Les descriptions que Vitruve [6.3, 4], Varron [*De ling. Lat.* 4] et Festus [*De signific. verb.*], ont données de l'atrium deviennent extrêmement claires dès que l'on a vu quelque ruines de maisons antiques, sur-tout celles de la ville de Pompéi; mais avant que l'on en eût decouvert aucune, il était difficile de comprehendre ces auteurs. Cependant Palladio avait deviné la forme, la construction, ainsi que les principales parties de l'atrium, et il en fit l'application aux edifices modernes d'une manière si ingénieuse, qu'elle peut être regardée en quelque sorte comme une invention nouvelle." The *locus classicus* for Palladio's atrium designs is the convent of the Carità in Venice: "I have endeavoured to make this house like those of the ancients; and therefore I have made a Corinthian atrium to it" Palladio, *The four books of architecture,* II.VI: cf. Wittkower, *Architectural principles in the age of humanism*, pp. 78–81.

27. Cf. Gell & Gandy, *Pompeiana*: "the French, during their occupation of Naples, laid open the walls around the city [continues in footnote: 'the walls in October 1812; the tombs in the March following'], the greater portion of the Street of the Tombs, with the Forum and Basilica. . . . At this period Mons. Mazois . . . began his splendid work, which promises if ever finished, to leave little to be desired upon the subject of the architectural details of ornaments" (pp. x–xi), "the excavations are conducted in a regular manner, rather with the laudable intention of laying open the city than of searching for treasures" (p. xii).

27. Bologna, The rediscovery of Herculaneum and Pompeii, p. 79.

28. Most concisely summarized in F. Saxl & R. Wittkower, *British art and the Mediterranean* (Oxford, 1969), pp. 78–79: "Neo-Greek Architecture", see also J. M. Crook, *The Greek revival: neo-classical attitudes in British architecture 1760–1870* (London, 1972), pp. 96–7: "thus the Greek Revival [in Britain] was launched within the context of the Romantic landscape."

29. Also conveniently summarized in Saxl & Wittkower, *British art and the Mediterranean,* p. 73–74: "The rise of a new style in decoration"; see also M. Praz, *On neoclassicism* (London, 1969), ch. 3, The antiquities of Herculaneum.

30. I have discussed this question in M. Goalen, Schinkel & Durand: the case of the Altes Museum, in *Karl Friedrich Schinkel: a universal man*, ed. M. Snodin (1991) pp. 27–35.

31. Mazois, *Les ruines de Pompéi*, vol. i, p. 5. Impatience with the products of the Academy of Naples is repeated at vol. ii, p. 62, n. 4: "l'académie de Naples a mis au jour, en 1808, un volume grand atlas contenant environ cent planches de peintures et de mosaïques sans explication. C'est là tout ce qui a été publié à Naples sur Pompéi."

32. *Ibid.*, vol. i, p. 6.

33. *Ibid.*, vol. iii, introduction, p. x.

34. *Ibid.*, vol. ii, p. 78.

35. *Ibid.*, pp. 76–7.

36. *Ibid.*, p. 79.

37. *Ibid.*

38. Mazois had not been a *pensionnaire* of the Académie de France at the Villa Medici (he had followed his friend A. Leclère, a winner of the Grand Prix, to Rome in 1808 but had moved to Naples after only a brief stay) although, through the good offices of the director of the Villa Medici, he had lodged at *S. Trinità dei Monti* during the engraving of plates for the *Ruines de Pompéi*; see the biography of Mazois in *Pompéi: travaux et envois des architectes Français au XIXe siècle* (Paris, 1980), pp. 291–2. There is a list of *envois* representing Pompeii between 1818 and 1937 in L. Mascoli, P. Pinon, G. Vallet, F. Zevi, Pompéi ou "L'antiquité face à face", in *Pompéi: travaux et envois des architectes Français au XIXe siècle* (Paris, 1980), pp. 82–83.

39. *Ibid.*, pp. 35 f.: "Les envois de Rome".

40. e.g. F-E. Callet in 1823–24: *Ibid.*, pp. 115–27.

41. e.g. P-É. Bonnet in 1859: *Ibid.*, pp. 178–84.

42. Although monumental urban groupings had continued to be a subject of study: e.g. H-P. Nénot, Delos, 1882; Victor Laloux, Olympia, 1883; Albert Tournaire, Delphi, 1894; Emmanuel Pontremoli, Pergamon, 1895: L'École Nationale Supérieure des Beaux-Arts, *Paris—Rome—Athens: le voyage en Grèce des architectes Français aux XIXe et XXe siècles* (Paris, 1982), pp. 258–65, 266–74, 306–13, respectively.

43. *Ibid.*, pp. 314–323.

44. A. Vidler, L'Acropole moderne, in *Tony Garnier: l'oeuvre complète*, (Ouvrage publié à l'occasion de l'exposition "Tony Garnier (1896–1948)"; Paris, 1989), p. 71 speaks of: "un tradition en crise, un modernisme avançant masqué sous l'académisme".

45. P. Pinon, Le béton et la Méditerranée, in *Tony Garnier: l'oeuvre complète*, p. 104.

46. "grand barbouillage de crayons, pompeusement qualifié de ville industrielle," *Compte rendu des séances de l'Académie des Beaux-Arts*, cited in Pinon, Le béton et la Méditerranée, p. 105.

47. Tusculum had been published by L. Canina, *Descrizione dell'antico Tusculo dell'architetto Cav. Luigi Canina* (Rome, 1841). For Garnier's *envoi*, see *Tony Garnier. L'oeuvre complète*, pp. 42–5. C. Pawlowski, *Tony Garnier et les débuts de l'urbanisme fonctionnel en France* (Paris, 1967), p. 65, cites Garnier's report on the *envoi*: "assez de ruines pour se faire une vision de cette ville très pittoresque et merveilleusement situé et pas assez, heureusement, pour faire une reconstitution".

48. *Pompéi: travaux et envois des architectes Français*, pp. 246–51. Chifflot was congratulated on the way in which: "les peintures ornementales qui couvrent les murs . . . sont exprimés avec une intensité, un éclat, une virtuosité remarquable". (*Compte-rendu de l'Institut,* 11 July 1903, cited *ibid.*, 246.) Garnier's own debt to Pompeii (and to Herculaneum) was noted by the academy: "[Garnier] s'est inspiré des plans de Pompéi et de ce qui est connu d'Herculanum . . . il a cherché à faire naître

l'impression qui produirait l'ensemble d'une ville antique" (Archives de l'Académie de France à Rome, 1904, cited in *Pompéi: travaux et envois des architectes Français*, p. 43.

49. L'École nationale supérieure des Beaux-Arts, *Paris–Rome–Athens*, pp. 324–31 (Delos) and 332–37 (Priene).

50. The publishing history is discussed in Centre Georges Pompidou, *Tony Garnier: l'oeuvre complète* (Paris, 1989), pp. 45–7.

51. Discussed in *ibid.*, p. 105 and illustrated on pp. 110–13.

52. Vidler, L'Acropole moderne, p. 77 and n. 18.

53. Vidler, L'Acropole moderne.

54. MS, Procès-verbaux de l'Académie des Beaux-Arts, 20 June 1901, cited in D. D. Egbert, *The Beaux-Arts tradition in French architecture* (Princeton, NJ, 1980), p. 91, n. 18.

55. Le Corbusier, *Towards a new architecture* (London, 1946), pp. 51–3.

56. J. Petit, *Le Corbusier lui-même* (Geneva, 1970), p. 28.

57. G. Gresleri, *Le Corbusier, viaggio in oriente* (Venice, 1984), pp. 326–35 reproduces Le Corbusier's drawings and photographs from 1911; p. 65 reproduces the plan of Pompeii from Le Corbusier's 1909 edn of Baedeker's *L'Italie des Alpes à Naples*, showing where he had made drawings and where photographs. Le Corbusier draws and photographs (p. 334) the outdoor *triclinium* of the House of Sallust with the treillage so admired by Mazois (Fig. 10.9).

58. Le Corbusier, *Towards a new architecture*, pp. 169–72.

59. Or rather Ch-E. Jeanneret. Jeanneret had not yet adopted the pseudonym Le Corbusier for all his activities: his articles on architecture, though, had appeared under this pseudonym since the first, October 1920, issue of *L'Esprit Nouveau*.

60. *Almanach d'Architecture Moderne* (Paris, 1925), described in its advice *au lecteur* as the *"livre d'or"* of the pavilion. A copy of the pavilion was reconstructed in Bologna; see G. Gresleri, *L'Esprit Nouveau* (Milan, 1979).

61. Le Corbusier, *Précisions sur un état présent de l'architecture et de l'urbanisme* (Paris, 1930), p. 186.

62. Le Corbusier, *L'almanach d'architecture moderne* (Paris, 1925), p. 145.

63. Vitruvius 6.7.4.

64. Compare Le Corbusier's description of the House of the Silver Wedding, above p. 195, with the following passage discussing the Pavillon de l'Esprit Nouveau: "We have pursued researches on polychromy designed to show that control of light that is the root of our architectural research. . . . Physiology of sensations; red, blue, yellow, etc., fixed sensations. Shadow, penumbra, full light: the same. One composes architecturally thus. . .. Light is the root of architectural organisation" (Le Corbusier, *L'almanach d'architecture moderne*, p. 145).

65. M. I. Finley, *Aspects of antiquity* (Harmondsworth, 1972), p. 13.

11

"Slouching towards Rome":
Mussolini's imperial vision

Luisa Quartermaine

Non si può concepire la storia d'Italia separata da quella di Roma.

"One cannot conceive the history of Italy separate from that of Rome." So begins an essay written by a 14–year-old Italian schoolboy in 1939. The essay goes on to explain that the material power Rome exercised over the world implied a spiritual supremacy expressed in a unified legal system as well as a common language and a "universal" culture, so that Romanity and Humanity could be seen as interchangeable concepts. "Even today", the essay concludes:

> in line with her tradition and according to her true mission and the purity of our race, the new Rome sets the foundations of a new civilization. History, great teacher of life (*maestra di vita*) teaches us that whenever Italy decays, all horizons darken, but when Italy is reborn in a new season, the whole sky burns bright with the light of her civilization.

I found these handwritten pages inside a pamphlet entitled *Civiltà Romana*, one of several commissioned by the Istituto Nazionale di Cultura Fascista[1] from Pietro de Francisci, and it is clear that, in order to cope with an unpalatable subject, the poor schoolboy had looked for inspiration in this pamphlet (from which most of his ideas were lifted).

Fascism initially presented itself as a movement which was above political parties, being concerned above all else with promoting national unity and strength. Rome provided a convenient model for organization and combat. Four large marble maps placed on the wall of the Basilica of Maxentius in Rome recalled the progressive conquests of the ancient Roman empire and implied that history might repeat itself. That the two "histories" (the Roman and the contemporary) should mirror each other had been a familiar theme since the 1920s with publications such as Tito Vezio's "Due marce su Roma"

203

(two marches on Rome): Julius Caesar's and Benito Mussolini's.[2]

The value of Roman history as a source of inspiration for contemporary Italy had been pointed out by Mussolini himself in a lecture delivered in 1926 at the University for Foreigners in Perugia. The lecture had a significant title: "Roma antica sul mare" (the seapower of ancient Rome).[3] Both the date, and the delivery of the lecture to a foreign audience, are important. Mussolini, by then in the fourth year of his government, had just emerged from the crisis of the so-called "Aventine secession". The name was derived from the famous incident involving the struggle between the Roman plebs and the patricians in the 5th century BC; it referred to the decision taken by parliamentary deputies opposed to fascism to leave the chamber of deputies *en masse* in protest against the killing by fascist thugs, in June 1924, of the socialist member of Parliament Giacomo Matteotti. Their aim was to provoke a "destabilization", and eventual overthrow of fascism, but Mussolini's reaction to the crisis (which lasted for over six months) and to four different attempts made on his life, was to concentrate power in his own hands and to move towards an extreme form of authoritarianism. This process was effectively completed by the end of 1926.

It was Mussolini's intention that internal social and political integration should be followed by expansion in Africa. The conviction strongly held by Mussolini that Italy's destiny lay in East Africa, and above all in the Mediterranean, necessitated that, as he put it, the Mediterranean be "converted from an Anglo-Saxon lake into a Latin sea".[4] Mussolini himself justified his intentions by linking the future of Italy to its past (namely Roman history) and, in particular, by relating his own policy of expansion to the successful attempts made by Rome to extend by sea the superiority already gained on land.

His lecture clearly had propaganda value in this context, and the topic chosen fitted this pattern. After tracing the origin of Rome's strength to her maritime interests, Mussolini pointed out that the Roman empire, although at its peak under Augustus, "was really born during those years of the launching of the first Roman battle fleet".[5] He then recounted in general terms the outline of the three Punic wars, until the destruction of Carthage by Scipio the Younger.

In the lecture there were also minor, yet pointed, references to episodes that echoed contemporary events. There was mention, for instance, of discussions among the Romans of the pros and cons of war, and the Romans who favoured war were referred to as "interventisti", a word with a familiar ring for some in the audience; Mussolini had been himself among the "interventisti" in similar discussions preceding the First World War. The drop in value of the Roman *as*, related to financial constraints after the first Punic war, was also cited in the lecture, perhaps a reminder of the contemporary economic difficulties which sparked off, at the end of 1926, Mussolini's political revaluation of the lira, the so-called *quota 90*. But, above all, behind the historical reminiscences were the political inclinations and intentions of its author and especially his determination to forge a new type of Italian. As Mussolini explained:

It would no longer be a question of grumbling against the sceptical, mandolin-playing Italians, but rather of creating a new kind of man who was tough, determined, strong-willed, a fighter, a latter-day legionary of Caesar for whom nothing was impossible.[6]

The Italian conquest of Africa had started well before Mussolini's time. It spread over a period of 60 years, and developed in three different stages: the years between 1870 and 1896 saw the Italian occupation of Eritrea and Somalia. This was stopped abruptly by the defeat at Adua. Tripolitania was conquered as a result of the war with Turkey in 1911–12, and finally, in 1935, Italy took Ethiopia and proclaimed the empire on 9 May.

Scipio and the battle of Zama became a popular theme throughout fascism to celebrate such victories and was a subject also exploited through the medium of cinema. In 1936 *Lo Schermo* (a well known film periodical of the time) published an anonymous article under the title "Il cinema per l'impero" (cinema for the empire) which made clear how cinema could serve the regime through a film which:

> could describe Rome, not the papier-mâché Rome of historical films, but the rugged, rural, and warlike Rome that conquered the world and from there moved on to represent the new vision of the empire on the seven fated hills of Rome, underlining the Caesar-like as well as human and socially revolutionary qualities of Mussolini's creation.[7]

Among the films which best portrayed the spirit of this article is *Scipione l'Africano* by Carmine Gallone, an ambitious film which aimed at succeeding both as spectacle and as political propaganda. It was planned just before the African campaign (and shot immediately after the final victory) with the involvement of Paoluccio di Galboli, President of ENIC and of LUCE (L'Unione Cinema Educativo), and through him of the ministries of popular culture, of the interior and of war (which sent infantry and cavalry troops to help as "comparse" or walk-on actors). The film took seven months to make (from August 1936 to March 1937), a long period by comparison with the average film. Although the film was not shot in Africa, but near Sabaudia, according to Luigi Freddi (director general for cinematography), Gallone had at his disposal enormous resources: 10 million lire, 12,000 infantry and cavalry, the studios of Cines and Titanus (the most important film companies), and of Cinecittà, which was then just beginning operations. Music was by a well known Italian composer, Ildebrando Pizzetti, and a "zoom" for special effects came from Britain, lent to Gallone by Alexander Korda. There were also 38 elephants on set.[8] Why such a display of money and resources? Because, as Luigi Freddi explained in an article in *Il Popolo d'Italia* (Mussolini's newspaper): "no other subject could signify better than this historical event the intimate union between the glory of the past and the brave achievement of our era".[9]

A parallel between the Roman and the fascist conquest in Africa was thus established through the film. Moreover, in showing that the Carthaginian people were less civilized than the Roman – thus "justifying" the presence of Rome in northern Africa – *Scipio* justified by analogy Mussolini's presence in Ethiopia. As the same Luigi Freddi claimed, rather rhetorically:

> The political aim of *Scipione l'Africano* is not banal propaganda, it is the expression of the transcendent continuity in our history which transmits into the Black Shirt legionary the living and vibrant echo of the legionary at Zama.[10]

Another and more practical purpose of the film was, no doubt, to galvanize the Italian cinema industry, an operation which was crucial after the economic sanctions imposed against Italy by the League of Nations in 1935. This economic purpose was not lost on Mussolini who, when previewing the film, admired along with its historical qualities, the fact that it was "achieved with the exclusive use of Italian people and resources".[11] He was, however, less convinced about other virtues in the film, which he found conspicuous by their absence; he declared the film too solemn a reconstruction of Roman history to be entertaining. He also disliked the main actor and commented: "Had he [Scipio] been as wet as this actor looks, I do not think he would have won many battles!"[12]

Even so, no other film received the official sanction granted by the regime to *Scipione l'Africano*: in the same summer of 1937 – predictably – it won the Mussolini Prize at the Venice Film Festival and the whole of the June–July issue of *Bianco e Nero* (one of the most prestigious film journals) was devoted to it. The film was also recommended for viewing in schools where pupils were encouraged to write essays with titles based on the film. Some of these essays were printed in the August 1939 issue of *Bianco e Nero* with an introduction by Giuseppe Bottai in which he noted that for the students the hero of the film:

> becomes the substitute for another hero . . . In fact, it is the latter that occupies entirely the minds of the viewers and into which the former dissolves. For the children, it is not Scipio who is the Roman hero, it is Mussolini. Through a subconscious power of transposition, Scipio's actions become Mussolini's. The analogy becomes identity.[13]

The reasons are not difficult to understand. The film opens with a shot the Roman forum where Scipio is talking to a mass of people. His speech here (and more so those he delivers later in the film, in Sicily, to the soldiers ready to embark for Carthage), as well as his manner, rhetoric, and intonation, are all clearly reminiscent of Mussolini's. He is applauded by the people, is seen mixing with them, is seen talking to his own children, in images that show him as father and protector of the nation. In shots devoted to the preparation of the war the voluntary troops that gather from all parts and march through the countryside strongly recall the 1922 march on Rome. The battle itself, however, with thousands of "real" troops (not to mention the 38 elephants) is the climax of the story. The shout after the victory, "We have avenged Cannae", is intended to mean "We have avenged Adua" (the infamous Italian defeat in Africa in 1896).

But *Scipione l'Africano* was not successful as a film. Certainly it was not the great "imperial film" that the regime had hoped for; it represented not the reality of conquest, but the myth of conquest, not the reality of empire, but the dream of an African empire, as a panacea. By 1943, in *Difesa dell'intelligenza*, Alberto Savinio was warning against the unqualified use of history or, as he put it:

> the bad advice given by imitation . . . those silly suggestions offered by badly written, badly read and badly interpreted history. Only intelligence can demonstrate the stupidity of wanting to repeat the war between Rome and Carthage.[14]

Meanwhile, regimentation and militarization had become increasingly the norm of fascist propaganda, particularly during the conquest of Ethiopia, for which the regime looked again for inspiration as well as justification to imperial Rome. In order "to help the Italian people to understand and keep alive their very essence [*spirito*]",[15] in 1936, the Accademia dei Lincei began a comprehensive study on the age of Augustus with essays on religion, art and literature as well as the political and juridical system. One of the works to be published as a result of this initiative was *Augustus and his empire* (issued in 1937), followed two years later by *Civiltà Romana*, both by Pietro de Francisci. He explained that, because fascism was "above all the rediscovery of those essential and universal principles of Italian civilization", only through the knowledge and the proper understanding of the history of Italy could it prosper. He wrote:

> I know from experience that there are men who believe in fascism as the spiritual foundation of a new humanism. . . . They also firmly believe that a constructive revolution cannot come out of nothing, but is a projection of new directives added to old elements alive in the blood and soul of a nation. . . . These men feel the need to go back to the origins and simple facts that form the basis of our history and of our spirit.[16]

The Italian people were, accordingly, encouraged to see in fascism, "a continuity reflected in the special mission assigned once again to Italy to offer people their true humanity".[17] The great Augustus, "one of those men who subsume in themselves the story of mankind and whose actions operate in history as a living force",[18] was the first of a long list of great men, Mussolini the last. This is the underlying theme of *Augustus and his empire*. The book begins with the observation that some historical events are of such significance as to signal the end of a period of civilization and the beginning of a new one. One such event, which affected the whole of central and southern Europe, was the changing of Rome from a republic to an imperial power. The book then describes the importance of Rome as founder of a worldwide juridical system and later as the centre of Christianity, which (almost by an act of Providence) followed the same roads opened by the empire. The advent of imperial Rome was the historic moment that informed not only early Christian and medieval history, but modern history as well; and, last but not least, the history of Mussolini's Rome.

The message implicit in the text surfaces in the conclusion of the pamphlet in all its fascist rhetoric:

> This is the ideal ground in which are rooted each of the fundamental elements which fascism, Roman in wisdom and energy, renews, develops and co-ordinates. Never before, like today when confronted with the Mussolinian achievement, solid, wholesome and weighty in its structure, and lucid, balanced and far-sighted in its ideals, have we been aware of the perennial worth of many spiritual values which had their seeds in the empire of Rome and which the Duce, the victorious achiever, has transformed . . . throughout our national life. And not only in national life – this can be said without provoking further a certain anti-Romanism which is becoming fashionable over the Alps – but also universal. In the old tired Europe, befuddled with apocalyptic visions called up by false prophets, a voice was heard . . . This voice is the voice of someone who has no equal in the world today, and who comes, once again, from Rome.[19]

Other aspects of Augustus' policies, which were prominent in the text, had a propaganda value. Above all he was (like Mussolini) presented as having reconstructed society and state after an era of civic disruptions and of civil wars caused by egotism, greed and the general disintegration of moral standards. If Augustus was successful, it was partly through his policy of gradual, yet revolutionary changes which allowed him by degrees to acquire the *imperium proconsulare, infinitum, maius*, and which enabled him, later, to receive the title of *Imperator*. He had in this way started a truly monarchical regime which, under the appearance of unchanged republican institutions, in practice operated above them. Augustus, in this way, became not only the supreme, but the indispensable head of the state. This transformation had been possible only because of the general consensus and support of the people. (Like the school children mentioned before by Giuseppe Bottai,[20] we are meant all the way through to read Mussolini for Augustus.)

Among the changes introduced by Augustus were the organization of a regular navy and the construction in Rome of imposing monuments. These were intended partly to restore the ancient religious values (which included the rehabilitation of the institution of the family as the essential organizational "cell" of Roman society and the promotion of births), partly to focus the attention of the Roman people on their nobility and on the divine origin of the Julian dynasty. Mussolini had similar aspirations.[21]

History and tradition interpreted in this way were ideal grounds for the next battle fascism was to fight, that of the supremacy of the race. The publication of these pamphlets coincided with closer political co-operation between Italy and Germany, and the introduction in Italy of anti-Semitic laws. This might explain why emphasis was placed in the pamphlet on Augustus's "innovative" legislation regarding citizenship, devised to ensure that the Roman people remained a distinct, select and aristocratic race. Mark Antony's attachment to Cleopatra is much criticized in the book, but his "sins" consisted not in having left his rightful wife, but in having broken with tradition: in having "distanced himself from the habits, laws, beliefs of his fathers"; in having "adopted the customs and symbolism of eastern countries"; in having "lived with a foreigner whom he called Isis or, at times, Selene"; in having "donated to foreigners lands and provinces belonging to the Roman people".[22] In contrast to Antony, Octavian represented the true Latin character. His *pietas*, wisdom and clear vision of things and events, his disdain for Dionysus and affection for Apollo (symbol of constant harmony), gave him a special place in the estimation of fascist leaders who stressed the link between his policies and fascist ideology. As *Civiltà Romana* once again explained:

> No other civilization could surpass the one that, from Rome, had twice spread into the world: imperial and Christian Rome. . . . That civilization is alive in us [Italians] not only through the continuity of the race and of our tradition, but also through our past "experience". Italy and imperial Rome must be considered as one entity.[23]

Having established the value of the Italian tradition, the next concern was its preservation. C. Cogni, one of the most forceful (not to say fanatical) supporters of racial policies, in *I valori della stirpe Italiana* stressed that:

> every Italian who is aware of the sublime racial value of Roman and Italian blood should seek to unite with the person who carries the best and most splendid of the ancient Roman blood.[24]

This "person" is soon afterwards described as "good, healthy, tall, strong, and capable of breastfeeding".[25] Above all, she must cultivate the feminine and avoid becoming an intellectual:

> The woman who gets tired of her femininity and focuses on her own intellect, becomes a poor person capable only of selling candles, having no better light to shed.[26]

Marriage and the rôle of women were subjects of lively debate in fascist Italy. The policy of the regime was to force women back into the home in their traditional rôle of wives and mothers and, as the regime moved towards war, the Roman myth of the mother of heroes and of the soldiers of the nation became ever more apt.[27]

'"War is to men what childbirth is to women" was one of Mussolini's better known phrases; he believed that women were incapable of synthesis and thus of any great spiritual creation. They were made to obey and could carry no weight in political life. Their pressing duty, confirmed repetitively by the popular women's magazines, was "to give without ever asking for anything in return, and to negate themselves for the lives of others and always under the tutelage of their husbands", though they were allowed to be administrators of what the school textbooks referred to as their "little kingdom". Some basic study of Italian and French, history and geography was allowed, provided it was limited to "only enough to add a little culture to their qualities as housewives . . . and in this way, as a model women, to contribute directly to the demographic campaign promoted by the fascist regime".[28]

As early as May 1926 the fascist deputy Vittorio Cian had expressed concern about the possible grave consequences that "the female invasion of the educational system would have on the ethics and subsequent military fibre of the nation, with their non-combative instinct, their patience, their willingness for compromise rather than self-assertive conflict". He deplored the notion, "which until yesterday was accepted more or less universally, of the equality of the sexes".

For Giovanni Gentile (responsible for the reform of the educational system) females were inferior both physically and spiritually to males. As Tracy Koon has explained, he believed that one of the problems in the education system was the influx of female teachers into secondary schools and universities. Although women could be elementary school teachers "because of their obvious maternal qualities", they were to be discouraged from teaching at higher levels, where teachers should possess "well marked characteristics of virility". Women, claimed Gentile, did not possess the originality of thought or that "iron spiritual vigour" the school demanded.[29]

What Italian women could provide was beauty. This at least according to another pamphleteer, Giovanni Marro who, in *Physical and spiritual qualities of the Italian race* (published in 1939), following the example of Leon Battista Alberti, compares man to a Doric column and woman to a Ionic one. Marro believed he could prove "scientifically" that morphological beauty brings with it that "power of synthesis" which is "one of the strongest characteristics of the Italian race",[30] and traces the "scientific reasons" for the supremacy of the Italian race, to Vitruvius and to his so-called *quadrato degli antichi*, (the well known image of a man contained in the square). Convinced that this is the first document of "rational anthropometry", intended to demonstrate man's harmonious proportions, Marro goes on to explain "from archaeological evidence" that white, middle-height people are those who fit the formula of Vitruvius best. He also "demonstrates" that the quality of the race is affected by its environment and by historic tradition in a continuum of aims and values harmonically produced and organized.[31] This is why, according to Marro, Italy and Rome, "have been and are one *stirpe* [race] in their *facere* and *pati*, in their fortunes, in everything".

Already in the early years of the regime, the fascist intelligentsia had advocated a policy of cultural isolation ostensibly to protect the "pure Latin spirit" from contamination by other "inferior" cultures – notably those of English-speaking origin. It was only in the late 1930s, however, that the glorification of the Latin race, in a crescendo of platitudes, became commonplace. Marro believes that history has demonstrated clearly that among all the forms of civilization derived from the same white root, the first place is undoubtedly occupied by the Italian race. This for Marro is the result of its "innate tendency towards progress" and its "ability to destroy inferior morphological aspects, while maintaining or acquiring the superior ones".[32] It can best be seen in the personality of the Italian people, and in their form of communication: their language. The Italian language – Marro argues – is aesthetically pleasing, economical in the way the words are uttered, harmonious in its architecture; it is the purest among the languages derived from Latin, which means that it is the legitimate heir of the spiritual and cultural patrimony of the Latin people.

From language as a way of communication Marro, with an unprecedented flight of imagination, moves to the other form of communication for which the Roman and the Italian were second to none: roads (including the "liquid roads" or sea-lanes used by the Italian maritime republics). In fact Marro believes that Italy itself, because of its geographical position and of its shape, is nothing more than a road, or better a bridge, linking Europe to Africa. This, Marro explains, is the reason why the Italian people have in their blood the urge for speed and mobility; hence their desire to dominate over land, sea and air.[33] The reference to the recently acquired empire and to the intensive road programme planned to connect it directly to Rome, is here implicit.

If quoting Rome meant not simply reproducing it, but making use of the text and reading it to some purpose, then nothing better than the stone and marble of architecture could express the lasting qualities of harmony, strength, and stability. "In my opinion, the greatest of all arts is architecture, because it comprises them all", said Mussolini.[34] Moreover, we are assured by Mussolini himself that Italians could take confidence from the knowledge that he was promoting the very best in national architecture. As he stated: "The architecture of Mussolini's era must reflect the masculinity, the force and the pride of the revolution".[35] And again:

> My ideas are clear, my orders precise. I am absolutely certain that they will become reality. In five years from now, Rome will appear wonderful to all the world: vast, orderly, powerful as she was at the times of her first empire under Augustus. You must clear the trunk of the great oak tree . . . all that grew around during the years of decadence must disappear . . . you will also free the majestic temples of Christian Rome . . . the thousand-year old monuments of our history must stand out in isolation as giants. . . . The third Rome will then spread over the hills, along the sacred river as far as the Tyrrhenian sea.[36]

It is clear from this declaration that in architecture, as in art and politics, the regime based its programme on three ideological tenets: the classical world, Christianity and fascism. This is the meaning of the three symbols, Minerva, a cross and a *fasces* contained in a drawing presented for a competition of propaganda posters held in 1937. Yet architecture also reveals one of the contradictions of fascism, namely its stress on both revolution and "order". The concept of order (borrowed from architecture itself) signifies a coherent, recognizable morphological system: it implies classicism and tradition, but in architecture "order" also implies emphasis on classification and typology, a hierarchy of qualities interpreted with nationalistic pride. The fascist revolution in Italy needed architecture to bequeath a new image to history and to offer contemporary society a new rallying point. It was embodied initially in the myth of dynamism promoted by the futurists, but then abandoned to follow a classical, grandiose style, naïvely and roughly inspired by *romanitas*. Hence its insistence on monumentalism, on the use of "noble" material, and its decision to end metal and reinforced concrete construction.

The dividing line between quotation (the following of a model and entrusting oneself to the security of its intrinsic authority), and evocation (the filtering of the traditional in a new concentrate capable of arousing memory and producing analogous but different effects) is narrow. Marcello Piacentini, one of the most prominent architects of the regime, sought vainly to square this particular circle:

> I see our contemporary architecture in a setting of great composure and perfect measure. It will accept the new proportions permitted by new materials while always subordinating them to that divine harmony which is the essence of our arts and of our spirit.[37]

Rome, and the extension of architecture into town planning, provided the sacred goal for an ideal pilgrimage. Simplicity, unity and elegance were the desired ingredients; a blend of "classical" and functional architecture based on strict symmetry and balance of masses, together with the cunning perspective dictated by Renaissance discoveries. Giorgio de Chirico's *Piazze d'Italia* conveys the spectral and metaphysical aura of such planned cities. Areas of some towns were partly realized (as in Turin, Milan or Brescia); others (such as the plan for the Esposizione Universale in Rome) were destined to remain a grand architectural Utopia. But Mussolini's ideal city, like its Renaissance predecessor, far from being revolutionary, was ultimately a deeply conservative conception and the result of a divided consciousness. The perception of space evoked grandeur: vast public squares, wide, straight streets and grandiose buildings with triumphant voids, offered no living space for humble people; indeed, they were possible only with the relocation of the urban population.

Italy's entry into the war was to leave Mussolini's great project for EUR unfinished. Ironically, the area was a popular film-setting in the post-war period, and became a living city only in recent times, after bourgeois alterations to the "purity" of the original design made it both tolerable and practical. Purity may have been lost in this process of accommodation, but a humanity of use (and, to some extent, of scale), was regained. It is a daunting judgement on fascist ideals that exactly such pragmatic compromise should prove the only possible way to mediate between those two worlds – the actual and the ideal – which the regime had sought to unite through rhetoric alone.

Notes

1. The Istituto Nazionale di Cultura Fascista (formerly Istituto Nazionale Fascista di Cultura) started in 1925 as a response to the challenge of the anti-fascist intellectuals led by Benedetto Croce. It aimed at creating a national consciousness based on fascist principles and achieved through a network of political indoctrination and a capillary, popular propaganda. During the Second World War it increased its activities by sponsoring lectures, films, concerts and exhibitions. It ceased to exist in 1943.
2. Published in *Mussolinia: Periodiche Mensili*, Biblioteca di Propaganda Fascista (Mantua, 1922).
3. The lecture was later to appear in print in a pamphlet by the same title, edited by the Ufficio Storico della R. Marina.
4. See speech of 18 March 1934, in M. Muggeridge (ed.), *Ciano's diplomatic papers: 12 June 1936–April 1942.* (London, 1948), pp. 60–61.
5. B. Mussolini, *Roma antica sul mare*, in *Ciano's diplomatic papers*, ed. M. Muggeridge (London, 1948), p. 6.
6. A. E. Ludwig, *Colloqui con Mussolini* Milan (1950), p.iii; summarized by R. de Felice, *Mussolini il duce, II Lo stato totalitario, 1936–1940* (Torino, 1981), p. 89; also reported in D. Thompson, *State control in fascist Italy: culture and conformity 1925–43* (Manchester & New York, 1991), p. 99.
7. "Il cinema per l'impero" in *Lo Schermo*, June 1936, quoted in C. Carabba, *Il cinema del ventennio nero* (Florence, 1974), p. 128.
8. G. P. Brunetta & J. A. Gili, *L'ora d'Africa del cinema italiano* (Rovereto, 1990), p. 112, n. 103.

9. L. Freddi, *Il cinema* (Rome, 1949), vol. i, p. 328.

10. *Bianco e Nero*, I, nos 7-8, July-August 1937, quoted in Brunetta & Gili, *L'ora d'Africa*.

11. Quoted in Freddi, *Il cinema*, vol. i, p. 327.

12. "Se avesse avuto la faccia molle di quello là, non so se ne avrebbe mai vinta una [di battaglia]", quoted by Freddi, *Il cinema* vol. i, p. 400. Freddi also reports that the film appeared to Mussolini to be instructive more than entertaining.

13. *Bianco e Nero*, III, no. 8, July-August 1939, quoted in Brunetta & Gili, *L'ora d'Africa*, p. 99.

14. A. Savinio, Difesa dell'intelligenza, 30 Agosto 1943, in *Sorte dell'Europa* (Milano, 1977).

15. P. de Francisci, *Civiltà Romana* (Rome, 1939), p. 8.

16. *Ibid.*, p. 7.

17. *Ibid.*, p. 8.

18. P. de Francisci, *Augusto e l'impero* (Quaderni, 1937), p. 6.

19. *Ibid.*, pp. 31-2.

20. Giuseppe Bottai, fascist journalist and from 1926 to 1943 at the centre of political life. Founder of the "corporations" for which he was under-secretary and minister. He was also Minister for Education and governor of Rome.

21. Fascism introduced a succession of special laws (*leggi eccezionali*) which, through imposition of order, discipline and hierarchy, had transformed the residual liberal state into an authoritarian one, and could be compared to the measures taken by Augustus. In particular: the law of 24 December 1925 dealing with the power and prerogatives of the Head of Government, set Mussolini officially above all ministers and effectively concentrated all executive powers in his hands; the law of 31 January 1926 withdrew citizenship from any Italian abroad suspected of activities detrimental to the regime. Both Mussolini and Octavian were against celibacy, and encouraged large families.

22. de Francisci, *Augusto e l'impero*, p. 15.

23. de Francisci, *Civiltà Romana*, pp. 10-11.

24. C. Cogni, *I Valori della Stirpe Italiana* (Milano, 1937), p. 151.

25. *Ibid.*, p. 151.

26. *Ibid.*, p. 154.

27. Cf. G.Biondi & F. Imberciardoni . . . *Voi siete la primavera d'Italia . . . l'ideologia fascista nel mondo della scuola 1925-1943* (Turin, 1982), p. 157, n. 2.

28. *Casa e Lavoro*, Anno II, No. 4, August 1930, 160. A special school for domestic science was opened in Rome in 1930 with the purpose of "preparing young girls for their future rôle of wives, mothers and fascist women, women who love their homes . . . and improve day by day to become worthy of the mission that our Duce has assign to them in a renewed Italy". (Cf. "La scuola superiore fascista di economia domestica di Roma", in *Casa e Lavoro*, Anno II, no. 7, November 1930, p. 240).

29. T. H. Koon, *Believe, obey, fight: political socialisation of the youth in fascist Italy, 1922-1943* (London, 1985), p. 49.

30. G. Marro, *Caratteri fisici e spirituali della razza Italiana* (Rome, Istituto Nazionale di Cultura, 1939), p. 15.

31. Plinio Marconi had already arrived at the same conclusions with respect to architecture; in 1933 he affirmed that "Dominant in the Italian spirit . . . [was] balance, the

ability to synthesize, and the capacity to combine the most disparate elements of life into a higher unity: this means the ability to operate within the bounds of reality and, without excluding any elements of life, to encompass them all in an harmonious unity which is complex, yet perfectly clear." (Architettura italiana attuale, in *Architettura*, special issue for the Milanese Triennale, quoted by L. Patetta, *L'architettura in Italia 1919–1922* (Milan, 1972), pp. 243–4).

32. Marro, *Caratteri fisici e spirituali della razza Italiana,* pp. 23.
33. *Ibid.*, p. 62.
34. A. E. Ludwig, *Colloqui con Mussolini* (Milan, 1932), p. 203.
35. Speech delivered in Campidoglio (Rome) in 1925 and reported in *Manifesto per l'architettura nazionale* (Manifesto for national architecture), cited in Patetta, *L'architettura in Italia*, p. 192.
36. "L'insediamento del Primo Governatore di Roma", in *Capitolium,* I, fasc. 10, January 1926, p. 596.
37. M. Piacentini, *Architettura d'oggi* (Rome, 1930), cited in F. Borsi, *The monumental era: European architecture and design 1929–1939* (London, 1986), p. 25.

Index

Abrams, P. 10
Ackerman, J. S. 163, 167
Adshead, S. D. 64
Africa 13, 14, 16, 107, 204–6
agriculture 5, 15, 27, 128, 138–9, 151–79
  suburban 154–7
Agrippa 50
Alberti, Leon Battista 185, 187, 210
Alexandria 14
Allison, Penelope 42, 63
Amorgos 112
Ampolo, C. 141
Andreau, Jean 2, 9, 10, 20, 40
Antioch 14
anti-Semitism 209
Antony, Mark 209
Aphrodisias 112
Apuleius 50
Apulia 16
aqueducts 161, 171
Arcadia 17
architecture 3–6, 64, 79–106, 184–202,
  211–13
Ardea 125
Aristotle 170
Arles 14
army, Roman 4, 17–18, 121–2, 129–32
Arthur, P. 11
Arval Brethren 141–2
Ashby, T. 64
associations, city 31, 32
Athens 11, 112, 126
Augustus 6, 51, 172, 207–209
Axius, Q. 151–2

Bacchanalia 145, 147
Badian, E. 131
Baiae 115, 153
Barker, G. W. 10
bars 3, 43–6, 53
Becker-Nielsen 10
Bedon, R. 10
Bologna 13, 19
Bologna, Ferdinando 187
Bottai, Giuseppe 206, 208
Bouchet, Jules 184
Bowersock, G. W. 109
Britain 9, 18, 107, 121
brothels 3, 51–5
Bruhns, Hinnerk 11
Bücher, K. 9, 31
Burnham, B. C. 9

Caere 126
calendar 138
Caligula 50
Calza, Guido 4, 81, 83, 85, 91, 95, 97
Campania 4, 11, 16, 18, 123, 143
capitalism 11, 12, 28–36
Capogrossi Colognesi, Luigi 3, 27–37
Carandini, Andrea 168
Carneiro, Robert 122, 124
Carthage 14, 204–6
Castell, R. 164
Castrén, P. 40
Cato 29, 161, 169, 171
Catullus 153
Caudium 127
Cherchel 19

Chevallier, R.   10
Chifflot   190
Childe, V. Gordon   1
Cian, Vittorio   210
Cicero   19, 56, 115, 126, 136–7, 151–2, 156, 159, 162, 166, 172
Claudius   45, 50, 112, 115
Claudius Pulcher, Appius   151–3
Claudius Pulcher, Cn.   14
cleanliness, street   50–1
Clitumnus, shrine of   136
Cogni, C.   209
colonization, Roman   126
Columella   158, 160
Commodus   81, 88
consumer city   1–4, 6, 9, 11–12, 15, 19, 22, 133
Corinth   2–3, 12–14
Cornell, T. J.   121–34
Costabile, F.   114
cults
    rustic   5, 135–50
    health   143–4, 147
Cumae   110, 111, 126
Cyrene   116

De Caro, Stefano   41
Decima   125
De Chirico, Giorgio   212–13
De Francisci, Pietro   203, 207
De Franciscis, Alfonso   40
Degrassi, A.   127
Delaine, Janet   3–4, 79–106
Della Corte, M.   40, 43, 46
De Simone, Antonio   41
Dessau, H.   16
Diana   13
Di Galboli, Paoluccio   205
Diocletian   18, 156
Diodorus   14
Dionysius of Halicarnassus   126
doorways   3, 66, 70–5
Durkheim, Emile   2, 10

economy   11–22, 27–36, 56–7, 128–33, 151–79
Egypt   30, 31, 132
elites   4, 5, 11, 12, 15–17, 20, 27, 33, 107–20, 133, 146, 156, 162–5
Engels, Donald   2, 9, 12–14
Eschebach, H.   42, 43
Ethiopia   205–7

Etruria   123, 126, 143, 145

fascism   6, 203–13
feudalism   27–33
Ficana   125
Finley, M. I.   1–3, 9–12, 27, 56, 162, 167, 181, 184, 198
Fiorelli, G.   46
fortifications   123–7
Foxhall, Lin   169
Frank, Tenney   40
Freddi, Luigi   205, 206
Frier, Bruce   12
Fustel de Coulanges, Numa-Denis   198

Gabba, E.   16, 124, 127
Gallone, Carmine   205
Gandy, John   181
Gardner, E. A.   64
Garnier, Tony   190–3
Gassner, Verena   41
Gell, Sir William   181
Gellius, Aulus   161
Gentile, Giovanni   210
Gibbon, Edward   17
Goalen, Martin   5, 181–202
graffiti   3, 52, 66, 68–70, 72
Gralfs, Bettine   41
Greeks   1–2, 4, 10, 27, 28, 107–17, 123, 126
Gros, P.   9
guilds   32

Hadrian   111, 112, 115, 116
Hannibal   127
Hanson, J. E.   65, 76
Harmand, J.   167
Harris, W. V.   128, 130
Hartog, F.   2, 9
Haverfield, F.   64, 76
Heitland, W. E.   162, 163
Hellenism   2, 4, 108–17
Herculaneum   4, 181, 186–7
Hillier, B.   65, 76
Hingley, R.   15
Holton, R. J.   9
hoplites   29, 123; see also army
Horace   37, 153, 156
Hulot, Jean   190

ideology   4, 55–6, 168
Industrial City   190–2

inscriptions 109–17, 127
Irelli, Cerulli 41

Johnson, Samuel 17
Jones, A. H. M. 132
Jones, John 198
Jongman, W. 9, 12, 21, 41, 173
Julius Agricola 121
Juvenal 50

Keay, Simon 10
Kleberg, T. 45, 46
Koon, Tracy 210

La Torre, G. F. 43–4, 46
Latium 123, 125, 143
Laurence, Ray 3, 63–78
Lavinium 125, 126
law and order 49–50
Le Corbusier, C. E. J. 193–8
Leontini 126
Letta, C. 147
Leveau, Philippe 9, 14, 15, 167
Ling, Roger 40
Livy 125, 127, 130, 131, 145
Lloyd, J. A. 10
Locri 110, 111
Lomas, Kathryn 1–7, 107–20
Lucania 16
Lupercalia 141
Lycia 17

MacDonald, W. C. 73
Maffei, Scipione 181
Magna Graecia 107–20, 126
Maiuri, A. 40, 41, 43
Marro, Giovanni 210–11
Martial 50, 153, 155, 159
Marx, Karl 1, 5, 10, 11, 14, 22
Matteotti, Giacomo 204
Maxentius 95
Mazois, François 181, 183, 186–90, 192–3, 198
medieval city 1, 28–33
Meiggs, Russell 79, 81
Mesopotamia 30
Meyer, Eduard 27
migration, rural–urban 127–8, 139
Millett, M. 16
Moeller, W. O. 41
Momigliano, Arnaldo 27
Mommsen, Theodor 50

Mouritsen, H. 4, 40
Murray, Oswyn 2
Mussolini, Benito 6, 204–15

Naples 110–12, 114–16
Nappo, Salvatore Ciro 41
Naxos 126
Near East 1, 30–2
Nemi 144
Nero 45
Nissen, H. 2
North, J. A. 5, 135–50

Oakley, Stephen 124
organizer city 15–17
Osborne, R. 11
Ostia 4, 79–106, 107
Ovid 140–2
Ozenfant, Amédée 197

Paestum 110, 111
pagi 14, 20, 124, 139, 147
Palladio, Andrea 185–7
Panhellenion 116
Parilia 140–1
"patrician city" 33
Patterson, J. R. 10
Pausanius 184
Pavolini, C. 99
Percival, John 165, 167
Pergamum 165
Persius 153
Petronius 19, 21
Phainippos of Athens 12
phratries 112, 115
Piacentini, Marcello 212
Piacenza 19
Pietrabbundante 124
Pinon, P. 10
Pirenne, Henri 1, 10
Pizzetti, Ildebrando 203
Plautus 45
"plebeian city" 33–4
Pliny the elder 155, 158, 171
Pliny the younger 20–1, 136, 158, 159, 162, 164, 170
Plutarch 14
polis 1–2, 10, 27, 28, 123
Pompeii 3–5, 12, 19, 21, 39–78, 107, 121, 164, 166, 172, 181–4, 186–90, 193–5, 198
popinae 45, 46; see also bars
Poseidonia 126

processor city   17–19
prostitution   50, 52; *see also* brothels
publicani   131–2
Purcell, Nicholas   5, 151–79
Puteoli   115, 116

Quartermaine, Luisa   6, 203–15

racism   209–11
Raper, R. A.   43, 65
religion   5, 135–50
rentier class   1, 11, 14, 15, 19, 20; *see also*
   elites
Rhegium   110, 111, 113, 116
Rich, J.   2, 9
Rihill, T. E.   10
Rivet, A. L. F.   167
roads   211
Robigalia   140, 141
Rodbertus, Johann Karl   31
Romanization   4, 15–17, 107–20
Rome   4, 28–32, 56, 57, 107, 123, 125–8,
   146, 203–15
Rossi, Pietro   2, 9, 10
Rossiter, J. J.   167
Rostovtzeff, M. I.   40, 162
rusticity   135–50

Samnium   16, 123–4, 126–7
Sartori, F.   112
Satricum   125
Savinio, Alberto   207
Scheid, John   141
Schinkel, Karl   187
Scipio the Younger   204, 205
Scipione l'Africano   205–7
Selinus   190
Seneca   39, 55–6, 163
service city   2, 12–14
Sertorius   131
Servius Tullius   123, 125
Settefinestre   160, 166, 167, 169, 170
Sicily   126
Silvanus cult   142–4, 147
Skydsgaard, J. E.   167
slaves   28, 29, 170
Smith, Adam   5, 10
Snodgrass, A. M.   123
Sollers, Bellicius   21
Sombart, Werner   1, 5, 9
Sparta   116, 126
spatial analysis   3, 63–78

Spencer, Herbert   122
Squarciapino, M. Floriani   81–2
storage   169–70
Strabo   5, 18, 21, 108, 110, 113, 114, 116,
   126, 160
streets   3, 47, 49–50, 66–73
Strocka, Michael   41

Tacitus   18, 121
Tarentum   110, 113–14, 116
Tarquinii   126
taxation   13, 17–21
Tchernia, A.   13
Terence   56
Theadelphia   14
Thelepte   13
Thulin, C. O.   20, 21
Tiberius   45, 50
Torelli, M.   9
town planning   63–78
Toynbee,   A. J.   128
trade   11, 13, 14, 17–19, 56, 130–2, 155
traffic   47, 51
Tsujimura, Sumiyo   47
Tusculum   190, 191

Ulpian   52
Umbria   16
urban–rural relations   5, 10–12, 15, 17–
   19, 28, 135–79
urbanization   16, 122, 127–8

Van der Poel, H. B.   42
Varone, Antonio   41
Varro   19, 21, 56, 151–6, 158, 159, 161,
   166, 186
Veii   126
Velia   110, 111, 113, 115
Vespasian   45, 50
Vezio, Tito   203
Vibo   110, 111
Vicetia   21
vici   15, 18–20, 124, 139, 147
Vidler, Anthony   193
villas   5, 15, 17–22, 28, 151–79
Vindolanda letters   131
viticulture   156–7
Vittinghoff, F.   10
Vitruvius   64, 160, 166, 184–7, 211

Wacher, J.   9, 15
Wallace-Hadrill, Andrew   2, 3, 9, 10, 12,

19, 39–62, 166
Wallerstein, I.   10
warfare   4, 28, 121–34
water management   171
Weber, Max   1–3, 5, 9–12, 15, 19, 22, 27–37
White, K. D.   167

Whittaker, C. R.   3, 6, 9–26
Wilson, A. G.   10
Wiseman, Peter   172
women, rôle of   209–11
Woolf, G.   16

zoning, socio-economic   64–5